Augustus T. Wirgman

The Constitutional Authority of Bishops in the Catholic Church

illustrated by the history and canon law of the undivided church from the apostolic

age to the Council of Chalcedon, A.D. 451

Augustus T. Wirgman

The Constitutional Authority of Bishops in the Catholic Church
illustrated by the history and canon law of the undivided church from the apostolic age to the Council of Chalcedon, A.D. 451

ISBN/EAN: 9783337301866

Printed in Europe, USA, Canada, Australia, Japan

Cover: Foto ©Lupo / pixelio.de

More available books at **www.hansebooks.com**

THE CONSTITUTIONAL AUTHORITY OF BISHOPS IN THE CATHOLIC CHURCH

ILLUSTRATED BY THE HISTORY AND CANON LAW
OF THE UNDIVIDED CHURCH FROM THE
APOSTOLIC AGE TO THE COUNCIL
OF CHALCEDON, A.D. 451

BY THE REV.

A. THEODORE WIRGMAN, D.D., D.C.L.

LATE FOUNDATION SCHOLAR OF MAGDALENE COLLEGE, CAMBRIDGE
VICE-PROVOST OF S. MARY'S COLLEGIATE CHURCH
PORT ELIZABETH, SOUTH AFRICA

LONGMANS, GREEN, AND CO.
39, PATERNOSTER ROW, LONDON
NEW YORK AND BOMBAY
1899

VIRO : ADMODVM : REVERENDO

IACOBO : GREEN, A.M.

DECANO : MARITZBVR

QVI : PER : QVINQVAGINTA : ANNOS

FIDEI : CATHOLICÆ : REBVS : IN : ARDVIS

CONFESSOR : STRENVVS

ET : PASTOR : FIDELIS

VITÆ : SACERDOTALIS

SPECVLVM : ET : EXEMPLAR : PRÆBVIT

HOC : OPVSCVLVM

DEDICAT : AVCTOR.

PREFATORY NOTE

THERE are two points with regard to the following pages towards which I would venture to draw the attention of those who may read them.

In the first place, the main object of the investigation may seem academic rather than practical to Churchmen in England. From these I would crave patience, because questions which touch the daily practical working of the Free Churches of the Anglican Communion must necessarily seem at present merely academic to Churchmen whose organisation is still linked with the State. Secondly, I desire the indulgence of all my readers on account of the necessarily frequent repetitions of the same arguments and the same enactments, in slightly varying forms, which this book contains. It seemed to me impossible to avoid this in a consecutive historic examination of the mind of the

Church as expressed in the gradual evolution of its jurisprudence.

I trust, however, that I have avoided wearisome iteration in dealing with a somewhat difficult and complex subject.

I have made free use of our great English Canonist, Bishop Beveridge, and also of the Rev. W. Clark's translation of Bishop Hefele's standard work on the Christian Councils, besides other authorities acknowledged in the text.

I owe a debt of gratitude to Mr. A. W. Goodman, of Sedbergh School, who has taken the responsibility of seeing this essay through the Press.

A. T. W.

S. MARY'S RECTORY,
PORT ELIZABETH, SOUTH AFRICA,
Christmas, 1898.

CONTENTS

CHAPTER I

THE DEVELOPMENT OF CONSTITUTIONAL EPISCOPAL AUTHORITY IN THE APOSTOLIC AGE

	PAGE
The Church, a Divine Society	1
The Apostolic Ministry is from God	3
It possesses the *Sacerdotium*	4
S. Augustine as sacerdotal as S. Cyprian	4
The Historic Backbone of the Church	5
Need of due historic proportion	6
The Mosaic Polity fulfilled in the Catholic Church	7
Life through the Church as a visible Polity	9
Belief in the Church precedes Baptism	9
The Constitutional Authority of Bishops	10
Difficulties created by Roman Despotism	11
The difficulties of Eastern Christendom	11
Anglican difficulties	12
Need of a centre	13
The Ministry of the Apostolic Church	14
Influence of the Levitical Hierarchy upon the Apostles	15
Both Ministries called of God	16
The Church independent of the State	17
The Primacy and Centre of the Levitical Polity	17
Our Lord's guidance of the Apostles	18
The true principle of Primacy	19
S. Peter's Primacy does not involve Supremacy	20
The true Primacy of S. Peter	21
Scriptural evidence of his Primacy	21
S. Peter's judgment on Ananias and Sapphira	23

CONTENTS

	PAGE
"Tibi dabo claves"	24
Professor Ramsay on S. Peter's Primacy	25
The Apostolic Mission to Samaria	26
Its importance as a new departure	26
It was led by S. Peter as the Primate Apostle	27
Position of S. James at Jerusalem	28
S. Peter at Antioch	29
The Gentiles at Antioch and S. Peter	29
Primacy of S. Peter over the whole Church	31
The Council of Jerusalem	32
S. Peter's Primacy at the Council	32
True significance of the presidency of S. James	32
S. Peter's Primacy not effaced by S. Paul	34
The beginnings of Diocesan Episcopacy	36
A Second Apostolic Council	36
Late date of i. Peter	38
S. Peter survived S. Paul at Rome	39
Primatial authority in the Apostolic Age	40
Note A.—The Mosaic Polity and Ritual finds fulfilment in the Catholic Church	41
Note B.—The Levitical Ministry not the delegates of the people	43
Note C.—The Primacy of S. Peter	44
Note D.—The reading καὶ οἱ ἀδελφοί	46
Note E.—The principle of Primatial authority in the Apostolic Age	47

CHAPTER II

THE WITNESS OF THE SUB-APOSTOLIC AGE TO THE CONSTITUTIONAL AUTHORITY OF BISHOPS, AS LIMITED BY THE PRINCIPLE OF PRIMACY WITH REGARD TO THE UNIVERSAL EPISCOPATE, AND BY THE COUNCIL OF PRESBYTERS WITH REGARD TO EACH DIOCESE

Constitutional authority manifest in the first century	53
Human elements in the Divine visible Polity	55
The Church organised upon the basis of the civil organisation of the Empire	56

CONTENTS xi

	PAGE
The Pagan and Christian organisations	57
Development of the localised Episcopate	58
The Primacy of S. John at Ephesus	59
The Primacy of S. Clement of Rome	60
The Roman Church not Presbyterian	61
Primacy of the Roman See	62
S. Clement writes in the name of the Roman Church	63
Authoritative tone of his letter to the Corinthians	64
Evidence of the Pastor of Hermas	65
S. Clement and "the cities abroad"	66
As Primate he sends the message to them	67
S. Clement no mere "foreign secretary"	68
But the *Persona Ecclesiæ* of the Roman Church	68
S. Clement on the Rulers of the Church	70
S. Clement's analogy from the Threefold Levitical Ministry	71
And from the Roman Army	71
Absence of a Bishop does not involve Presbyterianism	72
Limits of the rights of Laymen	74
Summary of S. Clement's witness	75
S. Ignatius of Antioch	76
S. Ignatius on the Threefold Ministry	77
Constitutional authority of the Bishop	77
S. Ignatius testifies to the universal rule of Bishops	79
The necessity of the Threefold Ministry	80
A valid Eucharist implies the Bishop's consent	81
S. Ignatius on the Roman Primacy	81
The Apostolic Ministry and the Laity	83
The Priests are the Bishop's councillors	83
The Bishop acts with his Priests	84
The Bishop is the lyre, the Priests are its strings	85
The Bishop not an Autocrat, but a Constitutional Ruler	85
Distinction between the three Orders	86
Note A.—The legitimate Primacy of the Roman See	87
Note B.—The Unified Church	94

CHAPTER III

The Constitutional Authority of Bishops as Developed in the Period of the "Ecclesia Pressa" before the Edict of Milan, and the Evidence for the Exercise of Patriarchal and Metropolitical Rights by the Chief Sees of Christendom

	PAGE
Prominence of the Metropolitan	103
Provincial decisions not final	104
Constitutional rights of Bishops, Clergy, and Laity	105
The case of Marcion	106
The Paschal Controversy	107
Action of Pope Victor	108
His excommunication resisted	109
True position of the Primate of Christendom	111
Its due limitations	111
View of S. Irenæus	112
Rome the centre of unity	113
The Patriarch of Alexandria	115
His dealing with Origen	116
Interdependence of Patriarchal Sees	117
Synod at Antioch against Novatian	118
Paulus of Samosata	119
First Council of Antioch against Paulus	120
Proceedings against Paulus	121
He is deposed by the Council of A.D. 269	122
Paulus evicted by Aurelian	123
Œcumenical Epistle of the Council	124
Addressed to Rome and Alexandria	124
Dionysius and Felix of Rome condemn Paulus	127
Legitimate Primacy of Rome	128
S. Cyprian on the Episcopate	129
Constitutional rights of the individual Bishop	130
Each Bishop shares in the universal Episcopate	130
The Ius Liturgicum	132
S. Cyprian and Pope Stephen	133
No one is Episcopus Episcoporum	133
S. Cyprian admits a legitimate Roman Primacy	134
His statements on the subject	136

Neither Ultramontane nor Protestant	137
S. Cyprian guards the rights of the Priesthood and Laity	138
He consulted his Clergy and Laity	140
Rome and Carthage at one on this point	141
The assenting voice of the Laity in Synod	142
S. Cyprian as Primate	143
The Bishop acts first as Diocesan	144
The Apostolic Canons mainly Ante-Nicene	145
Canon xxxv. on Metropolitans and Primates	146
The Greek and Latin Versions of these Canons	146
Canon xxxv. refers to Primatial Authority generally	148
Significance of the Phrase, "Of each nation"	149
Canon xxxviii. on Provincial Synods	150
Canon lxxiv. on the trial of Bishops	151
Penalty of contumacy	152
The Apostolic Constitutions	153
Priests and Deacons not to act without the Bishop	154
Bishop's constitutional veto	155
Consecration of Bishops	156
Consecration by one Bishop irregular	156
Note A.—The Provincial Synods on the Paschal Question	158
Note B.—On the formation and sub-division of Dioceses	159
Note C.—Communion with the Roman See not essential to Catholic Communion	161
Note D.—S. Cyprian and the modern Papal theory	163

CHAPTER IV

THE CONSTITUTIONAL AUTHORITY OF BISHOPS, AND THE RIGHTS OF PATRIARCHS AND METROPOLITANS AS FINALLY DEVELOPED BETWEEN THE EDICT OF MILAN (A.D. 313) AND THE COUNCIL OF CHALCEDON (A.D. 451).

Patriarchs and Primates	169
Desire of Constantine for Church Unity	169
The Church and the Empire	170
Increased power of the Roman Patriarch	171
Evil results of the union between Church and State	173
The period of Œcumenical Councils. The Council of Elvira	174

	PAGE
Its 53rd and 58th Canons	174
The Spanish Primacies	176
The Donatist Schism	177
Consecration of the Primate of Carthage	178
His Patriarchal position	180
The Council of Arles	181
Its relations with the Roman Patriarch	182
It forbids Episcopal intrusions	183
It regulates the consecration of Bishops	184
The Council of Ancyra	185
Case of a Bishop not accepted by his Diocese	185
A modern instance	186
Need of centralising the Anglican Communion	188
Dangers of Provincial autonomy	189
Council of Neocæsarea	189
Council of Nicæa	190
Who summoned it?	190
The idea of a legitimate Primacy of Rome	193
Probability that Sylvester was consulted	194
And presided by his Legates	195
In accordance with historical probability	195
And Church Order	196
The appointment and confirmation of Bishops	198
The power of the Metropolitan in Canon iv.	198
The process of Election	199
The Clergy elect, the Laity assent	201
Nullus invitis detur	202
The Confirmation and Consecration	202
Power of excommunication in Canon v.	203
Powers of a Bishop limited	206
He is responsible to the Universal Episcopate	208
An Appeal lies against his Sentence	209
Episcopal authority not autocratic	209
The Bishop's veto is not absolute	209
The rights of Patriarchal Sees in Canon vi. Special privileges of Alexandria	211
The Roman Patriarch	212
Primate, but not Monarch	212
The Patriarch of Antioch	214
The lesser Primacies	215

	PAGE
The rights of the Metropolitan	217
The seventh Nicene Canon	218
The See of Jerusalem	218
Raised ultimately to a Patriarchate	220
The Translations of Bishops and Clergy forbidden by Canon xv.	221
But allowed for a reasonable cause	222
Allowed only *permissu superiorum*	223
And not by the will of individuals	226
Nor for personal ends	226
Canon xvi. on unlawful Ordinations	226
Canon xviii. on Deacons	227
S. Athanasius and Pope Julius	229
The Eusebians and Pope Julius	230
Reply of Pope Julius to the Eusebians	231
The Council of Antioch *in Encæniis*	232
Its ninth Canon	234
Its definite provisions	235
Rights of Metropolitans and Bishops	235
Appeal to a Higher Synod	236
Limit of Appeals	237
The Metropolitan not *Iudex solus*	238
The Council of Sardica	239
Its decision on Appeals	239
Canon iii.	241
Canon iv.	243
Canon v.	243
The Appeal to Rome	243
The Gallican view untenable	244
Motives of the Sardican Fathers	245
Real meaning of these Canons	248
Definition of the Appeal to Rome	248
The Council of Sardica not Œcumenical	249
Patriarchal jurisdiction defined by its Decrees	250
The Emperor Gratian gives coercive jurisdiction to the Roman See	251
The case of Apiarius	252
The Second Œcumenical Council	253
The Meletian Schism	254
The second Canon of Constantinople	255
The third Canon	256

	PAGE
It was disputed in the West	257
Effect of the second Canon in defining the Patriarchates of the East	258
Canon vi.	259
Appeal to Patriarchal Synod	259
Not to the Civil Power	260
The African Code of Canons	261
Canons of 4th Council of Carthage	262
The *Ius Cyprium*. Its true significance	264
As applied to the Church of England	265
The Council of Chalcedon	266
Its importance as an Œcumenical Council	266
Canon ix. The Appeal to the Patriarch	267
Canon xxviii.	268
The Prerogative of Constantinople	269
The title of Patriarch	270
The title of Archbishop	270
Justinian's enactments	271
The Metropolitan tried by the Patriarch	271
Value of Primitive principles	272

CONCLUSION

Note A.—Chorepiscopi	273
Note B.—The authority of Law and Custom	274

CONSTITUTIONAL AUTHORITY OF BISHOPS

CHAPTER I

THE DEVELOPMENT OF CONSTITUTIONAL EPISCOPAL AUTHORITY IN THE APOSTOLIC AGE

THE Gospel of Christ announces to us the true τέλος of human life, and reduces to definiteness and exactitude the indefinite nobility of the Platonic ideal of being "as like to God as is possible."[1] In order to guide us towards this end, the Gospel is embodied and enshrined in a Visible Society—an outward system whereby the "means of grace" lead us to the realisation of the "Hope of Glory." For this reason no question concerning the structure or discipline of the Visible

---

[1] Φυγὴ δὲ ὁμοίωσις Θεῷ κατὰ τὸ δυνατόν. (Theæt. 176 a.) Καὶ ἐπιτηδεύων ἀρετὴν εἰς ὅσον δυνατὸν ἀνθρώπῳ ὁμοιοῦσθαι Θεῷ. (Rep., 613.) It may be urged that the words ὁμοίωσις δὲ δίκαιον καὶ ὅσιον μετὰ φρονήσεως γενέσθαι (Theæt. 176) constitute a definition of the likeness of God. But righteousness, holiness, and wisdom were practically and fully defined by the Incarnate Christ alone.

Society can be relegated to the region of purely historical or archæological inquiry.

We may reasonably set aside in this category questions concerning the laws or polity of Republican or Imperial Rome. But there is a direct spiritual import in all questions concerning the laws and polity of the Catholic Church. It is our duty to elucidate them in a spirit of judicial and impartial investigation, and we must employ every resource placed at our disposal by the methods and discoveries of history and archæology, without forgetting that we are on sacred ground, because the Catholic Church is the Body of Christ.

A failure, conscious or unconscious, to recognise this primary fact, caused Dr. Hatch to fall into serious errors in dealing with the origin and development of the Christian Ministry.

It is foreign to the principles of this inquiry to deal with an argument which compresses the scriptural evidence upon the Christian Ministry into the limits of a single page;[1] which doubts the authorship of the Pastoral Epistles,[2] and declines to discuss the ecclesiastical polity of the New Testament, apart from certain strange theories which the author has formed of the Ministry in the sub-apostolic age.

When we are virtually told by this author that

[1] Hatch's *Bampton Lectures*, p. 48.   [2] Ibid., p. 82.

Christ did not form a Visible Society, that *all* Christians did not regard membership of the Church as essential, that they gradually coalesced into societies, that the functions as well as the nomenclature of the Christian Ministry were derived from Pagan and Judaic sources, that a Bishop was merely a "chief almoner," destitute of spiritual or pastoral authority, we have chaos instead of the divinely appointed order and method of the City of God. We postulate in these pages the simple fact that the Apostolic Ministry was developed from above, and not from below; from God, and not from the people. When an author asserts that the Church and its Ministry "is divine as the solar system is divine,"[1] it logically follows that the Head of the Church is divine as Buddha is divine, and that the Catholic faith in the Incarnate Christ is "a fond thing vainly invented."

We are also compelled to traverse absolutely the conclusions of another author, who, whilst he opposes Dr. Hatch on historical grounds, and truly calls the Apostolic Ministry of the Church "that ministerial order—threefold, unequal, historic"—which he believes "to have been initiated, accepted, adopted by the Holy Apostles,"[2] immediately proceeds to deny the

---

[1] Hatch, *Bampton Lectures*, p. 20.
[2] Dean Lefroy, *The Christian Ministry*, p. 189.

logical consequences of the facts which he admits. To deny the "*sacerdotium*" of that Threefold Ministry which he owns to be Apostolic, in the face of the fact that it is the connecting link between the *sacerdotium* of our Lord and the *sacerdotium* of all the members of His Body the Church, is utterly contrary to the testimony of Christian antiquity. To attempt the proof of this denial from Tertullian and S. Irenæus, whilst stating that "Apostolic truth had been adulterated"[1] in S. Cyprian's day, so that the testimony of S. Cyprian is inadmissible; to urge inconsequently that S. Augustine (a much later writer) is a witness we must accept, because "it is clear that S. Augustine did not accept the theory of the official derivation of grace," and "it is no less clear that he did not believe in the principle of Apostolic Succession,"[2] is so strange and strained an effort of human reasoning, that we must be pardoned if we decline to pursue its fallacies in detail. It is enough to say that Dr. Hatch saw clearly enough that "the Augustinian theory of the nature of the Church" was as sacerdotal as S. Cyprian's, and was absolutely opposed to his own theories. Dr. Hatch understood the plain meaning of S. Augustine. It is evident that Dean Lefroy preferred to read his own meaning

[1] Dean Lefroy, *The Christian Ministry*, p. 383, n. [2] Ibid., p. 394.

into S. Augustine's words, and declined to accept what S. Augustine meant to teach.[1]

We are compelled unwillingly to allude to these inadequate and heretical theories of the origin and development of the Christian Ministry, in order to clear the ground and to make it quite plain that these pages are written from the Catholic standpoint. We do not desire to deal with theories but with plain facts—facts illuminated and illustrated, directly or indirectly, from the Catholic consent of the Undivided Church. The Divine origin and authority of the Threefold Apostolic Ministry is a root fact embedded in the life and history of the Catholic Church. It has been called "the historic backbone of the Church." But it is more than this. It is the divinely appointed channel of sacramental life and grace. It is the guardian of the faith, discipline, and worship of the Visible Kingdom of Christ on earth. By virtue of the authority of their Apostolic descent, the Ministers of Christ

---

[1] Fortunately Dean Lefroy quotes the passage—it is the well-known place referring to confirmation: "Nos autem accipere quidem hoc donum possumus pro modulo nostro; effundere autem super alios non utique possumus, sed ut hoc fiat Deum super eos a quo efficitur invocamus." (S. Aug. *De Trin.*, xv. 26.) The meaning is plain. The Apostolic Ministry is not the *source* but the *channel* of the gift of the Holy Ghost. Therefore the Prayer of Invocation is used before the laying on of hands to emphasise this truth, and thus this prayer is always considered to be the form of Confirmation, as the imposition of hands is its matter.

are the stewards of His Mysteries and the organs of His Body. The Apostolic Ministry, in its threefold order, pertains to the *esse*, and not merely to the *bene esse* of the Church. It adapted itself progressively to each stage of the development of the life of the Church, as an integral factor of that life, as it expanded century by century.

We can learn usefully from Dr. Hatch the lesson of due historic proportion. We need to remember carefully the varying characteristics of each passing century of the life of the Church. "Different centuries have been marked in ecclesiastical, as in social history, by great differences in the drift and tendency of ideas."[1] We recognise the wide gulf which separates S. Clement of Rome from S. Leo the Great, and our eyes can measure the yet wider gulf between S. Leo the Great and Leo XIII. But we shall find that certain common and essential principles lie behind the vast outward differences that sever the various distinctive periods of Church history.

Even the huge and unwieldy fabric of the modern Papacy veils from sight inner principles of ecclesiastical polity and order which the Rome of Leo XIII. holds in common with Constantinople and Canterbury. To question this fact would be

[1] Hatch, *Bampton Lectures*, p. 10.

to deny the possibility of the corporate reunion of the Catholic Church. We shall endeavour to investigate these principles as the true elucidation of the present inquiry.

In the first place, we must bear in mind that the Catholic Church of the Day of Pentecost was developed from the Church of the Old Covenant, and that the world-embracing Israel of God under the New Covenant is a legitimate historic development, expansion, and fulfilment of that narrower and more exclusive Israel which S. Paul views as the *root* of the Church of Christ.[1] Our Lord "came not to destroy but to fulfil,"[2] and the Mosaic polity of type and shadow finds its analogy and fulfilment in the divinely ordered polity of the Catholic Church.[3] S. Paul resisted the false Judaisers of his time, but there is a true Judaism of fulfilled type and prophecy and order in the Catholic Church of to-day which cannot be set aside, if we would view the Apostolic Ministry—the Christian *sacerdotium*—and the ecclesiastical discipline of the kingdom of God from its right standpoint.

---

[1] Rom. xi. 18. We may add that our Lord's High-Priestly prayer (S. John xvii. 6–8) points distinctly to His disciples as already forming a corporate Body, which can be viewed as the link between the Old Covenant and the Church of Pentecost. So Hengstenberg, *Christology of Old Testament*, vol. iv. p. 58.

[2] S. Matt. v. 18.   [3] See Note A.

In the next place, we may note that the Church came *first*, and Christians *afterwards*. The Church, as a visible polity and society, was not created by the tendency of Christians to associate together, and form organisations framed on maxims of human wisdom and experience.[1] The continuity of the Israel of the New Covenant with the Israel of the Old Covenant, is a fact which forbids the idea that the Church was created by Christians. Our Lord did not come down from heaven merely as a teacher of certain new religious ideas, which men could assimilate at their will, and then embody them at their leisure by forming associations for the purpose of propagating the new doctrines they had learnt from Him. The Church, as expanded at Pentecost, is the divinely ordered society into which converts were admitted by Holy Baptism as the *ianua Sacramentorum*. The branches could not create the Vine, nor could

---

[1] "Miraculous powers were given to the first preachers of Christianity, in order to their introducing it into the world; a Visible Church was established in order to continue it, and carry it on successfully throughout all ages. Had Moses and the Prophets, Christ and His Apostles, only taught, and by miracles proved, religion to their contemporaries, the benefit of their instructions would have reached to but a small part of mankind. . . . To prevent this, appears to have been one reason why a Visible Church was instituted, to be like a city upon a hill . . . to be the repository of the oracles of God; to hold up the light of revelation in aid of that of nature, and propagate it throughout all generations to the end of the world."—Bishop Butler's *Analogy*, ii. 10.

the members the Body. The baptismal interrogation of S. Cyprian's day sums up the truth concisely, "*Dost thou believe in eternal life and the remission of sins, through the Holy Church?*"[1]

Belief in the visible polity and organisation of the Church, as the divinely ordered Society and Kingdom, necessarily preceded enrolment upon its list of free citizens, and admission to the privileges of its membership.[2]

The careful preparation of catechumens included the distinct teaching that all must believe in the Church, as the *Civitas Dei*, who desired to exchange the bondage of sin for the freedom of her franchise.

The question of the constitutional authority of Bishops in the Catholic Church is one which

---

[1] "Credis in vitam æternam et remissionem peccatorum per sanctam Ecclesiam?" S. Cyprian, Ep. lxx. 2.

[2] We may note here some remarkable words of the Archbishop of Canterbury (Dr. Temple) on Individualism and Catholicism. "Men speak as if Christians came first and the Church after; as if the origin of the Church was in the wills of the individual Christians that composed it. But, on the contrary, throughout the teaching of the Apostles we see that it is the Church that comes first and the members of it afterwards. Men were not brought to Christ, and then determined that they would live in a community. . . . In the New Testament, on the contrary, the Kingdom of Heaven is already in existence, and men are invited into it. . . . Everywhere men are called in; they do not come in and make the Church by coming. They are called in to that which already exists; they are recognised as members when they are within; but their membership depends upon their admission, and not upon their constituting themselves a body in the sight of the Lord."—*Twelve Sermons Preached at the Consecration of Truro Cathedral*, pp. 17–20.

vitally affects its organisation. We purpose to investigate this question under the guidance of the preliminary considerations and principles which have already been stated. We shall keep in mind the facts which belong to the life and polity of the Church, and endeavour to discover from the evidence of history how they were manifested in the gradual development of its government.

It will be necessary to set aside resolutely the prejudices and prepossessions which result from the present unhappy divisions of Christendom. We must be capable of examining dispassionately the claims of a visible Primacy, without losing our hold upon the claims of the Invisible Head.[1] We may recognise to the full the independence which belongs to individual Bishops, without admitting the theory that the Catholic Church consists of a number of autocephalous dioceses wherein each Bishop does that which is right in his own eyes, without let or hindrance. The unhappy fact that the historic Primacy of Christendom has degenerated into a despotism, which, under certain conditions, claims to be infallible, need not cause us

[1] No one will accuse Dean Stanley of ecclesiastical prepossessions. He did not hold the Catholic doctrine of the Ministry of the Church, and yet he could write thus of the Pope's position: "Even those who entirely repudiate his authority must still regard him as the chief ecclesiastic of Christendom. If there is such a thing as a body of clergy at all, the Bishop of Rome is certainly the head of the profession."—Stanley, *Christian Institutions*, p. 220.

to forget the inherent infallibility of the Catholic Church, or permit us to destroy the constitutional order of her government by allowing the divinely ordered equality of Bishops to degenerate into anarchic diocesan independence.[1]

The fact that the Primate of Latin Christendom has become an unconstitutional despot has reacted unfavourably upon the Primates of Eastern and Anglican Christendom. In the East the Patriarchal See of Constantinople is overshadowed by Byzantine traditions of undue subserviency to the civil power. This begat mischief enough in the centuries immediately preceding the fall of Constantinople; and the independence of the Primate of the East has suffered still further from the fact that a Moslem Sultan stepped into the place of a Christian Emperor. In our own day the future of Eastern Christendom is bound up with the political power and religious zeal of Russia, which may, at no distant date, replant the Cross upon the desecrated

---

[1] The danger alluded to is no visionary one. The lack of the Provincial system, and of Metropolitical authority, is deeply felt in the American Church. At the present time we see in the Australian Church the un-Catholic anomaly of the Synod of the Diocese claiming power to reject the Canons of Synods General and Provincial. In South Africa we have seen a Bishop claiming the right of an absolute *veto*, beyond the scope of any appeal, upon the decrees and resolutions of the Synod of his Diocese, although the claim was subsequently disallowed by the House of Bishops.

Church of S. Sophia, and restore the ancient glories of the See of Constantinople. The Patriarch of New Rome would then recover the primatial rights accorded to him by the Council of Chalcedon, freed from the centrifugal tendencies which modern political changes have impressed upon the rulers and people of the Orthodox Church of the East.[1]

The difficulties which encompass the true development of the Primacy of Canterbury are different in degree and kind.

It is true that the Tudor tyranny was worse than the Byzantine, even under the Sultan. "The Commander of the Faithful" might now and again hang a Patriarch, but he did not crush the spiritual liberties of the Church under the forms of law, as Henry VIII. did. The present-day difficulty, however, is that the Henrician forms of law still encompass the throne of Canterbury,

[1] "The Greeks of to-day have no common blood. They include Cappadocians, Isaurians, Pisidians, Albanians, as well as Greeks by race. . . . They are united by nothing except the forms of the Orthodox Church. For old Rome as its centre was substituted the new Rome of Constantine. The political changes of the present century have even destroyed in appearance the unity of the Church; but still the idea remains, and every Greek looks forward to a future unity of the Church and its adherents, with free Constantinople as its metropolis." (Ramsay, *The Church and the Roman Empire*, p. 467.) Professor Ramsay's view of the religious aspirations of the Greeks may be modified by recent events, which have tended to cause thoughtful Greeks to view Russia as the sole hope of Eastern Christendom.

although its jurisdiction has developed from an insular Primacy to the virtual Patriarchate of a world-wide communion.[1] To the two Established Provinces of Canterbury and York are linked the unestablished and Free Churches of America and Greater Britain, and to the disestablished Churches of Ireland and Scotland, by a common acknowledgment of the Primacy of Canterbury. The problem before our ecclesiastical statesmen is to consolidate the Anglican Communion upon the true principles of Apostolic discipline and Catholic order. The vigour of the Anglican protest against the Papal conception of a single, infallible, spiritual monarch of Christendom has naturally weakened our hold upon any centralised system of Church government. The rule of the individual Bishop has been emphasised amongst us at the expense of the due authority of the Metropolitan and the Provincial Synod; whilst our central Primatial authority is necessarily somewhat vague and indefinite. This may be traced to a want of distinct ideas in the minds even of those who urge its claims, and most strongly

---

[1] "The successor of S. Augustine is coming to be regarded as the Patriarch in substance, if not in name, of the Anglican Churches throughout the world; the proud title, *papa alterius orbis*, has a far more real meaning now than when it was conferred many centuries ago." (Bishop Lightfoot, *Report of Wolverhampton Church Congress*, p. 13.)

realise the need of a centre, carefully guarded from the possibilities of future despotism. It may be given to us to restore the ancient and primitive ideal of the Patriarch, the Metropolitan, and the Diocesan Bishop in their true relations, as expressed and manifested in Synods General, Provincial, and Diocesan. Unless we do so we are face to face with the danger of disintegration. We have made a beginning. The Primacy of Canterbury can become a Patriarchate just as readily as the Lambeth Synod can develop into a decennial General Council of Anglican Christendom. We must return to first principles, and the present inquiry may in some measure aid us to do so.

We must deal in the first place with the evidence of Holy Scripture.

We are met, first of all, with the fact that the Apostles and their converts on the day of Pentecost were brought up in the Church of the Old Covenant, with its strict discipline and orderly hierarchy. Dr. Hatch recognises this fact, but unfortunately overweights it with a theory which derives the second order of the Threefold Apostolic Ministry from the Jewish elders,[1] and at the same

---

[1] "It seems certain upon the evidence that in these Jewish communities . . . there existed a governing body of elders, whose functions were partly administrative and partly disciplinary. With worship and teaching they appear to have had no direct concern. . . .

"The elders of the Jewish communities which had become Christian,

time denies that the Christian Priesthood had originally any concern with worship and teaching. We may fitly leave a theory so subversive of the fundamental conceptions and ideas of the Christian Ministry to refute itself, and we may safely turn from theory to fact. We may inquire briefly what influence the facts of the Levitical hierarchy and polity were likely to have upon the minds of the Apostles, without forgetting the all-important factor of the teaching they received from our Lord during the Great Forty Days. We may justly infer that our Lord, who "came not to destroy but to fulfil," would incorporate into the wider polity of the Catholic Church whatever leading ideas and principles of permanence might be embedded in the Church of the Old Covenant.

We note first of all that the Levitical hierarchy was of Divine appointment, and that the Aaronic priests were not merely delegates of the nation as "a kingdom of priests." This fact is emphasised by the writer of the Epistle to the Hebrews in the words, "No man taketh this honour" (*i.e.* the Apostolic Ministry) "unto himself, but he that is called of God, as was Aaron."[1] The Ministers of

were, like the elders of the Jewish communities which remained Jewish, officers of administration and discipline. The origin of the Presbyterate in those Christian communities which had been Jewish is thus natural and simple."—Hatch, *Bampton Lectures*, pp. 58-61.

[1] Heb. v. 4. See Note B.

the New Covenant, like the Ministers of the Old Covenant, are called of God, and are not called as delegates of the people. The representative character of the Apostolic and Aaronic priesthood is emphasised all the more clearly, because they were appointed *by God* to represent God to the people and the people to God.

The priesthood of the people was not permitted to usurp the functions of the divinely appointed priesthood either under the Old or the New Covenant. The usurpation of the functions of the Aaronic priesthood by Korah, and its punishment, showed that the Aaronic priesthood and the priesthood of the people were parallel facts, with a clear distinction between them. S. Jude's allusion to "the gainsaying of Korah"[1] shows that the same sin could be committed against the Apostolic priesthood as was formerly committed against the Aaronic priesthood, and that the wider and more glorious priesthood of the people under the New Covenant did not involve or permit any invasion of the special functions of the divinely appointed Threefold Apostolic Ministry.

The disciplinary distinction between the divinely appointed priesthood of ministry and sacrifice and the general priesthood of the people was thus

[1] S. Jude 11.

continued under the New Covenant as it was under the Old Covenant.

The Apostles were taught by our Lord to "render unto Cæsar the things that be Cæsar's, and unto God the things that be God's."[1] The Catholic Church was not to be subservient to secular governments in spiritual matters. This root-principle of true ecclesiastical life and order was not unfamiliar to the Apostles. It came from the heart of the Levitical polity. Uzzah's hand must not be laid on the Ark. King Uzziah is stricken with leprosy for usurping the priestly function, and Israel is taught that secular hands are not to be laid on things sacred. The principle of the separation of secular and sacred jurisdictions is laid down by Jehoshaphat: "And, behold, Amariah the chief priest is over you in all matters of the Lord; and Zebadiah the son of Ishmael, the ruler of the house of Judah, for all the king's matters."[2]

The Chief Priest's jurisdiction extended over the priests and the Levites who were more immediately in relation to his primacy, and in dealing with "the matters of the Lord" he had primarily to enforce discipline over his subordinates. The slackness of Eli's discipline over his sons, *as priests*, constituted the offence which was punished by the

---

[1] S. Matt. xxii. 22.   [2] 2 Chron. xix. 11.

removal of the honour of the priesthood from his branch of the house of Aaron. The ecclesiastical polity of the Old Covenant made Jerusalem a centre of spiritual discipline and organisation, as well as a centre of worship. The Apostles would have the lofty ideal of the City of God before them, "a joy of the whole earth," with a visible and well-disciplined organisation, fitted to wider purposes than that of the Jewish national Church in which they had been brought up—a kingdom of law and order, a true home of the liberty of Christ's freedmen, who are sheltered from the tyranny of evil by the very order and method and discipline which encompasses them as citizens of the Kingdom of Christ.

In dealing with the evidence of the New Testament upon the subject of the organisation of the Catholic Church, we must never lose sight of the fact that the Apostles were guided by our Lord's teaching during the Great Forty Days, concerning "the things pertaining to the kingdom of God."[1] It follows, therefore, that the indications we can trace of the beginnings of that jurisdiction, which

---

[1] Acts i. 3. "If the things which He spake were things pertaining to a kingdom, they must have been things pertaining to rule, to offices, to organisation, to means of transmission, as well as to matters pertaining to internal and spiritual religion."—Preb. Sadler, Comm. *in loc.*

The Apostles had received their previous training and discipline before the Crucifixion, as is graphically described in that book of original thought, *Pastor Pastorum* (Latham).

in after ages took more definite shape in the authority exercised by Patriarchs, Metropolitans, and Councils, must be considered as part and parcel of the constitutional organisation of the Church. When it is stated that Bishops are equal *iure divino,* and that the primacy exercised by Patriarchs and Metropolitans is only *iure ecclesiastico,* and therefore of less moment and authority, it is unwise to forget that *ius ecclesiasticum* has its origin in the regal power of Christ in His Church, and that the authority of Patriarch and Metropolitan is necessary to the orderly government of the kingdom of Christ.[1] It will not be necessary in these pages to discuss the Scriptural evidence for the Petrine claims, or the Vatican definitions of the *Petri privilegium* as inherent in the Roman See.

The fact that these claims are unsupported by Apostolic authority, Scriptural and historical evidence, and the general *consensus* of the teaching of the undivided Church, need not compel us to reject the idea of a *Primus inter pares* in the Apostolic College, or of a similar Primacy of Christendom, purged from the theories which found their expression in the false Decretals and the

---

[1] "All the twelve Apostles were equal in mission, equal in commission, equal in all things, *except priority of order, without which no society can well subsist.*"—Abp. Bramhall, *Just Vindication of the Church of England,* chap. v. pp. 152, 153.

"Priest-King" theory of Hildebrand and Innocent III.[1]

We may seem to be stating a truism, but sometimes truisms need stating and re-stating. The usual aim of the most Catholic-minded anti-Papal controversialists is to content themselves with the comparatively easy task of rebutting the Papal claims, and avoiding any constructive theory of polity upon which the corporate reunion of Christendom can be based. We hear little of the constant appeal of the Anglican Reformers to an unfettered Œcumenical Council, and very little practical effort is made to convince Catholics in communion with the See of Canterbury of the danger of their centrifugal tendencies. We do not incur the risk of admitting the Vatican doctrine of S. Peter's supremacy, in admitting to the full his Primacy of honour and order,[2] and in maintaining that the principle of such a Primacy

---

[1] "The Papacy is, as it were, the Eucharist of Christ's government in His Church."—Rivington, *Authority*, p. 21.

"Though we would grant the See of Rome her ancient Primacy, yet we cannot accept it as it is now offered, transformed into a *quasi*-sacramental Headship."—*Primary Charge of Bishop King*, p 28.

[2] The Vatican Decree condemns those who hold this Primacy of honour, and leaves no *via media* between Ultramontanism and Ultra-Protestantism. "If any one shall say that Blessed Peter the Apostle . . . received a Primacy of honour only . . . let him be anathema" (Vatican Decrees). If the arguments of the following pages seem to any to concede too much in the direction of a Petrine Primacy, it is satisfactory to know that the view here upheld lies under the anathema of the Vatican Council.

of Christendom does not conflict with the corporate rights of Bishops as the successors of the Apostles.

We pass by the controversy occasioned by our Lord's words to S. Peter in S. Matt. xvi. 17–19, S. Luke xxii. 31, 32, and S. John xxi. 15–17, save that we must deal briefly with the consequences which appear to have their origin in the words, "*tibi dabo claves,*" and in "the special pastoral charges" of the "*Pasce oves.*"[1]

The Primacy of S. Peter during our Lord's life on earth, as viewed in the light of the passages cited above, was necessarily confined to a personal prominence, and a priority in order as shown in the lists of the Apostles. We trace it in his speaking in their name, and in his association with S. James and S. John, as first amongst the chosen three. We naturally look into the dawn of Church history after the Day of Pentecost for the development of the Primacy of S. Peter, after our Lord's teaching during the Forty Days. What shape did it assume then?

(i.) In the interval between the Ascension and Pentecost he takes steps for the election of an Apostle to fill the vacancy in the Apostolic College

---

[1] S. Peter "holds the first place in all the lists; he has a precedence of responsibility and of temptation. . . . Above all, he receives special pastoral charges."—Bishop Lightfoot, *S. Clement*, p. 481. See also Note C.

left by Judas the traitor.[1] The method of the election is abnormal, but the procedure of S. Peter in notifying the vacancy and ordering the election, is in the main that which all Primates and Metropolitans follow at the present day. The narrative of Acts i., vers. 15, 21, 22, is the foundation of the Canon Law of Christendom which deals with the action of Primates and Metropolitans when Episcopal vacancies occur within their provinces.[2]

(ii.) He preaches the first Missionary Sermon on the Day of Pentecost, and thereby unlocks the door of the Catholic Church to the Jews, thus fulfilling in one sense our Lord's promise, *tibi dabo claves* (Acts ii. 14 and 28).

(iii.) He works the first miracle of the Church, at the gate of the Temple (Acts iii. 6).

---

[1] "Two persons appear to have been fixed, under the direction of S. Peter, by the assembled believers, of whom one was chosen to the Apostolate by God through the casting of lots. The person so chosen was admitted into the Apostolical College—by what process is not stated in detail. Our translation states that he 'was numbered with the eleven Apostles.' The Greek appears to imply considerably more; it is συγκατεψηφίσθη."—Gladstone, *Ch. Principles*, v. p. 209.

[2] The Primate or Metropolitan issues the mandate to the vacant Diocese to elect a godly priest as their Bishop, and with his com-provincial Bishops confirms the election, and consecrates the Bishop-elect. This procedure is followed by the unestablished and disestablished Churches in communion with Canterbury. See Irish Church (Const. cap. vi.), Scottish Church (Canon iii.), American Church (Canon xix.), South African Church (Canon iii.), Australian Church (General Synod Determ. i.), Church of New Zealand (Canon i.), Church of West Indies (Canons iii. and v.), Canada (Province of Rupertsland, Canon vi.), and compare the procedure laid down with its foundation in Canon iv. (Conc. Nicæn.).

(iv.) He again preaches to the Jews as the leader of the Apostles (Acts iii. 12).

(v.) When he is summoned before the Sanhedrin with S. John he speaks officially for the whole Church (Acts iv. 8).

(vi.) He exercises coercive jurisdiction as the *Primus inter pares* of the Apostolic College in the case of Ananias and Sapphira.[1] It is not quite legitimate to parallel this judgment of S. Peter's, which was exercised on offending Christians, with S. Paul's denunciation of Elymas the sorcerer, who was outside the pale of the Church. Both judgments were followed by direct supernatural penalties, but there is a difference of a very distinct kind between them. One was an exercise of ecclesiastical discipline, in which solemn sentence is pronounced by the Primate Apostle, with the result that "great fear came upon the whole Church" (Acts v. 11). The other was the outward and manifest victory of the true religion in the person of S. Paul over the false religion in the person of the Magian impostor. Both S. Paul and the Magian were endeavouring to gain the ear of Sergius Paulus. The true parallel here is the rivalry between Moses and the Court-magicians of

---

[1] "After the first gift of grace comes the first visitation of anger in the punishment of Ananias and Sapphira. Peter asserts his Primacy here also, and the guilt is punished."—Bishop Lightfoot, *S. Clement*, vol. ii. p. 489.

Pharaoh, and not the solemn ecclesiastical judgment of S. Peter in the case of Ananias and Sapphira, or his subsequent judgment on Simon Magus.

(vii.) S. Peter is for the second time the spokesman and representative of the Church before the Sanhedrin (Acts v. 29).

(viii.) He opens the door of the Church to the Gentiles, and for the second time exercises the prerogative of the promise *tibi dabo claves* (Acts x. 34–48).

(ix.) He sums up the debate in the Council of Jerusalem, and S. James, as Bishop of Jerusalem, and, in that capacity, President of the Council, refers to S. Peter's words as the basis of his judgment and of the decree of the Council (Acts xv. 7–25).

(x.) S. Paul, at the beginning of his ministry, went up to Jerusalem "to visit Cephas" (ἱστορῆσαι Κηφᾶν), ἱστορῆσαι is somewhat emphatic. "A word used," says Chrysostom, "by those who go to see great and famous cities" (Lightfoot in Gal. i. 18).[1]

S. Paul acknowledged no Primacy of infallible authority in S. Peter. The relations of S. Paul to S. Peter at Antioch (κατὰ πρόσωπον αὐτῷ ἀντέστην,

---

[1] ἱστορέω τινά = *personam aliquem insignem coram cognosco, de facie.* Grimm, *N. T. Clavis*, p. 211. "Paul says he went up to see Peter (evidently regarding him as the leading spirit in the development of the Church)."—Ramsay, *S. Paul the Traveller*, p. 381.

Gal. ii. 11) are enough to cause reasonable theologians to reject the Papal theory of the Petrine claims.

But this passage shows that S. Paul visited S. Peter officially as the Primate Apostle. It makes for the Patriarchal and Metropolitical authority of the *Primus inter pares*, just as much as the episode at Antioch makes against the Hildebrandine view of the Papacy.

(xi.) We find S. Peter exercising a Primate's duty in visiting the Churches. "Peter passed through all quarters" (Πέτρον διερχόμενον διὰ πάντων), Acts ix. 32. No one can accuse Professor Ramsay of viewing the Apostolic age from a purely ecclesiastical standpoint. Yet he traces in this passage the leadership of S. Peter,[1] and infers that this leadership is also to be traced in the journey of S. Peter and S. John to Samaria for the purpose of ministering Confirmation to the Samaritan converts of S. Philip the Deacon. This mission of S. Peter and S. John to Samaria has been utilised by Anti-Papal controversialists in a fashion which, to say the least, is strained. It may be perfectly true that we cannot imagine the College of Cardinals sending Pope Leo XIII. and Cardinal

[1] "It appears from *Acts* that Peter was the leading spirit in these journeys of organisation, which knit together the scattered congregations in Judæa and Samaria."—Professor Ramsay, *S. Paul the Traveller*, p. 42.

Vaughan on a mission to America, for instance, to deal with some question of importance.¹ But although the mission to Samaria is conclusive as an argument against the Petrine *monarchy*, it is no argument against the Petrine *primacy*, when its issues are considered at their true value. Once more we may be permitted to remark that the worst way to combat the un-Catholic and unscriptural *Petri privilegium* is to ignore the Scriptural witness for Primatial authority in the Apostolic age. The mission to Samaria was a momentous departure. Hitherto the Church had been a purely Jewish community, which superadded the doctrines of Christ to a strict adherence to the Temple worship and Mosaic ritual.

Was the Church to expand into the Catholic ideal of Pentecost, or was it to remain a Jewish sect rigidly centred upon the Temple worship at Jerusalem?² The Hellenist pressure had already

---

[1] "That the subject Apostles should send their supreme Pontiff and also one of their fellow-subjects on a joint mission—that is incredible."—Puller, *Primitive Saints and the See of Rome*, p. 117.

[2] The Primitive Church had clung to Jerusalem, and lived there in a state of simplicity and almost community of goods, which was an interesting phase of society, but was quite opposed to the spirit in which Jesus said, "Go ye into all the world and preach the Gospel to the whole creation." For the time it seemed that the religion of Christ was stagnating into a sociological experiment (Ramsay, *St. Paul the Traveller*, p. 41). This view is substantially true, although a modification of it is strongly urged by Mr. Simcox (*Early Church History*, p. 6).

caused the choice and ordination of the seven Deacons. The teaching of the Archdeacon S. Stephen (to adopt a later nomenclature) was the first assault upon the idea that the Catholic Church should be permanently fettered with Jewish swaddling clothes. The persecution after his martyrdom scattered abroad the Christians of Jerusalem, who "went everywhere preaching the Word" (Acts viii. 4). The Hellenist Deacon S. Philip was unfettered by the narrow traditional hatred which severed Jew and Samaritan. The Samaritan received the Gospel of Christ. The news must have been a shock to the innate prejudice of the Church at Jerusalem.

Here was the parting of the ways, so soon to be emphasised still further by the baptism of Cornelius and the final decision of the Council of Jerusalem in favour of Gentile liberty and co-equality with the Jew in the Catholic Church. We cannot imagine that this crisis did not cause anxious debate amongst the Apostles at Jerusalem. S. Peter, as *primus inter pares*, would naturally advocate the ratification of S. Philip's work in Samaria in the most formal and authoritative manner possible. The most natural course was adopted. S. Peter and the Apostles decided that the mission to Samaria was so important that the Primate Apostle should undertake it himself, and that he should be accompanied by S. John, as the next available in Apostolic rank, since the local episcopate of Jerusalem belonged to S. James, who was therefore stationary.[1]

It is safe to say, without risking anachronism, that the position of S. James at Jerusalem was the Apostolic prototype of the monarchical and localised episcopate which we find in the Ignatian Epistles.[2]

There was, however, another far-reaching consequence of the martyrdom of S. Stephen besides the conversion of the Samaritans. Some of the scattered Christians, "men of Cyprus and Cyrene," came to Antioch and taught the Gentile Greeks the

---

[1] It is thoroughly in accord with the idea of the Primatial and Metropolitical Office that the Bishops of a Province should request their Metropolitan to undertake a special office or mission of importance, and that he should associate one of their number with himself by their consent.

[2] The position of S. James in the Clementine romance, which may be dated at the end of the second century (according to Dr. Salmon, or even earlier, in Bishop Lightfoot's opinion), is undoubtedly that of Primate of Christendom. The Clementine Recognitions and Homilies are Ebionite in their doctrinal tone, and their author naturally insists on the Primacy of S. James and the Church of Jerusalem. The position of S. Peter is secondary. He has to send to S. James his Discourses and his Acts year by year. (Clem., *Homilies*, i. 20, and *Recognitions*, i. 72.) But it is possible that the Epistle of Clement to S. James, which gives an account of S. Clement's succession to S. Peter after the Apostle's martyrdom, may be dated as early as A.D. 220, and it may represent a tradition of S. James's Primacy as a natural sequence of events, since the writer of the supposed letter believed that S. James survived S. Peter. In this case the address to S. James as "Bishop of Bishops" is natural enough, although we believe that the tradition of S. James's Primacy is historically incorrect, since he was martyred before S. Peter and S. Paul.

Gospel of Christ.[1] The Apostolic Church at Jerusalem heard of this influx of Gentiles into the Church, and sent S. Barnabas (and subsequently S. Paul was summoned from Tarsus by him to aid in the growing work), the result of which action was that the Gentile Church of Antioch speedily almost rivalled in importance and influence the Mother Church at Jerusalem. Christendom then was divided into the Mother Diocese of Jewish Christians which had extended throughout all Judæa, and Galilee and Samaria,[2] and the Gentile Diocese of Antioch, which had outgrown its Jewish foundation. The primary question was to blend Jew and Gentile into one Catholic Church. We must not, however, pass by the very weighty tradition which is linked with the festival of the "Cathedra Petri" at Antioch.

S. Jerome considers that S. Luke's account of the Church in Antioch omits the previous planting of it in that city by S. Peter.[3] His authority is late, but he represents one of the firmest and most positively asserted traditions of Ecclesiastical History. The

---

[1] Acts xi. 20.   [2] Acts ix. 31.
[3] "Primum Episcopum Antiochenæ Ecclesiæ Petrum fuisse eumque Romæ translatum." (S. Jerome, Comm. in Gal. ii.) The Eusebian Chronicle makes the same statement. Πέτρος ὁ κορυφαῖος τὴν ἐν Ἀντιοχείᾳ πρῶτον θεμελιώσας ἐκκλησίαν. So also Euseb., H. E. iii. 34. We may note (without giving undue weight to its authority) that the Paschal Chronicle says :—τετάρτῳ ἔτει τῆς εἰς οὐρανοὺς ἀναλήψεως τοῦ Κυρίου, Πέτρος ὁ Ἀπόστολος ἀπὸ Ἱεροσολύμων ἐν Ἀντιοχείᾳ τῇ μεγάλῃ τὸν λόγον τοῦ Θεοῦ ἐδίδασκεν.

probable solution is that S. Peter founded the Church of the Jewish Christians in Antioch about four years after the Ascension, before " the men of Cyprus and Cyrene" had begun their mission to the Gentiles. This view will help to account for S. Peter's temporising with the Judaisers at Antioch. If he was the founder of their Church, and had been subsequently convinced by the baptism of Cornelius, and by other events, that the Church was destined to be Catholic and not merely Jewish, Antioch was the very place where he might be tempted to make concessions to the prejudices of those whom he had taught, before he had himself grasped the full consequences of the world-wide character of the religion of Christ. It has been recently held that this temporising of S. Peter and its rebuke by S. Paul may have taken place before the Council of Jerusalem.[1] This view is antecedently probable, and it seems difficult to believe that S. Peter would have acted in such a manner *after* the Council of Jerusalem. With regard to the bearing of that Council upon S. Peter's position, we may safely say that it does not militate against his Primacy, whilst it is conclusive against his Supremacy in the Vatican sense.

Whilst avoiding the anachronism of a local Primacy, which was an after-development of the

---

[1] Professor Ramsay, *S. Paul the Traveller*, p. 164.

subsequent local and territorial Episcopate, we may once more safely say that the Church, at the era of the Council of Jerusalem, may be roughly considered as consisting of the Mother Diocese of Jerusalem, where the beginnings of a local Episcopate are discerned in the position of S. James, and the Gentile Diocese of Antioch, which had expanded out of the local Jewish Church founded by S. Peter. The Primacy of S. Peter would be unquestioned at both centres. His leadership was needed to keep them from drifting apart. We may well believe that the organising genius of S. Paul saw that a Council was necessary to keep the Jewish and Gentile Christians in the unity of the One Flock and the One Shepherd.

If we accept the sequence of events which sets his resistance to the temporising policy of S. Peter before the Council of Jerusalem, we find that S. Peter's strong words on the side of freedom may be in some measure traced to the influence of S. Paul. The position of S. Peter as *primus inter pares* is in no way minimised by S. Paul's action at Antioch. A strong Bishop may at any time influence the policy of his Primate, and even overshadow him, as Laud, when Bishop of London, overshadowed by his commanding influence the last days of Abbot's Primacy.

When we deal with the action of the Council itself, we find the Primacy of S. Peter clearly in evidence. After much discussion, in which the Judaisers must have put forward their whole case, S. Peter intervenes with Primatial authority and decisive argument. He sets before the Council the plea which S. Paul had used to him at Antioch. S. Paul had pointed out that it was inconsistent in him to allow the Judaisers to force their law upon the Gentiles, whilst he himself, though a Jew, used his Christian liberty.[1] S. Peter tells the Council that the Church had no right to impose on Gentile Christians a yoke of ceremonial observances "which neither we, the Jewish Christians, nor our fathers were able to bear."[2] In his address S. Peter asserts his Primacy, by reminding the Council that "God made choice among you, that by *my mouth* the Gentiles should hear the word of the Gospel."[3] Then came the testimony of S. Barnabas and S. Paul, who were filled with the fresh experiences of the first great Missionary Journey.

And lastly we find S. James, as the local Head of the Mother Church at Jerusalem, pronouncing the formal judgment of the Council, and basing that judgment upon the previous words of S. Peter.[4]

---

[1] Gal. ii. 14.   [2] Acts xv. 10.   [3] Ibid. v. 7.
[4] Πέτρος δημηγορεῖ, ἀλλ' Ἰάκωβος νομοθετεῖ. S. Hesychius. Migne, *Patrol. Græc.* xciii. 1480. These words do not mean that S. James

It will be noted that the decree ran in the name of the Apostles and elders and brethren,[1] and not in the name of the Bishop of Jerusalem alone, as subsequent custom might lead us to expect, if the Council had been merely the Synod of one Diocese.

A recently published view of the Council goes so far as to deny that S. James was actually its President.[2] But whilst we have the narrative as it stands, we do not feel it possible to disturb the conclusion we have adopted, even on the authority of a name so weighty. But we note the view taken by Dr. Hort as conclusive against the airy confidence with which another writer has said that "the Council was to have been a pre-

legislated as Primate, and can be reconciled with the view we have taken.

[1] Acts xv. 23. The reading καὶ οἱ ἀδελφοί will be briefly considered in Note D.

[2] In his chapter on "The Apostles in relation to the Ecclesia," Dr. Hort comments as follows upon Acts xv. :—

"There is nothing in St. Luke's words which bears out what is often said that St. James presided over the conference at Jerusalem. If he had it is strange that his name should not be mentioned separately at the beginning, where we read only that the Apostles and elders were gathered together. In the decisive speeches at the end, the lead is taken by St. Peter, the foremost of the twelve. After Barnabas and Paul have ended their narrative, James takes up the word. . . . Then again the words which begin his conclusion, 'Wherefore my judgment is' cannot reasonably be understood as an authoritative judgment pronounced by himself independently. . . . It is just the same afterwards, the decision is said to be made by the Apostles and the elders with the whole Ecclesia."—*The Christian Ecclesia*, by F. J. A. Hort, D.D. (Macmillan).

cedent (on a small scale) for that of Nicæa; it was turned into a precedent for that of the Vatican —only we must remember that it was S. James who was Pope; S. Peter was no more than a liberal Cardinal."[1] We may safely conclude that the Council of Jerusalem is a witness to the historic Primacy of S. Peter, whom Dr. Hort unhesitatingly calls "the foremost of the Twelve."

The silence of the historian of the Acts concerning S. Peter's doings after the Council of Jerusalem does not involve the extinction of his Primacy, or the substitution of the Primacy of S. Paul for that of S. Peter. S. Luke centres his narrative in its later stages exclusively upon the lifework of S. Paul, but this does not countenance the theory of an effacement of S. Peter's Primacy. It is hard to accept a theory of this nature, when the fact of S. Peter's residence in Rome is considered, and its outcome as manifested in the tone and character of his first General Epistle. There are good reasons for believing that S. Peter survived S. Paul,[2] and lived at Rome some ten or twelve

---

[1] Simcox, *Early Church History*, p. 85. The Primacy of S. Peter is no more jeopardised by the position of S. James at the Council of Jerusalem, than the Primacy of Pope Anastasius was by the decree of the Council of Turin in A.D. 401, on the Ithacian schismatics who were to be reconciled on the terms set forth in "the former letters of Ambrose of blessed memory, and of the Bishop of the Roman Church." (*Concilia*, ii. 1383, ed. Coleti.) Here Milan comes before Rome in the decree of a Council of the Province of Milan.

[2] Dr. Hatch is not inclined to give undue weight to ecclesiastical

years after the martyrdom of the Apostle of the Gentiles, which we may date in A.D. 67.[1] But we must note some events which took place during the closing years of the life of S. Paul. The death of Festus, and consequent temporary vacancy of the Procuratorship, gave an opportunity to Hanan to bring S. James, the Bishop of Jerusalem, before the Sanhedrin, and according to Josephus, he was condemned to death by stoning.[2] He was succeeded by Symeon the son of Clopas, and during the interval between the first and second imprisonments of S. Paul, the Episcopate received a further addition by the consecration of S. Timothy

traditions. Yet he is inclined to accept the hypothesis of a long residence of S. Peter at Rome on account of the strength of traditional evidence; for he says, " It is difficult to suppose that so large a body of tradition has no foundation in fact." "Hatch on S. Peter," in *Encyclopædia Britannica*.

[1] Dr. M'Giffert, a modern Protestant writer, goes so far as to say that though "in the light of such early and unanimous testimony it may be regarded as an established fact that Peter visited Rome, it is equally certain that he cannot have gone there during Paul's lifetime. . . . And yet a somewhat prolonged residence and activity in Rome seems to be imperatively demanded by the traditions of the Roman Church, and by the universal recognition which was later given to the claim of that Church to be the see of Peter. It is true that there is no single witness to whom we can appeal with any degree of confidence, and it is true, moreover, that the tradition of a twenty-five years' episcopate is worthless. But the honour in which Peter's memory was universally held by the Christians of Rome, and the way in which his figure overshadowed that of Paul, can hardly be explained on merely dogmatic grounds. Nothing less than his leadership and personal domination in the Roman Church can account for the result."—Dr. M'Giffert's *History of Christianity in the Apostolic Age*, p. 591.

[2] The account of the martyrdom of S. James by Hegesippus (*apud*

as Bishop of Ephesus and S. Titus as Bishop of Crete. We do not mean to imply that S. Paul consecrated S. Timothy or S. Titus to the position of the Diocesan Bishops of the Ignatian age.[1] They may rather be considered as Apostolic delegates with Primatial jurisdiction, who moved from place to place, like the "Prophets" in the Διδαχή, while we may consider that S. John, in subsequent years, established Diocesan Episcopacy (in the Ignatian sense) in the Churches of Asia Minor. The Apostles, at the death of S. James, may have taken common measures to establish "the first-fruits of their ministry" as Diocesan Bishops. It is at least probable that they met in a second Apostolic Council to concert this measure.[2] But

Euseb. ii. 23), seems to show that he received the Ebionite and ascetic view of the life and character of the first Bishop of Jerusalem. His account of the martyrdom of S. James by stoning is confirmed by Josephus : καὶ παραγαγὼν εἰς αὐτοὺς τὸν ἀδελφὸν Ἰησοῦ τοῦ Χριστοῦ λεγομένου, Ἰάκωβος ὄνομα αὐτῷ, καί τινας ἑτέρους, ὡς παρανομησάντων κατηγορίαν ποιησάμενος, παρέδωκε λευσθησομένους. [Jos. *Ant.* xx. 9. 1.] Hegesippus regards the martyrdom of S. James as the immediate cause of the siege of Jerusalem. Origen says, ταῦτα δὲ συμβέβηκεν Ἰουδαίοις, καὶ ἐκδίκησιν Ἰακώβου τοῦ δικαίου. κ.τ.λ. (*Contra Celsum*, i. 47).

[1] "But though it may be thought an anachronism, and even a misleading one, to call them bishops, it seems plain that they were in the fullest sense vicars—that they were intended to be successors—of the Apostles."—Simcox, *Early Church History*, p. 129.

S. Timothy and S. Titus "respectively were stationed to act as the delegates of S. Paul in Ephesus and in Crete."—Gladstone, *Church Principles*, p. 213.

[2] The idea of a second Apostolic Council is partly based by Rothe upon his rendering of καὶ μεταξὺ ἐπινομὴν δεδώκασιν (Clem. Rom. *Ad Cor.* xliv.), "afterwards added a supplementary direction." The recent

the condition of the Church at the death of S. Paul seems to have been somewhat as follows :—
S. Peter, the Primate Apostle, lived at Rome with S. Mark as his "interpreter" for the Latin language.[1] The Church at Jerusalem under Symeon lost its

discovery of an eleventh century Latin MS. of a clearly primitive translation by Dom Morin strengthens Rothe's rendering. The Latin for ἐπινομὴν δεδώκασιν is *legem dederunt*. Bishop Lightfoot reads ἐπιμονήν = gave permanence to the office. But there is no MS. authority for this, and the sense of the passage does not suffer whichever view is taken. It is difficult to avoid seeing in the phrase "*prospiciente concilio*" of the Ambrosian Hilary (on Eph. iv. 12) an allusion to a second Apostolic Council. Rothe holds that the Council of the Apostles, which appointed Symeon to succeed S. James as Bishop of Jerusalem, "discussed larger questions than the appointment of a single Bishop, and that the constitution and prospects of the Church generally came under deliberation. . . . The centre of the system then organised was episcopacy, which at once secured the compact and harmonious working of each individual congregation, and as the link of communication between separate brotherhoods formed the whole into one undivided Catholic Church" (*Anfänge*, &c., pp. 354-392). We have quoted Bishop Lightfoot's paraphrase of Rothe's view, and since the Bishop does not adopt his theory, we may with more readiness accept his statement of it. If we reduce Rothe's theory to the establishment of a *local* Episcopate, we may very well accept it. We have already seen that the Primatial system, as well as the Episcopate, existed in germ in the Apostolic Age. We may very well believe that the idea of localised Primacies and Bishoprics emanated from Apostolic decision and direction.

[1] Μάρκος μὲν ἑρμηνευτὴς Πέτρου γενόμενος, ὅσα ἐμνημόνευσεν, ἀκριβῶς ἔγραψεν, οὐ μέντοι τάξει τὰ ὑπὸ τοῦ Χριστοῦ ἢ λεχθέντα ἢ πραχθέντα.— Papias, *Routh Rel. Sacr.* i. 13.

Even De Pressensé, writing from a strong Protestant standpoint, feels bound to admit that S. Peter resided at Rome. "The unanimity of tradition as to Peter's stay at Rome appears to us of weight. It is so much the more worthy of credence because several of the Fathers— for example, Tertullian and Irenæus—had no interest in establishing the Primacy of the Bishop of Rome."—*Early Years of Christianity*, vol. i., p. 214.

pre-eminence owing to the Jewish war, which was to end in the fall of Jerusalem and the destruction of the Temple in A.D. 70. S. John was organising and ruling the Church in Asia Minor, aided probably by S. Andrew and S. Philip, whose name is linked with Hierapolis[1] with some measure of certainty. The Neronian persecution, of which S. Paul was the most illustrious victim, seems to have been a localised outburst of hatred, organised by Nero and his courtiers to divert suspicion from himself as the real incendiary who caused the great fire at Rome. The attitude of the Flavian emperors was a policy deliberately hostile to all who confessed "the Name" of Christ, and struck deeper than Nero's savage attack upon an obscure and unpopular Jewish sect known as "Christians."

The First General Epistle of S. Peter seems to have been written under the pressure of the Flavian policy, and mainly on this account we postulate for it a later date than is commonly assigned to it.[2] It is addressed to the Gentile

---

[1] τὸ μὲν οὖν κατὰ τὴν Ἱεράπολιν Φίλιππον τὸν ἀπόστολον ἅμα ταῖς θυγατράσι διατρῖψαι. κ.τ.λ. (Euseb. iii. 39).

[2] The difference between the Neronian and Flavian policy may be briefly summed up as follows:—Nero persecuted the Christians for certain specified offences against Roman society (*odium humani generis*). Tacitus (*Ann.* xv. 44) gives an account of Nero's action, and the Christians were tried for serious offences connected with "the Name of Christ" (*flagitia cohærentia nomini*). Pliny's letter to Trajan and his reply show that the Flavian policy which Trajan continued was more thorough. Offences need not be proved. The mere acknowledgment

Churches of Asia Minor, and it is written from Rome.[1] The traces of his Roman residence are manifest from S. Peter's line of thought, and the general tone of this Epistle. It is virtually addressed to the Catholic Church as a whole, and it shows that the fisherman of Galilee has risen to the conception of the Church as a spiritual empire. Persecution for the name of Christ threatens the whole Church, and the Primate Apostle sets the spiritual empire of "the strangers and pilgrims," who are yet "the chosen generation" and the "royal priesthood," in battle array against the hostile world-empire of Imperial Rome. And then, in his Second Epistle, written shortly after the first, we find S. Peter calmly awaiting his inevitable martyrdom.

After the martyrdom of S. Peter, which we venture to date about A.D. 85,[2] S. John became the Primate

of the "Name" is a crime against the State. S. Peter's First Epistle points to this latter policy being in force when he wrote. Professor Ramsay's main reason for a later date for S. Peter's First Epistle is based upon this specific difference between the Neronian and Flavian policies. It is right to add that Professor Ramsay's view has been opposed by Dr. Sanday and Professor Mommsen. But there are other reasons for believing in a later date for this Epistle, based upon the uniform tradition of S. Peter's residence at Rome for a period of some length, as well as upon the internal evidence of the Epistle itself.

[1] The idea that S. Peter wrote from the literal Babylon is most conclusively disposed of by Bishop Lightfoot. (*S. Clement*, vol. ii. p. 492.)

"It is far advanced on the path that leads to the letter of Clement to the Corinthians."—Ramsay, *Church in Roman Empire*, p. 287.

[2] S. Clement mentions S. Peter and S. Paul as having suffered

Apostle by virtue of the pre-eminence accorded to him in the Gospels and Acts, even if other Apostles still survived. Before long he became the sole survivor of the Apostles, and personally guided the transition of the government of the Church from the Apostolate to the localised territorial Episcopate. An attempt has been made to deny the Johannine authorship of the Fourth Gospel upon the grounds that its author desires to present S. John as the victorious rival of S. Peter. An examination of the Gospel of S. John from this point of view is enough to refute this baseless theory.[1]

The principle of Primatial order and authority is clearly traceable during the Apostolic age.[2] We shall trace its development, subsequent to the

martyrdom (*Ad Cor.* c. iv.). But there is no reason for inferring from this reference the truth of the later tradition that they suffered at the same time. S. Clement, if we accept the theory that he was ordained by S. Peter, would naturally mention him first, and even if we reject this theory of S. Clement's ordination as Bishop, the Scriptural priority of order, and its outcome, would naturally lead him to mention S. Peter first. Dionysius of Corinth writes of S. Peter and S. Paul visiting Corinth and Rome "and having taught there suffered martyrdom," κατὰ τὸν αὐτὸν καιρόν (Euseb., *H. E.* ii. 25). But Bishop Lightfoot justly observes that "the expression κατὰ τὸν αὐτὸν καιρόν need not be pressed to mean the same day or the same year." The arguments of Professor Ramsay with regard to the internal evidence of 1 Peter demanding a much later date than is usually attributed to it are convincing. (*Church in the Roman Empire*, p. 284.)

[1] "The representative official precedence of S. Peter thus really underlies the whole narrative of the Fourth Gospel. The nearness of S. John to the Lord is a relation of sympathy, so to speak, different in kind."—Bishop Westcott, *S. John* (Introduction, p. xxiii.).

[2] See Note E.

death of S. John (A.D. 100), and the further relations of Bishops to their clergy and the laity in the Sub-Apostolic Age.

NOTE A.

The Mosaic Polity and Ritual finds fulfilment in the Catholic Church.

When, in process of time, the clergy adopted distinctive vestments at all times of their ministration, it is interesting to note that liturgical writers drew a parallel between the vestments of the Aaronic priesthood and those used by the Apostolic ministry. The principle of symbolism in worship has passed from the Old Covenant to the New, and reverence is preserved by the stately solemnity of the ritual of the Church. A thoughtful theologian, writing of the Apocalypse, states that "its description of things above is plainly a vision of the same truth which, in the Epistle to the Hebrews, is set forth argumentatively, that the whole Jewish ritual was an *example and shadow of heavenly things* (Heb. viii. 5). [Wilberforce *On the Incarnation*, p. 256.] "According to the mind of ancient expositors (on Heb. x. 1) the word σκιά would best be rendered here by *sketch* or *outline* (and not *shadow*), and the word εἰκών by *picture* (not *image*). There are three things considered here—i. The *reality* of the *future* good things in *Heaven* and in *Eternity;* ii. The εἰκών, or clear picture of them *in the Gospel;* iii. The σκιά, or dim outline of them *in the Law. Umbra in Lege; Imago in Evangelio; Veritas in cœlo.* (S. Ambrose on Ps. xxxviii.) Bishop Wordsworth *in loc.*

So S. Chrysostom : "Ἕως μὲν γὰρ ἂν ὡς ἐν γραφῇ περιάγῃ τις τὰ χρώματα, σκιά τίς ἐστιν. ὅταν δὲ τὸ ἄνθος ἐπαλείψῃ τις, καὶ ἐπιχρίσῃ τὰ χρώματα τότε ἐικὼν γίνεται. Τοιοῦτόν τι καὶ ὁ νόμος ἦν. (Hom. xvii. on Heb. x.)

Theodoret, Theophylact, and Œcumenius comment on the same text in the same sense.

S. Ambrose applies the same idea to the memorial Sacrifice of the Holy Eucharist. "Umbra in Lege, imago in Evangelio, veritas in cœlestibus. Ante agnus offerebatur, offerebatur et vitulus, nunc Christus offertur : sed offertur quasi homo, quasi recipiens passionem ; et offert se ipse quasi sacerdos, ut peccata nostra dimittat ; hic in imagine, ibi in veritate, ubi apud Patrem pro nobis quasi advocatus intervenit." (*De Officiis Ministrorum*, I. xlviii.)

The *outline* of the Law, glorious even when its distinctive ritual is administered by "the ministers of condemnation," is exceeded in glory by the bright colours of the full *picture* of the Gospel, which "the ministers of righteousness" administer. (*Cf.* 2 Cor. iii. 9.)

The principle here laid down is clearly expressed by Walafrid Strabo in the ninth century, in dealing with the Vestments. "Statutum est Concilio Bracarensi ; ne sacerdos sine orario celebret missam. Addiderunt in vestibus sacris alii alia, vel ad imitationem eorum quibus veteres utebantur sacerdotes, vel ad mysticæ significationis expressionem. Quid enim singula designent, quibus utimur nunc, a prioribus nostris satis expositum est. Numero autem suo antiquis respondent : quia sicut ibi tunica, superhumeralis linea, superhumerale, rationale, balteus, feminalia, tiara et lamina, sic hic dalmatica, alba, mappula, orarium, cingulum, sandalia, casula, et pallium. Unde sicut illorum extremo soli pontifices, sic horum ultimo summi tantum pastores utuntur." (*De Rebus Ecclesiasticis*, cap. xxiv.)

So, too, Ivo of Chartres, a twelfth-century writer: "Iste autem sacrarum vestium ritus per Moysen sumpsit exordium; quamvis Christiana religio plus intenta rebus quam figuris, sacerdotes suos non omnibus illis veteribus induit ornamentis." (*Sermo de significationibus indumentorum sacerdotalium*, &c.; Migne, Patrol. Lat. clxii. p. 520.)

NOTE B.

The Levitical Ministry not the Delegates of the People.

It is contrary to the primary sense of the Old Testament teaching to consider the Aaronic priests as the delegates of the people, for their *representative* ministry was derived from God, and their priestly functions involved far more than mere delegation. The view that they were delegates is apparently based on a single passage, where it is said that "the children of Israel shall put their hands on the Levites" (Numb. viii. 10). Commenting upon this text, Bishop Lightfoot says that "the Levites are, so to speak, ordained by the whole congregation. The nation thus deputes to a single tribe the priestly functions which belong to itself as a whole." (*Dissertation on the Christian Ministry*, p. 182.)

But, *pace tanti viri*, we may be permitted to remark that though Israel is called a nation of priests, it is inaccurate to say that "priestly functions" belong to the whole congregation. The priesthood of the whole nation finds its expression and direct representation in the "priestly functions" discharged by Aaron and his successors. The *Levites* discharged no "priestly functions," and even if we admit that the action of the congregation in laying hands on the Levites involved some sort of delegation, it can, at the most, have meant that the Levites discharged their special subordinate ministries as representing the people. God vindicated the Divine appointment of His priests by His judgment upon those who assumed that the priesthood of the nation could be manifested by self-appointed individuals. "There came out a fire from the Lord, and consumed the two hundred and fifty men that offered incense. The censers of these sinners against their own souls were made broad plates for a covering of the altar: to be a memorial to the children of Israel that no stranger, which is not of the seed of Aaron, come near to offer incense before the Lord; that he be not as Korah, and as his company." (Numb. xvi. 35, 38, 39, 40.)

The parallel truths of the general priesthood of the people (under the Old and New Covenant alike), and the special and representative priesthood, appointed by God to discharge "priestly functions," are alike to be accepted as a part of the Divine Revelation.

NOTE C.

The Primacy of S. Peter.

The "Pasce Oves" may very reasonably be interpreted as a charge given to the Primate Apostle, as the representative of the other Apostles, and the symbol of the unity of the Church. Bishop Moberly says of S. Peter: "Though his fall was great—greater than that of all who forsook their Lord and fled—yet was his restoration great too; for he was again chosen of them all to be the one to receive, as representing all, the great Pastoral Commission." (*Discourses on the Great Forty Days*, p. 190.)

The same idea pervades the well-known passage of S. Cyprian in his Treatise on the Unity of the Church:—

"Super unum ædificat ecclesiam, et quamvis apostolis omnibus post resurrectionem suam parem potestatem tribuat . . . tamen ut unitatem manifestaret, unitatis eiusdem originem ab uno incipientem sua auctoritate disposuit. Hoc erant utique et cæteri Apostoli quod fuit Petrus, pari consortio præditi, et honoris et potestatis, sed exordium ab unitate proficiscitur, ut ecclesia Christi una monstretur." (*De Unit. Eccl.*, 4, p. 212, ed. Hartel.)

Bishop Lightfoot has noted the later interpolations of this passage (*S. Clement*, p. 485). But we are not now concerned with anti-Papal arguments, so that it is not necessary to deal with the interpolations. We content ourselves with quoting the genuine text of S. Cyprian, and illustrating it with the following words of Archbishop Benson :—

"The Divine reality of such their unity had been taught especially in the respective charges of the Lord to Peter and to the Twelve. The authority and power committed is the same to each several Apostle. But for the sake of showing that many Apostles did not make many Churches, but one only, therefore the first declaration of the foundation of a Universal Church is couched in language addressed to one only—S. Peter. For that one occasion the words are to one, but the meaning is for ever to all." (*S. Cyprian, His Life, His Times, His Work*, by E. W. Benson, D.D., late Archbishop of Canterbury, p. 196.)

Archbishop Benson was firmly impressed by the power and Primatial position of the Throne of S. Augustine, which he so worthily filled. If his words do not directly involve the idea that Patriarchal and Primatial authority is as necessary to the unity of the Church now as it was in the Primitive Church, they certainly tend in that direction. The many Anglican authorities who admit to the full the Primacy of S. Peter, do not see with equal clearness that the principles involved therein are necessary to Church unity in every Province and in every Patriarchate of the Catholic Church.

NOTE D.
The reading καὶ οἱ ἀδελφοί.

The Textus Receptus has the reading οἱ ἀπόστολοι καὶ οἱ πρεσβύτεροι καὶ οἱ ἀδελφοί. Westcott and Hort, and the R.V., omit καὶ οἱ before ἀδελφοί, and Professor Ramsay accepts as probable Dr. Blass's theory that the word ἀδελφοί is an accidental corruption. We cannot follow this view. The consent of "the whole Church" to the decree of the Council is clearly expressed in Acts xv. 22. (Τότε ἔδοξε τοῖς ἀποστόλοις καὶ τοῖς πρεσβυτέροις σὺν ὅλῃ τῇ ἐκκλησίᾳ.)[1]

The consent of "the whole Church" is a subsequent necessary condition which renders the decree of a Council binding as a true and unerring definition of the "Faith once delivered to the Saints." It is in accordance with the relative positions of Bishops, Priests, and laymen in Synods, that *the decision arrived at* (δόγμα) by the Bishops, as possessing a *votum decisivum* to define the Faith, with the aid of the Priests, as *consenting* counsellors and assessors, should be promulgated with the concurrent assent (which does not involve *initiative* or *deliberative* rights in matters of faith and doctrine) of the laity. If we believe that the laity shared in the Pentecostal outpouring of the Spirit, and that "the whole Church" is the Spirit-bearing Body of Christ, the right of the laity to concurrent assent in the

---

[1] S. Chrysostom's comment on these words is worth noting: ἔδοξεν ἡμῖν γενομένοις ὁμοθυμαδόν, . . . ὥστε δεῖξαι, ὅτι οὐ τυραννικῶς, ὅτι πᾶσι τοῦτο δοκεῖ, ὅτι μετὰ ἐπισκέψεως ταῦτα γράφουσιν. (S. Chrys., *In Acta Apost.*, Hom. xxxiii.)

THE READING καὶ οἱ ἀδελφοί   47

decrees of Councils is a foregone conclusion. If Acts xv. 22 expresses this right, it is at the least reasonable to suppose that the formal decree would run in the name of "the Apostles and Elders and Brethren." The other reading seems quite meaningless, and the evidence for the word ἀδελφοί is too strong for it to be dismissed as an accidental corruption, whilst the evidence for the words καὶ οἱ is strong enough to demand its acceptance on the basis of admitting a reading which makes sense, instead of a reading that is unintelligible. The history of the Church and the logic of facts must sometimes be taken into consideration by textual critics.

The reading καὶ οἱ is adopted by Tischendorf, in which he follows E, G, H, and most cursives. It is omitted in the uncial codices A, B, C, D, and in the Codex Sinaiticus. But the corrector of the Codex Sinaiticus marked c inserts καὶ οἱ, and Scrivener observes "that one object of this corrector was to assimilate the Codex to MSS. more in vogue at his time." If this correction may be dated as that of a fifth or sixth century copyist, it is extremely unlikely that he would insert καὶ οἱ in the interests of the laity. The tendency of things ecclesiastical at that date was all the other way. It is therefore an admissible theory that he had access to some uncial MS. which is now lost.

NOTE E.

The Principle of Primatial Authority in the Apostolic Age.

We may note that Bishop Beveridge and Dr. Hammond, two of the most learned divines of the Caroline period, which closed the epoch of the Anglican Reformation, unhesitatingly refer the establishment of the principle of primatial authority to the Apostolic age. Bishop Beveridge says: " Sed mirari subeat, nec quidem immerito, qua tandem ratione hæc consuetudo in ecclesiam primo introducta sit, ut licet Episcopatus ubique gentium unus idemque sit, unus tamen in unaquaque provincia episcopus cæteris præesset, et maiorem, quam reliqui, auctoritatem haberet. . . . Quod si Concilia generalia et vetustiora Ecclesiæ statuta consulamus, nihil prorsus de prima huius consuetudinis institutione, vel etiam initio, in iis inveniemus. Incœpta est enim, vel instituta, priusquam universalia Concilia celebrari cœperint, quæ propterea eam nusquam instituunt, sed prius institutam ubique supponunt, et sua demum auctoritate confirmant."

Bishop Beveridge alludes here to the sixth Canon of Nicæa, which deals with Metropolitical and Primatial rights, on which he observes that " Synodus Nicæna Metropolitanorum iura τὰ ἀρχαῖα ἔθη, *antiquos mores* vocavit." He carefully guards himself against admitting that the principle of Primatial authority involves the theory of a Papal monarchy.

Referring to the thirty-fourth Apostolic Canon, he says: " Quo tamen non decernitur, ut in unaquaque gente unus Episcopus esset primus, sed ut omnes cuiusque gentis Episcopi τὸν ἐν αὐτοῖς πρῶτον, *illum, qui in iis primus est*, cognoscant et tanquam caput existiment. Ubi propterea pro concesso sumitur, quotcunque in ulla gente Episcopi erant, unum inter eos Primum fuisse, sive Primatem, eundemque reliquorum caput esse, atque ita proinde ab illis existimandum. Nulla itaque primæ huiusce rei institutionis vestigia videre est, quam nihilominus ab ipsis Ecclesiæ primordiis ubique gentium obtinuisse pro comperto habemus. Quapropter vix dubitare licet, quin aliquo saltem modo ad ipsos Apostolos referatur, qui si non ipsi hunc primatum instituerunt, instituendo tamen viam straverunt

PRIMATIAL AUTHORITY IN APOSTOLIC AGE 49

apertissimam." (Beveridge, *Cod. Canonum*, &c., tom. ii. pp. 60, 61.)

Bishop Beveridge here adopts the line of argument advocated in these pages. The principle of Primacy is plainly visible in the Apostolic age, and this principle involves the further grouping of Metropolitans under Patriarchs, one of whom is necessarily *primus inter pares*. He proceeds to strengthen his argument by noting how the world-wide Church adapted itself to the civil organisation of the world-wide empire of the Apostolic age. The civil Metropolis became the ecclesiastical Metropolis, because the Church in the mother city became naturally influential and important. As the Roman roads became highways for the Gospel, so the grouping of the Empire into civil "Dioceses" and "Provinces" formed the providential basis of ecclesiastical organisation. It was said of Pagan Imperial Rome that "the powers that be are ordained of God," and therefore the civil organisation of the Empire under those powers could unconsciously become the handmaid of the Catholic Church. Antioch, Corinth, Ephesus, and Thessalonica, to give notable instances, were, civilly, metropolitan cities, and became naturally metropolitan centres of Church organisation.

Bishop Beveridge notes that S. Paul's Epistles were written to metropolitan cities like Rome, Corinth, and Ephesus, or to the Church in a civil Province, as Galatia was: "Vel denique ad Primum in provincia Episcopum Metropoli præfectum, ut ad Timotheum et Titum" (p. 65). Bishop Beveridge believes that S. Timothy and S. Titus were Primates, which is much nearer to the ideas of their special position adopted by modern scholars than the view which made them local Bishops of Ephesus and Crete. He quotes S. Chrysostom to prove his view:

Δῆλον δέ ἐστιν ἐντεῦθεν, ὅτι ἐκκλησίαν λοιπὸν ἦν ἐμπεπιστευ-

D

μένος ὁ Τιμόθεος, ἦ καὶ ἔθνος ὁλόκληρον τὸ τῆς 'Ασίας. κ.τ.λ. (S. Chrys., *Hom.* xv. *in* 1 *Tim.*). He proceeds: "Idem dicendum est de Epistola ad Titum ; quem totius insulæ Cretæ Primatem fuisse, sive Primum Episcopum, ex ipsis Pauli ad eum verbis liquido constat, dicentis Τούτου χάριν κατέλιπόν σε ἐν Κρήτῃ, ἵνα τὰ λείποντα ἐπιδιορθώσῃ. κ.τ.λ." (Tit. i. 5). Bishop Beveridge lays stress upon the hundred cities of Crete, and the fact of its becoming an Ecclesiastical Province with Gortyna as its Metropolis. But even if we think that he does not sufficiently realise the fact that local Diocesan Episcopacy was not organised so early as he appears to imagine, the Primatial idea appears clearly enough in the position of SS. Timothy and Titus as Apostolic delegates in charge of Provinces of the Church. Bishop Beveridge sums up as follows: "Quamobren Apostoli, etiamsi singulas peragrare ut provincias, summam tamen ad Metropoles curam iure meritissimo contulerunt ad Romam Imperii caput, ad Antiochiam Metropolim Syriæ, ad Corinthum Metropolim Achaiæ, ad Ephesum Metropolim Asiæ, ad Thessalonicam Metropolim Macedoniæ, etc., ut e supradictis patet. Cum ipsi igitur Apostoli in Ecclesia propaganda tantam provinciarum et Metropoleon rationem habuerint, exemplo quidem licet non præcepto suo Metropolitanis et Primatibus in Ecclesia instituendis occasionem præbuerunt" (Ibid., ii. p. 69).

Bishop Beveridge may be considered by some moderns an out-of-date theologian. But he belonged to the days when it was truly said, "Clerus Anglicanus stupor mundi," and Bishop Hefele, the modern Roman canonist and theologian, paid him the just tribute of practically adopting his settlement of the controversy upon the date and authority of the Apostolic canons as final. (Hefele, *Councils*, vol. i. p. 452.)

The arguments of Dr. Hammond are formed upon the

same lines as those of Bishop Beveridge. He traces the metropolitical or Primatial authority of S. Timothy and S. Titus over their provinces. (*Works*, vol. ii. Oxford ed., p. 217.)

Dr. Hammond also shows how the Church adapted herself in Apostolic days to the Roman organisation of Provinces and their mother cities (pp. 221 and 222). It is remarkable that the researches of Professor Ramsay have led him to adopt practically the same conclusions. Dealing with the unifying efforts of the State Paganism of the Roman Empire, he says: "Everything that the imperial policy did in the provinces during the first century was so arranged as to encourage the unity of the entire Roman Province; and the priests of the imperial religion became by insensible degrees a higher priesthood, exercising a certain influence over the priests of the other religions of the province. In this way a sort of hierarchy was created for the province and the Empire as a whole; the reigning Emperor being the religious head, the Supreme Pontiff of the State, and a kind of sacerdotal organisation being grouped under him according to the political provinces. As time passed, gradually the Christian Church grouped itself according to the same forms as the imperial religion, not indeed through conscious imitation, but because the Church naturally arranged its external form according to the existing facts of communication and inter-relation. In Pisidian Antioch a preacher had unique opportunities for affecting the entire territory whose population resorted to that great centre. So Perga was a centre for Pamphylia, Ephesus for Asia. But the clerical influence of these centres was confined to the Roman district or province. In this way, necessarily and inevitably, the Christian Church was organised around the Roman provincial metropolis, and according to the Roman provincial divisions.

The question then is, when did this organisation of the Church begin? I can see no reason to doubt that it began with Paul's mission to the West. It grew out of the circumstances of the country, and there was more absolute necessity in the first century than later, that if the Church were organised at all, it must adapt itself to the political facts of the time, for these were much stronger in the first century. The classification adopted in Paul's own letters to the Churches which he founded, is, according to provinces, Achaia, Macedonia, Asia, and Galatia. The same fact is clearly visible in the narrative of *Acts*; it guides and inspires the expression from the time when the Apostles landed in Perga. At every step, any one who knows the country recognises that the Roman division is implied." (*S. Paul the Traveller*, pp. 134, 135, 136.)

CHAPTER II

THE WITNESS OF THE SUB-APOSTOLIC AGE TO THE CONSTI-
TUTIONAL AUTHORITY OF BISHOPS, AS LIMITED BY
THE PRINCIPLE OF PRIMACY WITH REGARD TO THE
UNIVERSAL EPISCOPATE, AND BY THE COUNCIL OF
PRESBYTERS WITH REGARD TO EACH DIOCESE.

THE development of the authority of the Historic Episcopate is clearly traceable in the Apostolic age. But we have also seen that it is an authority constitutionally limited by the principle of Primacy on the one hand, and by the central idea of the unity of the whole body of the faithful on the other.

The lesson of the Council of Jerusalem is undoubtedly that of constitutional authority. The Primate Apostle is no infallible autocrat of Christendom. The Apostles are not autocephalous and independent ecclesiastical monarchs. The Cyprianic maxim of co-ordinate responsibility is plainly manifest.[1] The "Elders" of the Second Thrones have their consultative voice, and the body of the faithful, "the whole Church," expresses its assent through the "brethren" who are associated

[1] Episcopatus unus est, cuius a singulis in solidum pars tenetur. (*De Unit. Eccl.*, ed. Benedict., p. 195.)

with the "Apostles and Elders" in sending forth the decree of the Council.

The result of the Council may not have been immediately manifest. Yet it virtually set forth the world-wide ideal of the Catholic Church of Pentecost. The spiritual Kingdom of our Lord was fashioned visibly by the wisdom and organisation which the Apostles learnt during the Great Forty Days, and we can, to some degree, measure that Divine Wisdom by its historical results. Nothing really good was to be cast aside. The faults of previous formative efforts in human organisation, whether in things spiritual or temporal, were alone to be discarded. "The finger of the Hand Divine," God's Holy Spirit of order and symmetry of method, was clearly traceable in the history of the world. And so the Catholic Church was fashioned out of the Church of the Old Covenant,[1] and the spiritual empire of the Lord Christ adapted its organisation to the "Dioceses" and "Provinces" of Imperial Rome.[2] The Visible

[1] After the Christian Churches had ceased to circle round Jerusalem, and had begun to take the form of a new spiritual empire wide as the Roman Empire itself, there grew up a conception that the new *Ecclesia Dei*, whose limits were the world, was the exact counterpart, though on a larger scale, of the old *Ecclesia Dei*, whose limits had been Palestine. (Hatch, *Bampton Lectures*, p. 138.) But the conception did not *grow up*, as Dr. Hatch imagines. It was rooted in the very idea of the Catholic Church as the visible Kingdom of God on earth.

[2] Peter de Marca says: "Apostolos orbem Ecclesiasticum in Provincias distribuisse ad exemplum dispositionis civilis." And he further

Church was not at war with human society as such. Its warfare was directed against "the world;" or, in other words, against *human society, organised apart from God*. Every sound element of human wisdom in statecraft and organisation was quickened with the Breath of Pentecost, and fashioned to the service of the City of God. The fact that we can trace there human elements in the organisation of the Church does not lead us to minimise the Divine powers inherent in her ministry and sacraments. This recognition of the human element does not drag down the Church to the level of an ordinary human organisation.[1] It rather uplifts the human into the region of the Divine. We are not afraid to make comparisons and trace resemblances between the polity of the Roman Empire and the polity of the Catholic Church. Each such resemblance shows us that certain details of wise organisation in an earthly kingdom were "good gifts" from "the Father of Lights," and were therefore worthy to be wrought into the Divine statecraft of the City of God.

---

adds: "Apostolos cum Ecclesias distribuerent in Provincias, in animo habuisse ut in eis corpus Episcoporum statueretur sub præsidentia Episcopi Metropoleos." (*De Concord*, VI. i.) The learned Gallican divine is here practically in agreement with the latest results of modern research as expressed by Professor Ramsay.

[1] Here is the fundamental error which dominates the careful, and otherwise most useful, historical researches of Dr. Hatch.

We must now deal with the circumstances which marked the close of the Apostolic Age.

The Church was organised upon the general lines of the civil divisions of the Empire. The hostility of the Empire to the Church was in accordance with the nature of things. The unity of the Empire was bound up with the idea of the various local cults being permitted to exist upon the sole condition of owning the supreme authority of the Emperor, in his religious capacity as "Pontifex Maximus," and recognising his Pagan hierarchy with its delegated authority in each Province. The civil power dimly began to perceive that the Catholic Church set up a rival organisation with absolutely exclusive claims to spiritual allegiance. The mere fact that this new organisation, with its unique spiritual powers, followed the lines of the organisation of the Empire, would intensify the growing hostility of the Pagan State to the Catholic Church. The commanding influence of the Church of Rome, organised and guided by the two great Apostles S. Peter and S. Paul, the one being the Primate Apostle and the other the Apostle of greatest intellect and power, was the parallel (to a certain limited extent) of the influence of the "Pontifex Maximus," a title which later Bishops of Rome shrewdly appropriated and utilised. The Pagan High Priest of the Provincial

WITNESS OF THE SUB-APOSTOLIC AGE 57

Metropolis found himself faced by the Metropolitan of the Christians, who wielded a mightier authority than his own—an authority kindled by the new enthusiasm of living spiritual forces, which caused the cold and effete State Paganism to shrivel in its presence. The fierce flame of the Neronian persecution burnt itself out in vain efforts to terrorise the disciples of the new Faith. The relentless legal warfare of the Flavian Emperors against the Christians was an equal failure. The Church held its own, with various periods of repose, when apathy and indifference suffered the laws against Christianity to become for a time dormant, until the final outburst under Diocletian was followed by the victory of Constantine and the Edict of Milan in A.D. 313. But we have anticipated the development of events. What was the organisation of the Church at the close of the first century? We have seen how it followed the lines of the Empire and became localised, when Apostolic missionary journeys resulted in the formation of organised centres of Church life.

The threefold Apostolic Ministry was first manifested in the Apostles, the Presbyter - Bishops appointed by them, and the Deacons. The Pastoral Epistles show us another stage in the life of the Church. The Apostolic delegates, S. Timothy and S. Titus, exercise an Apostolic jurisdiction apart from the unique gifts of the Apostles themselves. The "Prophets" of the Διδαχή[1] seem to hold an analogous position, whilst the Angels of the Seven Churches appear to be Bishops with local Sees, like S. James at Jerusalem. We find this local Episcopate firmly established all over Christendom by the days of S. Ignatius, and the commanding position of the See of Ephesus in the East is mainly due to its being the centre whence this localised Episcopate spread under the guidance of the last surviving Apostle.[2] We find no trace of autocephalous independent action on the part of

---

[1] The Prophets of the Διδαχή are called High Priests. Πᾶσαν οὖν ἀπαρχὴν ... δώσεις τοῖς προφήταις, αὐτοὶ γάρ εἰσιν οἱ ἀρχιερεῖς ὑμῶν. But the Prophet, as Ruler or Apostolic Delegate, is not *absolute*. He is to be honoured as ἀρχιερεύς, but the Presbyter-bishops and deacons exercise the *same ministry*, and are to be honoured *together with* the Prophets and Teachers who occupy the first rank in the Apostolic Ministry. ὑμῖν γὰρ λειτουργοῦσι καὶ αὐτοὶ τὴν λειτουργίαν τῶν προφητῶν καὶ διδασκάλων· μὴ οὖν ὑπερίδητε αὐτούς· αὐτοὶ γάρ εἰσιν οἱ τετιμημένοι ὑμῶν μετὰ τῶν προφητῶν καὶ διδασκάλων. (Διδαχή, xiii. and xv.)

[2] S. Irenæus tells us that S. John survived until the reign of Trajan. Ἀλλὰ καὶ ἡ ἐν Ἐφέσῳ ἐκκλησία ὑπὸ Παύλου μὲν τεθεμελιωμένη, Ἰωάννου δὲ παραμείναντος αὐτοῖς μέχρι τῶν Τραϊανοῦ χρόνων, μάρτυς ἀληθής ἐστι τῆς τῶν ἀποστόλων παραδόσεως. (*Contr. Hær.*, iii. 3, 4.) S. Clement of Alexandria, in a well-known passage, tells us something of S. John's exercise of his Primacy. Ἐπειδὴ γὰρ τοῦ τυράννου τελευτήσαντος ἀπὸ τῆς Πάτμου τῆς νήσου μετῆλθεν εἰς τὴν Ἔφεσον, ἀπῄει παρακαλούμενος καὶ ἐπὶ τὰ πλησιόχωρα τῶν ἐθνῶν, ὅπου μὲν ἐπισκόπους καταστήσων, ὅπου δὲ ὅλας ἐκκλησίας ἁρμόσων, ὅπου δὲ κλήρῳ ἕνα γέ τινα κληρώσων τῶν ὑπὸ τοῦ Πνεύματος σημαινομένων. (*Quis Dives*, &c., c. 42.) The Muratorian fragment tells us that S. John wrote his Gospel "at the urgent entreaty of his fellow disciples and Bishops" (cohortantibus condiscipulis et Episcopis suis). (*Canon Muratorianus*, ed. Tregelles, p. 17.) We may date this fragment on the Canon at about A.D. 170.

these localised Bishops. The Seven Churches of Asia looked to the Bishop of Ephesus as their Metropolitan. Its importance as the civil metropolis would naturally make it the headquarters of S. Timothy, whose position as Apostolic delegate would probably devolve upon him the care of all the Province of Asia. But though Ephesus stands first on the roll of the Asian Sees,[1] the Metropolitan of Ephesus is addressed in the Apocalypse by one higher than himself. He is bidden to listen to the inspired voice of the Apostle S. John, whose unique position as the last of the Apostles lent an authority to his guidance and governance which none else could challenge whilst he yet lived. But the years rolled on, and the old age of S. John forbade his active intervention.

A dispute arose in the Church at Corinth when certain presbyters were unjustly deposed by the

[1] We have already noted that the importance of Ephesus as the Church centre of the province of Asia came from the fact that S. John grouped around him some of the surviving Apostles and disciples of the Lord in addition to the weight of his personal presence. These are the "condiscipuli" of the Muratorian fragment which we have already quoted.

"When after the destruction of Jerusalem S. John fixed his abode at Ephesus, it would appear that not a few of the oldest surviving members of the Palestinian Church accompanied him into 'Asia,' which henceforward became the headquarters of Apostolic authority. In this body of emigrants, Andrew and Philip among the twelve, Aristion and John the Presbyter among the other personal disciples of the Lord, are specially mentioned." (Bishop Lightfoot, *Colossians*, p. 45.)

people. The inhabitants of the Provinces had learnt to bow to Imperial Rome. The Roman Christians were a powerful and well-organised body, with the prestige of the Primate Apostle and S. Paul still with them. Linus, the friend of S. Paul, had been appointed by the Apostles, Bishop of the central city of the ancient world.[1] Cletus had followed Linus, and now S. Clement was Bishop of Rome. In the name of the great and influential " Church of God which sojourneth at Rome," he wrote to " the Church of God which sojourneth at Corinth,"[2] a letter of kindly and authoritative reproof on account of their recent dissensions. We need not minimise the Primatial position of the writer of this letter, or the authoritative tone of the letter itself, in order to guard against the assumptions of the Vatican Decrees. There is no trace in S. Clement's letter that he claimed to inherit S. Peter's Apostolic Primacy, and if, as seems certain, his letter was written before the death of S. John, the most that can be claimed for him is that since the last surviving Apostle was silent from the infirmities of old age,

---

[1] Bishop Lightfoot, after an exhaustive examination of the evidence upon the subject, finally adopts the order of succession which is followed here, which is the same as that which appears in the Latin Canon of the Mass. (*S. Clement*, vol. i. 201-345.)

[2] Ἡ ἘΚΚΛΗΣΙΑ τοῦ Θεοῦ ἡ παροικοῦσα Ῥώμην τῇ Ἐκκλησίᾳ τῇ παροικούσῃ Κόρινθον. κ.τ.λ. (*S. Clement*, i. 1.)

the next available person to deal with the Corinthian difficulty would be the Bishop of the Imperial city. We do not forget that this very Epistle of S. Clement has been used to deny S. Clement's own position as Bishop of Rome,[1] and the doctrine of the Historic Episcopate as a fact of Church life and history. But we are not now concerned with theories that involve forced interpretations of ancient documents, and a total isolation of their testimony from the general tone of their contemporary environment. It is just as wilful an anachronism to imagine that the Church of Rome in S. Clement's day was Presbyterian,[2] as it is to believe that S. Clement wielded the authority claimed by a mediæval Pope. The undoubted fact that the Primacy of Rome appears in S. Clement's Epistle to be centred in the Church rather than in the individual who presided over it, does not really

---

[1] The theory of some modern critics that Linus, Cletus, and S. Clement were "fellow presbyters" who governed at the same time a Presbyterian Church of Rome, instead of being Bishops who succeeded each other in regular order is unhesitatingly condemned by Bishop Lightfoot. (*S. Clement*, vol. i. p. 67.)

[2] When Mr. Simcox says that he is "certain that the Churches founded by the Apostles were originally presbyterian," he is either confused and confusing, or does not use the word "presbyterian" in its customary sense. In the same sentence he states that in the Apostle's days the Episcopate existed, *but unlocalised*. The Presbyterianism of Calvin could not coexist with any Episcopate at all, localised or unlocalised. (*Early Ch. Hist.*, p. 214.)

militate against that legitimate conception of Primacy which has existed in the Church from the days of the Apostles to our own. The Primate owes his position to the See which he occupies, and not to his own personal qualities of leadership. The Church of Rome, in the first and second centuries, derived its authority from its Apostolic foundation, and from the position of the Imperial city in its relation to the provinces, and also to what S. Ignatius calls "the presidency of love."[1] We note first of all the authoritative and Primatial tone of this Epistle of S. Clement, which Bishop Lightfoot describes as "urgent and almost imperious." The Bishop goes so far as to say: "It may seem strange to describe this noble remonstrance as the first step towards papal domination. And yet, undoubtedly, this is the case."[2] Upon the principle of *corruptio optimi pessima* we can agree with the Bishop. S. Clement's Epistle is an authoritative assertion of the true principle of Primacy and Church order, as against autocephalous action at Corinth, which terminated in disorder. The Vatican decrees, which refer to the Pope's position in Christendom, are perversions and exag-

---

[1] S. Ignatius, *Epistle to the Romans*, i. προκαθημένη τῆς ἀγάπης. "The Church of Rome, as it is first in rank, is first also in love." Bishop Lightfoot *in loc.*

[2] Bishop Lightfoot, *S. Clement*, vol. i. p. 70.

gerations of the legitimate Primacy of Rome,[1] which amply justify all Catholics who decline to accept them, because they are at variance with the doctrine and discipline of the Primitive Church.

The fact that S. Clement's name does not appear in the letter only emphasises the truth that the Bishop of Rome was so identified with the Primacy of the Church over which he ruled, that he wrote in its name.[2] As the *persona ecclesiæ* his primacy was identified with the Church of Rome rather than with any idea of his personal succession to the Primate Apostle.[3] He claims no personal *Petri privilegium* as centred in himself. At the most he alludes to "the good Apostles," S. Peter and S. Paul, as personally known to him, and as "the noble examples which belong to our generation."[4]

---

[1] See Note A.

[2] This practice continued for a considerable time. In A.D. 165 Pope Soter wrote to Corinth in the name of the Roman Church. (Euseb., iv. 23.)

[3] S. Jerome says that S. Clement "scripsit *ex persona ecclesiæ Romanæ* ad ecclesiam Corinthiorum valde utilem epistulam, et quam in nonnullis locis etiam publice legitur," &c. (*De Viris Illustribus*, c. 15.) The fact that S. Clement does not call himself Bishop of Rome is no argument against his being so. Within about a hundred years of his death S. Clement of Alexandria uses the title "Apostle" to describe his position as Primate of the Apostolic See of Rome. Καὶ μὴν ἐν τῇ πρὸς Κορινθίους ἐπιστολῇ ὁ ἀπόστολος Κλήμης . . . λέγει. (S. Clem. Alex., *Strom.*, iv. 17-19.)

[4] τοὺς ἀγαθοὺς ἀποστόλους. (S. Clem., *Ad Cor.*, vi.) "Such an

S. Clement does not exclude the idea that the ministry of S. Peter and S. Paul at Rome constituted it the one Apostolic See of the West, and that the residence of the Primate Apostle at Rome would, after the fall of Jerusalem, make the Roman Church the centre of Christendom.[1] The authoritative tone of his letter to the Corinthians is based upon a tacit assumption of this fact, as well as of the other fact which has already been noted, namely, the position of Rome as the capital of the world. It is difficult to construct any other hypothesis to account for the authority claimed in this letter.[2] But although the Primacy of the Roman Church was the historic cause of the Primacy of the Roman Bishop, we need not minimise unduly the position of S. Clement and his successors in the "Cathedra Petri." Although

epithet may be most naturally explained on the supposition that Clement is speaking in affectionate remembrance of those he had known personally." Bishop Lightfoot *in loc.*

[1] "The later Roman theory supposes that the Church of Rome derives all its authority from the Bishop of Rome as the successor of S. Peter. History inverts this relation and shows that, as a matter of fact, the power of the Bishop of Rome was built upon the power of the Church of Rome." (Bishop Lightfoot, *S. Clement*, vol. i. p. 70.)

[2] The recently recovered portion of this Epistle (in the MS. discovered at Constantinople by Bryennios) adds to this tone of authority. δέξασθε τὴν συμβουλὴν ἡμῶν, καὶ ἔσται ἀμεταμέλητα ὑμῖν (c. 58).

Ἐὰν δέ τινες ἀπειθήσωσιν τοῖς ὑπ' αὐτοῦ δι' ἡμῶν εἰρημένοις, γινωσκέτωσαν ὅτι παραπτώσει καὶ κινδύνῳ οὐ μικρᾷ ἑαυτοὺς ἐνδήσουσιν. κ.τ.λ. (c. 59).

Χαρὰν γὰρ καὶ ἀγαλλίασιν ἡμῖν παρέξετε, ἐὰν ὑπήκοοι γενόμενοι τοῖς ὑφ' ἡμῶν γεγραμμένοις διὰ τοῦ ἁγίου πνεύματος. κ.τ.λ. (c. 63).

the "Cathedra Petri" did not minister unique personal immunities and prerogatives to its occupant, it conveyed dignity and primacy to the Church over which he presided, and by degrees his position as the first in rank of all the Patriarchs and Primates of Christendom was acknowledged without question. There is an allusion to S. Clement's position with regard to the other Churches of Christendom in the *Pastor* of Hermas, which throws some light on the subject. The date of Hermas is uncertain, but if we accept the later date, which makes him the brother of Pope Pius (A.D. 140),[1] there is no reason for rejecting Bishop Lightfoot's view of him as a younger contemporary of S. Clement, whose death may be placed at A.D. 100. The evidence of Hermas on Church organisation is the evidence of a man who had seen the earlier nomenclature of the Apostolic age crystallise into the Bishops, Presbyters, and Deacons of the Ignatian epistles; but he uses the

[1] "Pastorem vero nuperrime temporibus nostris in urbe Roma Hermas conscripsit sedente cathedram urbis Romæ ecclesiæ Pio episcopo fratre eius" (*Muratorian Fragment on the Canon*). So, too, the *Liberian Chronicle*, "Sub huius (Pii) episcopatu frater eius Ermes librum scripsit," &c. Hermas may very well have known S. Clement as a young man, and, *pace* Dr. Salmon, who rejects the Muratorian statement, he may have accommodated the ecclesiastical condition of affairs as seen in the *Pastor*, to that which obtained in his youth, rather than to that which existed when his brother Pius was Bishop of Rome. We need not quote instances of such treatment in allegories or romances.

earlier language to suit the date he has fixed for his visions and allegories. He speaks of Presbyters and Deacons, and of "Church rulers,"[1] who form the highest order of the Ministry. In his Vision he sees the Church personified as a woman[2] ("a pre-existing, divinely-created idea," as Professor Ramsay so fitly remarks), and she commits to his charge a book which she tells him to copy. Again she meets Hermas, and tells him she has other words to add. "But when I finish all the words, all the elect will then be acquainted with them through you." Hermas is thus to be the mouthpiece of a message from the personified Church to all the elect. It is a message *urbi et orbi*. "You will write, therefore, two little books, and you will send one to Clement and the other to Grapte. *So Clement shall send it to the cities abroad, for this charge is committed unto him*, and Grapte shall instruct the widows and the orphans, while thou shalt read it to this city together

---

[1] Hermas, *Vis.* iii. 9, 7; *Sim.* ix. 26, 2; ἐρεῖς οὖν τοῖς προηγουμένοις τῆς ἐκκλησίας. *Vis.* ii. 2, 6.

[2] "Hermas states the view held by the early Church as to its own origin. The Church appears as an old woman, 'because she was created first of all, and for her sake was the world made.' The Church was for Hermas a well-articulated organism, and not a collection of individual Christians, with no bond of union beyond certain common rites and beliefs; yet its organisation was not constructed by the early Christians, but was a pre-existing divinely created idea, independent of the existence of actual Christians to embody it in the world." (Ramsay, *Church in R. E.*, p. 362.)

with the presbyters who preside over the Church."[1]

Grapte, evidently a deaconess, has to instruct the order of widows, and to teach this revelation to the orphans in the exercise of her subordinate ministry. Hermas himself shares with the priests of the city the duty of reading the revelation to the Christians in Rome. Thus the message is proclaimed *urbi*. But S. Clement, the Primate of Christendom, sends it forth *orbi* to the cities abroad, and to all the elect (τοῖς ἐκλεκτοῖς πᾶσι) who dwell outside Rome, and have to receive, through Hermas, the message of the personified Church. The visions of Hermas may not touch a very high level of thought and power. We may rate their spiritual value as low as we please, without invalidating their incidental testimony to contemporary Church life and organisation.

This passage is a clear testimony to the Primatial position of S. Clement. We decline to recognise in it merely the fact that S. Clement was the medium of communication between the Church of Rome and the rest of Christendom. To see in this passage a bald statement that S. Clement

[1] "Ὅταν οὖν ἀποτελέσω τὰ ῥήματα πάντα, διὰ σοῦ γνωσθήσονται τοῖς ἐκλεκτοῖς πᾶσι. Γράψεις οὖν δύο βιβλιδάρια, καὶ πέμψεις ἓν Κλήμεντι καὶ ἓν Γραπτῇ. Πέμψει οὖν Κλήμης εἰς τὰς ἔξω πόλεις· ἐκείνῳ γὰρ ἐπιτέτραπται· Γραπτὴ δὲ νουθετήσει τὰς χήρας καὶ τοὺς ὀρφανούς· σὺ δὲ ἀναγνώσῃ εἰς ταύτην τὴν πόλιν μετὰ τῶν πρεσβυτέρων τῶν προϊσταμένων τῆς ἐκκλησίας. (Hermas, *Vis.* ii. 4.)

was merely "the foreign secretary" of the Roman Church is a minimising of evidence which leads to historic disproportion. It is hard to believe that Hermas, the brother of Pope Pius, would minimise the dignity of his brother's office by describing his brother's most illustrious predecessor as a sort of "foreign secretary" or correspondent of a governing Synod of Presbyters. The personality of S. Clement is too strong for such a view, even if we modify it so far as to suppose that the letter to the Corinthians was sent forth as the joint production of a Synod of the Roman Church over which S. Clement presided. The letter is evidently the work of one man, and bears no traces of emendation by members of a Synod, even if it were submitted to such a body before it was finally despatched to its destination.

The manifest unity of authorship which is evident in the letter shows the strength of S. Clement's position as *persona ecclesiæ*. His position was such that he was enabled to write this letter in the name of the Roman Church, and with the full weight of its authority. Dr. Hammond's theory,[1] that the Church in Rome was divided into a Petrine and Pauline party, with Linus as the Pauline Bishop and S. Clement as the Petrine, — both parties being fused afterwards during

---

[1] Hammond, *De Episcopatus Iuribus* (ed. 1651), p. 257.

S. Clement's episcopate — is not a tenable hypothesis. The monarchical episcopate was developed at Rome under the Apostles, and the order of the early Bishops (in the succession which we have already indicated) must be accepted as historic. But no doubt a Petrine and a Pauline party existed at Rome, and S. Clement united them and welded them together.[1] The commanding influence exercised by S. Clement finds its natural expression in his letter to the Corinthians. It was read in the public worship of the Corinthian Church for many years, and, as Eusebius tells us, in very many Churches elsewhere as well,[2] and the 85th Apostolical Canon (Coptic v. 5)[3] orders it to be read in Churches as quasi-canonical. Naturally this epistle has been the battle-ground of controversy upon the subject of Church organisation. The bulk of these controversies may be dismissed as foreign to our subject,[4] although we

[1] "Not separate organisations, but divergent tendencies and parties within the same organisation—this would be the truer description. Under such circumstances Clement was the man to deal with the emergency. At home and abroad, by letter and in action, in his doctrinal teaching and in his official relations, his work was to combine, to harmonise, and to reconcile." (Bishop Lightfoot, *S. Clement*, vol. i. p. 98.)

[2] ἐν πλείσταις ἐκκλησίαις ἐπὶ τοῦ κοινοῦ δεδημοσιευμένην πάλαι τε καὶ καθ' ἡμᾶς αὐτούς (*Ecc. Hist.* iii. 16). S. Jerome's testimony to the same effect has already been cited.

[3] Only fifty of the Canons called "Apostolical" have any claim to be considered Ante-Nicene. But this does not touch the argument.

[4] We may note in passing that eminent Lutherans like Mosheim and

may note in passing that S. Clement uses the nomenclature of the Pastoral Epistles with regard to the Presbyter-Bishops and Deacons. But, like Hermas, he sets above these "the Rulers" of the highest order of the Threefold Ministry, who are also termed "distinguished men" where the allusion evidently refers to Apostolic delegates, like S. Timothy and S. Titus, or to the Bishops who were the immediate successors of the Apostles.[1]

Neander have condemned as spurious S. Clement's testimony to the Apostolic succession and organisation of the Church, which begins with cap. 40. This condemnation is due to the inherent difficulty which besets persons who examine the Fathers from the standpoint of a foregone conclusion. Whatever stands in the way of that conclusion must be got rid of by an arbitrary process of *ci-devant* criticism. The real learning of Mosheim and Neander does not save them in this instance from themselves. *Cf.* Mosheim, *De Reb. Christ.*, p. 156; and *Eccl. Hist.*, vol. i. p. 80, where he says that "this Epistle seems to have been corrupted and interpolated," &c.

Bishop Lightfoot says that "Neander attacked the passage (c. 40) on the ground of its sacerdotalism. But the attack had no other basis than the writer's own subjectivity, and notwithstanding his great name, it has fallen into merited oblivion." (*S. Clement*, vol. i. p. 363, on Neander's *Church History*, vol. i. p. 272.)

[1] S. Clem., *Ad Cor.* c. i. ὑποτασσόμενοι τοῖς ἡγουμένοις ὑμῶν, καὶ τιμὴν τὴν καθήκουσαν ἀπονέμοντες τοῖς παρ' ὑμῖν πρεσβυτέροις. Also c. xxi. τοὺς προηγουμένους ἡμῶν αἰδεσθῶμεν, τοὺς πρεσβυτέρους ἡμῶν τιμήσωμεν. Both places refer to "Rulers" who were superior to Presbyters. We tcannót adopt the forced interpretation which would render "Presbyers" in these passages "*older men*," and *not* the Presbyters of the Church. With these "Rulers" we must identify the ἐλλόγιμοι ἄνδρες of c. xliv. There is clear evidence in this chapter of the chain of Apostolic Succession. The Apostles themselves appointed Presbyters, and then made provision for the continuance of the succession by means of Apostolic delegates, like S. Timothy and S. Titus, and Bishops, like S. Clement himself, and those constituted by S. John in Asia Minor. These ἐλλόγιμοι ἄνδρες ordained Presbyters and appointed them to their

The highest order of the Ministry, according to the plain sense of S. Clement, had the power of ruling and of ordination. The principle of Apostolic Succession is clearly laid down. The Apostolic Ministry is developed from above.[1] The mind of S. Clement is imbued with the Roman conception of law and order, and he sets forth the idea that it is the will of God that definite ministries should exist, and the duty of obedience to ecclesiastical authority, by means of the analogy of the Threefold Ministry of the High Priest, Priest, and Levite of the Old Covenant; whilst the layman is to abide by "the layman's ordinances."[2] He instances the discipline and subordination of ranks in the Roman army as a model for due subordination. "All are not Prefects, nor rulers of thousands, nor rulers of hundreds, nor rulers of fifties."[3] We may perhaps trace in this passage the ideal of spheres of work with the consent of the Church. The ejected Corinthian Presbyters apparently belonged to both classes, some of them being ordained by the Apostles themselves and some by their immediate successors.

[1] Οἱ ἀπόστολοι ἡμῖν εὐηγγελίσθησαν ἀπὸ τοῦ Κυρίου Ἰησοῦ Χριστοῦ, Ἰησοῦς ὁ Χριστὸς ἀπὸ τοῦ Θεοῦ ἐξεπέμφθη. Ὁ Χριστὸς οὖν ἀπὸ τοῦ Θεοῦ καὶ οἱ ἀπόστολοι ἀπὸ τοῦ Χριστοῦ· ἐγένοντο οὖν ἀμφότερα εὐτάκτως ἐκ θελήματος Θεοῦ. . . . κατὰ χώρας οὖν καὶ πόλεις κηρύσσοντες καθίστανον τὰς ἀπαρχὰς αὐτῶν, δοκιμάσαντες τῷ πνεύματι, εἰς ἐπισκόπους καὶ διακόνους τῶν μελλόντων πιστεύειν. (*Ad Cor.* xlii.)

[2] Τῷ γὰρ ἀρχιερεῖ ἴδιαι λειτουργίαι δεδομέναι εἰσίν, καὶ τοῖς ἱερεῦσιν ἴδιος ὁ τόπος προστέτακται, καὶ Λευΐταις ἴδιαι διακονίαι ἐπίκεινται· ὁ λαϊκὸς ἄνθρωπος τοῖς λαϊκοῖς προστάγμασιν δέδεται. (*Ad Cor.* xl.)

[3] Οὐ πάντες εἰσὶν ἔπαρχοι οὐδὲ χιλίαρχοι οὐδὲ ἑκατόνταρχοι οὐδὲ πεντηκόνταρχοι οὐδὲ τὸ καθεξῆς. (*Ad Cor.* xxxvii.)

ecclesiastical organisation that possessed the mind of S. Clement. The subalterns, or rulers of fifties, may have represented the Deacons, the centurions the Priests, and the tribunes or rulers of thousands the Diocesan Bishops, whilst the Prefects would represent Primates and Metropolitans, such as he was himself, as Bishop of the Imperial City, and of the Church first in rank amongst the Apostolic Sees.[1] It has been argued that the Corinthian Church was Presbyterian when S. Clement wrote this letter, because he does not mention the Bishop, but confines his reproof to the factious members of the Church who had unlawfully deposed their Presbyters. Bishop Lightfoot supposes that "there was a vacancy in the Bishopric at that time, or that the Bishop's office had not yet assumed at Corinth the prominence which we find a few years

---

[1] It is worthy of note that the very word "Eparch," which S. Clement here uses of a military office, also meant a civil "Prefect," and afterwards became an ecclesiastical equivalent for "Metropolitan." Εἰ δὲ πρὸς τὸν τῆς αὐτῆς ἐπαρχίας μητροπολίτην ἐπίσκοπος ἢ κληρικὸς ἀμφισβητοίη. κ.τ.λ. (Conc. Chalced. Can. ix.) Canon xvii. of the same Council directs that the ecclesiastical divisions shall follow the civil ones, thus stereotyping the ancient and primitive organisation, whereby the Roman Bishop's jurisdiction, as Patriarch over the Suburbicarian Churches, coincided with the civil jurisdiction of the Prefect of Rome. (See Cave, *Dissertation on Church Government*, chap. iii. par. 3.) The coincidence here noted is too remarkable to be lightly dismissed, when we consider that the principle of Primacy was rooted in the Apostolic age, and when we note that a writer so free from ecclesiastical bias as Professor Ramsay traces so clearly the correspondence between the organisation of the Church and of the Empire in the earliest days.

later in Asia Minor."[1] The first hypothesis is readily admissible. The absence of a bishop does not make the Church of any particular country Presbyterian or Congregational.[2] The Church in America had to exist for over a hundred years before the first American Bishop was consecrated, and the Church in South Africa had to wait nearly fifty years before Bishop Gray was consecrated. But the clergy of the Church in America and South Africa did not become Presbyterians because they were deprived of Episcopal ministrations. People argue about the Church of the first days in a way that would provoke a smile if the arguments were applied to times nearer to our own. We note in this Epistle of St. Clement the first distinctive mention of the layman as such. He has his duties and privileges, and special sphere

[1] Bishop Lightfoot, *S. Clement*, vol. i. p. 353. The independent and autocephalous action at Corinth, which called for S. Clement's Primatial rebuke in the name of the Roman Church, was most likely to take place during a temporary vacancy of the See. The deposition of the Presbyters must have been the conjoint work of certain other Presbyters and laymen combined, whom S. Clement reminds of S. Paul's former denunciation of Corinthian party spirit.

[2] We may go even further than this, and state plainly that even if the Apostles were not able to set in order all the Churches at once, and if on this account Corinth had no bishop, or (as it seems) Philippi when S. Polycarp wrote to the Philippians, it is no argument against the universal order of the Threefold Ministry *iure divino*. S. Epiphanius simply and naturally remarks that οὐ πάντα εὐθὺς ἠδυνήθησαν οἱ Ἀπόστολοι καταστῆσαι, and that for a while incompleteness of organisation may have been tolerated, owing to stress of circumstances, until χρεία γέγονε. (*Hær.* lxxv. 5.)

in Church order, which he must not overpass. He has no right to take part in deposing Presbyters, who have "blamelessly and holily offered the oblations,"[1] and we may reasonably infer that, since such depositions must have been based upon matters of doctrine and discipline, the layman has no authority to deal with such matters. "Let each in his own order make his Eucharist to God in gravity, abiding in a good conscience, not transgressing the appointed canon of his ministration."[2] Although these words apply primarily to the Eucharist as the central act of worship, and to the layman's exercise of his priesthood therein, through the divinely appointed Priesthood of the Apostolic Ministry, their application naturally has a wider scope. The "appointed canon" of the layman's ministration is the germ of the Canon Law of Christendom, which regulates and defines the position of the laity with regard to the Faith, Discipline, and

[1] Τοὺς ἀμέμπτως καὶ ὁσίως προσενεγκόντας τὰ δῶρα τῆς ἐπισκοπῆς (*Ad Cor.* xliv.). S. Clement compares the Church's Eucharistic "Liturgy" with the "Liturgy" of the Old Covenant. Even so unsacerdotal a writer as Harnack sees in this passage the Eucharist set forth as the chief function of the Presbyter-Bishop. It is idle to say that the earliest conception of the Christian Ministry was *unsacerdotal*. The *sacerdotium* is as plain here as it is in the Apostolic age. "Beyond a doubt the προσφέρειν δῶρα τῷ Θεῷ, *in the sense of offering sacrifices*, appears as the most important function of the episcopus." (Harnack, *Texte u. Untersuch.*, p. 144, n. 73.)

[2] "Ἕκαστος ἡμῶν, ἀδελφοί, ἐν τῷ ἰδίῳ τάγματι εὐχαριστείτω τῷ Θεῷ ἐν ἀγαθῇ συνειδήσει ὑπάρχων, μὴ παρεκβαίνων τὸν ὡρισμένον τῆς λειτουργίας αὐτοῦ κανόνα. (*Ad Cor.* xli.)

Worship of the Church, and is explained by "the layman's ordinances," to which S. Clement previously refers. To sum up the evidence of S. Clement's Epistle upon the subject which we are considering, we may say that, first of all, it bears witness to the principle of Primacy for which we have been contending, which is none the less strong because it is in the main incidental and indirect. It exhibits Professor Ramsay's clear ideal of the "Unified Church," which he aptly terms "the combination of imperial centralisation and local home rule, which is involved in the conception of a self-governing unity."[1] Next we note the principle of Apostolic succession, and the continuity of the Catholic Church with the Church of the Old Covenant, as witnessed by the analogy drawn by S. Clement between the Threefold Levitical Hierarchy of High Priest, Priest, and Levite, and the Threefold Apostolic Ministry of the Catholic Church.[2] Then we have the parallel between the Eparchs and subordinate officials of the Empire, and the due subordination of the officials of the

---

[1] Professor Ramsay, *S. Paul the Traveller*, p. 125. See also Note B.
[2] Lipsius well says (*in loc.*): "Non negare possum V. T. hierarchiam quæ vocatur, hoc loco ad Christianorum societatem accommodari."

"The new law of the Church" Clement "most characteristically connected with the two models of the political and military organisation of the Roman State, and the sacerdotal hierarchy of the Jewish Theocracy." (Pfleiderer, *Hibbert Lectures*, p. 252.)

Church, as a disciplined organisation of men under authority, from Primate to Deacon. And lastly, we have the beginnings of clear definition of the layman's rights and privileges by the "canon" of his ministration, and "the layman's ordinances" by which he is bound.

When we turn from S. Clement, the Roman Primate, to S. Ignatius, the Martyr of Antioch, we find ourselves in a totally different atmosphere. Bishop Lightfoot has vindicated the genuineness and authenticity of the Seven Letters of S. Ignatius of the Shorter Recension, as against the interpolations of a fourth-century writer in the Longer, and as against the exclusive claim of the three Curetonian letters in the Syriac.[1] We are not concerned with the learned controversy that has lasted since Voss Ussher and Bishop Pearson first vindicated the exclusive claims of the Shorter Recension. We accept as final the conclusions of Bishop Lightfoot. The Seven Letters were written under the strain and stress of approaching martyrdom, by a man journeying to Rome under sentence of death. They are filled with a glorious spiritual enthusiasm, and we do not expect to find in them any approach to S. Clement's lofty tone of authority and calm appeals to the spirit of

---

[1] The Curetonian letters are evidently extracts from a version of the genuine Seven Epistles.

order and organisation. And yet these Epistles have been a veritable battle-ground upon the question of the threefold order of the Apostolic Ministry.[1] The nomenclature of the Pastoral Epistles and of S. Clement's Epistle is changed in these writings of S. Ignatius. We hear no more of the Presbyter-Bishops. The word "Bishop" is reserved for the successors of the Apostles in the highest order of the Threefold Ministry. In subordination to them are the Presbyters and Deacons. We are not to suppose that S. Ignatius himself was the author of this changed nomenclature. He writes of the Ministry in its threefold order as a permanent factor in the life of the Church, and he assumes that the nomenclature used by him is a matter of universal usage, so that he need not explain or justify its use. To him the Bishop is the centre of unity. But the Bishop is not an irresponsible autocrat. His synod of priests forms his standing council of advice. The strange view

[1] When Calvin and others supplanted the Threefold Apostolic Ministry by a new ecclesiastical polity devised by the wit of man, they parted from the historical continuity of the Catholic Church, and endeavoured to conceal their novelties by denying the witness of history. Naturally the clear testimony of the Ignatian Epistles was one of their first objective points of attack. They assumed that Prelacy was a corruption of primitive order. Since the Ignatian Epistles witnessed for Episcopacy, they had to be treated as Luther treated the Epistle of S. James. Daillé's attack on these Epistles was the ablest. We are even grateful for its futile show of learning, because it evoked Bishop Pearson's *Vindiciæ Ignatianæ*.

of Dr. Hatch that two Bishops could co-exist in one city without schism[1] is directly negatived by S. Ignatius, and we find no trace in him of a congregational autocephalous episcopate.[2] The Bishops

---

[1] Dr. Hatch, in his *Growth of Christian Institutions*, maintained the curious view that in the early centuries "a Bishop, Presbyters, and Deacons existed for every Christian community" (*Ch. Inst.*, p. 16). "Every town, and sometimes every village had its Bishop" (*Ibid.*, p. 18). "There is no trace of the dependence of any one community on any other" (*Bampton Lectures*, p. 195). Cornelius and Novatian at Rome, as rival Bishops, were merely carrying on the usual custom of "free organisation," according to Dr. Hatch, and the transition to Diocesan Episcopacy and the law of "one Bishop for one city" was owing to S. Cyprian's influence (*Bampton Lectures*, p. 103). Even Harnack declines to follow him here (*Analecten zu Hatch*, p. 252). According to Dr. Hatch, the Bishops before S. Cyprian's day were merely Congregationalist Ministers, absolutely autocephalous, knowing nothing of the Imperial unity of the Church, and absolutely free from the germs of any Primatial or Metropolitical system. His view is *prima facie* unreasonable, and historically incorrect.

Such aberrations can only be explained by the unconscious anachronism which pervaded the mind of Dr. Hatch. He was tinged very palpably with the spirit of the Protestant Reformation, and he was unconsciously trying to justify its results, in matters of Church organisation, by viewing the early Church from a standpoint inherently alien to the ἦθος of Historical Christianity.

[2] S. Ignatius is warning the Philadelphians against division. Ὅσοι γὰρ Θεοῦ εἰσιν καὶ Ἰησοῦ Χριστοῦ, οὗτοι μετὰ τοῦ ἐπισκόπου εἰσίν· καὶ ὅσοι ἂν μετανοήσαντες ἔλθωσιν ἐπὶ τὴν ἑνότητα τῆς ἐκκλησίας, καὶ οὗτοι Θεοῦ ἔσονται, ἵνα ὦσιν κατὰ Ἰησοῦν Χριστὸν ζῶντες . . . εἴ τις σχίζοντι ἀκολουθεῖ, βασιλείαν Θεοῦ οὐ κληρονομεῖ. The privileges of the kingdom of God depend upon its unity. If a man is in schism he cuts himself off from his rights of inheritance within the kingdom. "Those who are of God" abide in the unity of the Church, which is manifested by each Bishop as a centre of unity for his Diocese, as representing a united portion of a united whole. This being the plain meaning of S. Ignatius, it follows that he enjoins one Eucharist, one Altar, and one Bishop. σπουδάζετε οὖν μιᾷ εὐχαριστίᾳ χρῆσθαι, μία γὰρ σὰρξ τοῦ Κυρίου ἡμῶν Ἰησοῦ Χριστοῦ, καὶ ἓν ποτήριον εἰς ἕνωσιν τοῦ αἵματος

WITNESS OF THE SUB-APOSTOLIC AGE 79

are linked together as units of a larger whole. The Primatial letter of S. Clement to the Corinthians is evidently alluded to, and S. Ignatius clearly testifies to the Primacy of the Roman Church.[1]

We have already touched upon the fact that the language of S. Ignatius presupposes the general nomenclature of Bishop, Presbyter, and Deacon, as being usual in his day to express the Threefold Apostolic Ministry. Writing in A.D. 110, or thereabouts, he speaks of "the Bishops established in the farthest parts,"[2] and his witness points to the

αὐτοῦ· ἓν θυσιαστήριον, ὡς εἷς ἐπίσκοπος, ἅμα τῷ πρεσβυτερίῳ καὶ διακόνοις. κ.τ.λ. (*Ad Philadel.*, iii. and iv.)

S. Ignatius could have found no room for the theories of Dr. Hatch, for they are of the essence of that very σχίσμα against which he was warning the Church.

[1] S. Ignatius reminds the Romans of their exhortations and admonitions εἰς τὰς ἔξω πόλεις, although he does not use the phrase, and it is improbable that he had seen the *Pastor* of Hermas. He says, ἄλλους ἐδιδάξατε (*Ad Rom.*, iii.), "Ye have hitherto been the instructors of others besides yourselves."

"In this case Ignatius would refer to the exhortations of the Romans, whether by letter or by delegates to foreign Churches. More especially we may suppose that he had in his mind the Epistle of Clement." (Bishop Lightfoot, *in loc.*)

[2] καὶ οἱ ἐπίσκοποι οἱ κατὰ τὰ πέρατα ὁρισθέντες. (*Ad Ephes.*, iii.) After recapitulating the evidence for the general establishment of the Episcopate, Bishop Lightfoot says that "though there are grounds for surmising that the Bishops of Rome were not at the time raised so far above their presbyters as in the Churches of the East, yet it would be an excess of scepticism, with the evidence before us, to question the existence of the Episcopate as a distinct office from the presbyterate in the Roman Church. With these facts before us, we shall cease to regard the expression (*Ephes.*, iii.) 'the Bishops established in the farthest parts' as a stumbling block." (Bishop Lightfoot, *S. Ignatius*, vol. i. p. 381.)

universal establishment of the Apostolic Ministry in its threefold order at the time of the death of the Apostle S. John. The fact that S. Ignatius does not address his Epistle to the Roman Church to the Bishop personally is no evidence against the facts we have stated.

Since our argument is not directed to prove the plain facts of Apostolic Succession and Episcopacy in general, we need not burden our pages with a detailed examination of the abundant evidence upon these points which is contained in the Ignatian Epistles. We may, however, quote two typical passages. "In like manner let all men respect the Deacons as Jesus Christ, even as they should respect the Bishop as a type of the Father, and the Presbyters as the council of God, and as the College of the Apostles. Without these (*i.e.* the three orders) no Church has a title to the name."[1] It is not recognised as a part of the One Visible Society which Christ founded, which is, as S. Ignatius calls it, "the Catholic Church," the covenanted sphere of the presence of our Lord Jesus Christ. Again he says, "Do ye all follow your Bishop, as Jesus Christ followed the Father, and the Presbytery as the Apostles; and to the Deacons pay respect, as

---

[1] Ὁμοίως πάντες ἐντρεπέσθωσαν τοὺς διακόνους ὡς Ἰησοῦν Χριστόν, ὡς καὶ τὸν ἐπίσκοπον ὄντα τύπον τοῦ πατρός, τοὺς δὲ πρεσβυτέρους ὡς συνέδριον Θεοῦ καὶ [ὡς] σύνδεσμον ἀποστόλων· χωρὶς τούτων ἐκκλησία οὐ καλεῖται. (*Ad Trall.* iii. 1.)

to God's commandment. Let no man do aught of things pertaining to the Church apart from the Bishop. Let that be held a valid Eucharist which is under the Bishop or one to whom he has committed it. Wheresoever the Bishop shall appear, there let the people be; even as wheresoever Christ Jesus may be there is the Catholic Church."[1] We have here the first use of the phrase "the Catholic Church," to express the Imperial unity and order of the "Ecclesia Dei" of the New Covenant. The idea which underlies the phrase is coeval with the Day of Pentecost, when the Church of the Old Covenant was broadened into the Catholic Church, of which our Lord Christ is the true and only Head. The individual Bishop is the centre of unity for his Diocese, as our Lord is the centre of unity for the whole Church. The unity of action of the Bishops finds its outward expression through their subordination to the collective Episcopate, which expresses its rule of mutual interdependence through the priority of order exercised by the Metropolitan, the Primate, and the Patriarch. Although S. Ignatius does not expressly mention this priority of order, we may

---

[1] Πάντες τῷ ἐπισκόπῳ ἀκολουθεῖτε, ὡς Ἰησοῦς Χριστὸς τῷ Πατρί, καὶ τῷ Πρεσβυτερίῳ ὡς τοῖς ἀποστόλοις· τοὺς δὲ διακόνους ἐντρέπεσθε ὡς Θεοῦ ἐντολήν. Μηδεὶς χωρὶς ἐπισκόπου τι πρασσέτω τῶν ἀνηκόντων εἰς τὴν ἐκκλησίαν. Ἐκείνη βεβαία εὐχαριστία ἡγείσθω ἡ ὑπὸ τὸν ἐπίσκοπον οὖσα, ἢ ᾧ ἂν αὐτὸς ἐπιτρέψῃ· ὅπου ἂν φανῇ ὁ ἐπίσκοπος, ἐκεῖ τὸ πλῆθος ἔστω, ὥσπερ ὅπου ἂν ᾖ Χριστὸς Ἰησοῦς, ἐκεῖ ἡ καθολικὴ ἐκκλησία. (*Ad Smyrn.*, viii.) See also Note B. upon the "Ecclesia Dei."

legitimately infer it from his reference to the Primacy of the Roman Church,[1] and we must not forget that the special circumstances of his letters do not naturally lead him to touch upon it. He is exhorting the laity to maintain Diocesan unity, and he vehemently insists on the Threefold Ministry as the guardian of this unity. He tells us that no Eucharist is valid except the Bishop celebrate, or license a priest to celebrate it for him. Here we see that the Bishop has cure of souls and jurisdiction in his Diocese.[2] His priests share his cure of souls, and celebrate the sacraments by his formal permission. We have in this passage also a definition of the position of the faithful laity. It is not so clear as that of S. Clement, which was doubtless before the mind of S. Ignatius as he wrote. But the indication is plain enough. The πλῆθος, or *Plebs Christiana*, holds fast to the Bishop as the

---

[1] S. Ignatius addresses his letter to the Romans to the Church, ἥτις καὶ προκάθηται ἐν τόπῳ χωρίου 'Ρωμαίων. This may be referred to the *potentior principalitas* which S. Irenæus assigns to the Roman Church (iii. 3, 2). The reason why the phrase "in the country of the region of the Romans" is used, instead of saying simply "the Church in Rome," may have applied to the special jurisdiction of the Roman Church over the Sub-urbicarian Churches of the region directly controlled by the Præfectus Urbis. The passage may thus refer to the general Primacy of Rome, as well as to the special jurisdiction over the neighbouring region. The Sub-urbicarian jurisdiction, though not named so early, may well have had its germ in the age of S. Ignatius. But the Primacy which he acknowledges is the "Primacy of love" (προκαθημένη τῆς ἀγάπης). (S. Ign., *Ad Rom.*, i.)

[2] Οὐκ ἐξόν ἐστι χωρὶς τοῦ ἐπισκόπου οὔτε βαπτίζειν οὔτε ἀγάπην ποιεῖν. (S. Ign., *Ad Smyrn.*, viii. *Cf.* Tert., *De Baptismo*, xvii.)

centre of unity, whether in worship, or in such share in deliberative assemblies as the phrase "the whole Church," in Acts xv., may fairly warrant. But the elevation of all three orders of the Apostolic Ministry above the layman by S. Ignatius is warrant enough that he did not contemplate any positive interference by the laity with matters of faith, doctrine, and discipline. The Bishop, according to S. Ignatius, is no feudal overlord. His priests are his official councillors, and not his vassals.[1] The Synod of the Diocese thus never became an assembly in which the Bishop is sole legislator and judge.[2] He presided as representing the collective responsibility of his own order. He could exercise

---

[1] The great Gallican canonist and theologian Du Pin is very clear on this point. He says : "Observandum est primis Ecclesiæ sæculis Episcopum nihil gravioris momenti fecisse sine consilio Cleri sui, ac maxime Presbyterorum. . . . Quippe apud antiquos forum erat Ecclesiasticum, in quo Episcopus et Presbyteri sedebant. Huius Synedrii meminere sæpius antiqui. Ignat. Epist. ad Magnesios ait Episcopum præsidere *loco Dei*, et Presbyteros *loco consessus Apostolorum*, eosdem Presbyteros Epist. ad Philadelphenses *Concilium Episcopi* vocat ; similiter Presbyteros *Præsidentes* appellat Tertullianus in Apologetico, *Præsident*, inquit, *apud nos probati quippe seniores hunc honorem non pretio sed testimonio adepti*." (Du Pin, *De Antiqua Ecclesiæ Disciplina*, p. 250, ed. 1691.)

[2] Du Pin is equally emphatic on the rights of the priesthood "in Synodis privatis" (*i.e.* in Diocesan Synods). "Apud omnes eruditos constat Episcopum olim nihil quidquam magni momenti sine Presbyterio egisse aut iudicasse, sicut nec Metropolitanum absque Synodo Provinciæ. Quin etiam in Conciliis Provinciarum sedisse legimus Presbyteros et cum Episcopis iudicasse, multo ergo magis in Synodis privatis cum Episcopo sedebant et iudicabant." (*De Ant. Eccl. Disc.*, p. 251.)

his authority as President, but he is responsible for its exercise to his Metropolitan and his com-provincial Bishops. The germ of all this constitutional exercise of authority is to be found in S. Ignatius. The more certain definition of its scope and limits was gradually developed with the growth of the Canon Law. It is worth while to give in detail the passages in which S. Ignatius expresses the constitutional relations between the Bishop and the Priests of his Diocese. Writing to the Philadelphians, S. Ignatius, after having said in the previous chapter, "Do nothing without the Bishop," emphasises the constitutional position of the Bishop by exhorting those who had taken part in divisions to return "to the unity of God and to the council of the Bishop."[1] The "council of the Bishop" means the Bishop with his council of Presbyters, as assessors with whom he is bound to advise, as a constitutional ruler. Submission to the Presbyters as well as to the Bishops is enjoined, when S. Ignatius tells the Ephesians "that being perfectly joined together in one submission, submitting yourselves to your Bishop and Presbytery, ye may be sanctified in all

---

[1] εἰς ἑνότητα Θεοῦ καὶ συνέδριον τοῦ ἐπισκόπου. (*Ad Philadelp.*, viii.) So also the Apostolic Constitutions, where the Presbyters are styled σύμβουλοι τοῦ ἐπισκόπου καὶ τῆς ἐκκλησίας στέφανος · ἔστι γὰρ συνέδριον καὶ βουλὴ τῆς ἐκκλησίας. (*Ap. Const.*, ii. 28.) The Bishop's licence to officiate is absolutely necessary for all ministrations in his Diocese, as S. Ignatius plainly indicates.

things."[1] In the same epistle he urges united worship, "to the end that ye may obey the Bishop and the Presbytery without distraction of mind, breaking one bread;"[2] because in the mind of S. Ignatius unity of worship and a valid Eucharist depend upon the unity of the Catholic Church, which is guaranteed by obedience to the Bishop and his constitutional advisers. We have an exact definition of the meaning of this relation of the Bishop to his Priests in the mind of S. Ignatius, where he aptly compares it to the strings fitted to a lyre. "Your honourable Presbytery," he tells the Ephesians, "which is worthy of God, is attuned to the Bishop, even as its strings to a lyre."[3]

The instrument is useless without its strings, and the strings must be fitted to the instrument, or else they in their turn are useless. This simile is the key to the whole position. The Bishop is not an absolute monarch. He does not administer discipline or give decisions without consulting his priests. Apart from them he does not act in autocratic isolation. The Priests, on the other hand, cannot act apart from him, for by virtue of his

---

[1] ἵνα ἐν μιᾷ ὑποταγῇ κατηρτισμένοι, ὑποτασσόμενοι τῷ ἐπισκόπῳ καὶ τῷ πρεσβυτερίῳ κατὰ πάντα ἦτε ἡγιασμένοι. (*Ad Eph.*, ii.)

[2] εἰς τὸ ὑπακούειν ὑμᾶς τῷ ἐπισκόπῳ καὶ τῷ πρεσβυτερίῳ ἀπερισπάστῳ διανοίᾳ· ἕνα ἄρτον κλῶντες. (*Ad Eph.*, xx.)

[3] τὸ γὰρ ἀξιονόμαστον ὑμῶν πρεσβυτέριον, τοῦ Θεοῦ ἄξιον, οὕτως συνήρμοσται τῷ ἐπισκόπῳ ὡς χορδαὶ κιθάρᾳ. (*Ad Eph.*, iv.)

Apostolic succession, which he shares with the universal Episcopate, he possesses *iure divino* the *potestas ordinis*, and the rights of the constitutional Ruler and Judge. The Priests can appeal to the universal Episcopate and the Catholic Church, as a whole, against any misuse of his powers by their Bishop. The canonical methods of such an appeal, in its graduated course from the Metropolitan and his Synod as its first stage, to the Patriarch, and ultimately to a General Council, will be hereafter discussed. Again, we find S. Ignatius calling the Presbytery "a worthy spiritual coronal" round the Bishop,[1] and saying that if obedience is due "to the Bishop, as to the grace of God," it is also due to the Presbytery "as to the law of Jesus Christ."[2] If obedience is due to the Bishop as representing our Lord, the Presbyters are as the Apostles, as the Council of God.[3]

The distinction between Bishop and Priest is always most definite and clear, and so is the Ignatian view of the Diaconate. The Deacon

---

[1] ἀξιοπλόκου πνευματικοῦ στεφάνου. (*Ad Magn.*, xiii.) Here we have an evident allusion to the custom of the Bishop sitting in the centre of his συνέδριον of priests.

[2] ὑποτάσσεται τῷ ἐπισκόπῳ ὡς χάριτι Θεοῦ καὶ τῷ πρεσβυτερίῳ ὡς νόμῳ Ἰησοῦ Χριστοῦ. (*Ad Magn.*, iii.)

[3] τῶν πρεσβυτέρων εἰς τύπον συνεδρίου τῶν ἀποστόλων. (*Ad Magn.*, vi.) *Cf.* τοὺς δὲ πρεσβυτέρους ὡς συνέδριον Θεοῦ, καὶ [ὡς] σύνδεσμον ἀποστόλων. (*Ad Trall.*, iii., and *Ad Smyrn.*, viii.)

belongs to the Apostolic Ministry in its threefold order. He has no part in the συνέδριον of the Priests, but he is the layman's superior, and the obedience enjoined to him in his ministrations[1] clearly marks off the Ignatian view of the layman's position, which is virtually the same as S. Clement's.

The Sub-Apostolic Age at its close thus manifests the constitutional relations of the Church and her Ministry, which were afterwards more definitely developed.

NOTE A.

The Legitima e Primacy of the Roman See.

The Primacy of the Roman Church, and the consequent Primacy of the Roman Patriarch, as the first in order and influence of the five Patriarchs of the Church, is an established fact of Church History. One of the most brilliant opponents of the modern Papal claims writes as follows:—
"After the destruction of Jerusalem, which during the first forty years after Pentecost had been the natural metropolis of Christendom, the Churches which had been constituted in the great cities of the Empire took the lead in the order of their civil precedence, with the Church of Rome

---

[1] *Cf. Ad Magn.*, vi.; *Ad Trall.*, iii.

necessarily in the first place. The See of Rome had also the glory of having been founded by the two great Apostles S. Peter and S. Paul, who were martyred outside the walls, and whose bodies were reverently treasured, and had in honour by the Roman Church. The Roman See was therefore very eminently an Apostolic See, and it was the only Apostolic See in the Western or Latin-speaking portion of the Church. In the East Apostolic Sees in some sense abounded. In the West there was but one, and that one was the Primatial See of the whole Church. No wonder that the Bishop of Rome was held in high honour, and was the natural person to take the initiative in movements affecting the whole body. But we must be careful not to exaggerate in this matter. There was a marked Primacy of honour and influence, but there was no Primacy of Jurisdiction." (*The Primitive Saints and the See of Rome*, by F. W. Puller, M.A., p. 22.)

By this last sentence we may infer that the author means no Primacy of Jurisdiction, *iure divino*, although the Pope, as Patriarch of the West, exercised a certain appellate jurisdiction in accordance with the Sardican Canons. But it must be remembered that beyond all Patriarchal jurisdiction, both in the East and West, lay an appeal to the collective Episcopate in General Council assembled. We shall examine at a later stage of our inquiry the instances of Papal jurisdiction which are commonly alleged as implying jurisdiction over the whole Church *iure divino*. There are certain collateral causes which have contributed to the Primacy of the Roman Church.

(i.) *The number of its clergy and people.* During the Decian persecution Pope Cornelius wrote to Fabius of Antioch of the forty-six priests, seven deacons, seven subdeacons, forty-two acolytes, &c., of the Roman Church, διὰ τῆς τοῦ θεοῦ προνοίας πλούσιός τε καὶ πληθύων ἀριθμὸς μετὰ μεγίστου καὶ ἀναριθμήτου λαοῦ. (Euseb. iv. 43.) And S. Cyprian writes to Pope Cornelius: "Et quamquam sciam, frater . . . florentissimo illic clero tecum præsidente, et sanctissimæ atque amplissimæ plebi legere te semper litteras nostras," &c. (*Ep.* 55 *ad Cornel.*)

(ii.) *Its wealth and charity.* We find Dionysius writing to Pope Soter about the middle of the second century of the abundant charity and gifts of the Roman Church to poorer Churches. He says: Ἐξ ἀρχῆς γὰρ ὑμῶν ἔθος ἐστὶ τοῦτο, πάντας μὲν ἀδελφοὺς ποικίλως εὐεργετεῖν, ἐκκλησίαις τε πολλαῖς ταῖς κατὰ πᾶσαν πόλιν ἐφόδια πέμπειν, . . . δι᾽ ὧν πέμπετε ἀρχῆθεν ἐφοδίων, πατροπαράδοτον ἔθος Ῥωμαίων Ῥωμαῖοι διαφυλάττοντες. κ.τ.λ. (*Ap. Euseb.*, iv. 23.)

(iii.) *The purity of its faith.* This was abundantly manifest in the Arian controversy, and also in the controversy between Pope Stephen and S. Cyprian on the rebaptism of heretics. Notwithstanding errors of method on the part of the Pope, the judgment of S. Cyprian and the African Bishops was not accepted by the Catholic Church as a whole, and the decision of Pope Stephen won its way to general acceptance. The defections of Liberius and Honorius are exceptions which prove the rule of Roman orthodoxy, whilst they guard us by anticipation against illegitimate claims of infallibility on behalf of the Chair of S. Peter.

(iv.) *Its services to the whole Church as a centre of unity.* We have the well-known passage of S. Irenæus, where he says of the Roman Church: "To this Church, on account of her superior pre-eminence, every Church must resort," &c. (S. Irenæus, *Adv. Hær.*, iii. 3.) We admit with Fr. Puller that *propter potentiorem principalitatem* does not convey the idea of supremacy *iure divino*, but it is a strained view of the passage to refer the *principalitas* solely to the secular rank of the Imperial City. We prefer, with Palmer, to refer *principalitas* to the pre-eminence of the Church as a centre of unity where Christians from all parts were constantly meeting, and thus were in a position to learn from the Roman Church and from one another the true balance of the Faith. S. Cyprian tells Pope Cornelius of the schismatics of his diocese who "dare to set sail, and carry letters to the Chair of Peter and to the principal Church whence sacerdotal unity has taken its rise" (S. Cyprian, Ep. 54).

We cannot well limit the meaning of *unde unitas sacerdotalis exorta est* to the probable fact that the Bishops of North Africa and Italy traced their Apostolic succession to the Roman See. It implies that the Church of Rome is a centre of unity for the whole Church. But it is not *de fide* that separation from the communion of the See of Rome involves separation from the communion and unity of the Catholic Church. The loyalty of the eminent canonist Du Pin to the See of Rome is beyond dispute. Yet he says that S. Cyprian and Firmilian were not out of communion with the Catholic Church, because they were excommunicated by Pope Stephen. "Quis audeat dicere," says Du Pin, "Athanasium et alios fuisse schismaticos, Arianos vero in Ecclesia, eo quod Liberius hos ad communionem suam admisisset, illos ab ea repulisset?" (*De Ant. Eccl. Disc.*, p. 257.)

(v.) *The imperial greatness of Rome as the centre of government.* We have already shown how the organisation of the Catholic Church was adapted to the organisation of the Roman Empire. This is of itself reason enough for the city of Rome to be the centre of Christendom. S. Cyprian assigns precedence to Rome on account of its greatness. "Quoniam pro magnitudine sua debet Carthaginem Roma præcedere" (Ep. 49). Du Pin puts this very clearly : "Porro si quæras cur potissimum Romana Ecclesia sit electa quæ primatum obtineret, responderi potest id factum, quia Romana urbs erat prima, nec alia congruentior ratio videtur reddi posse" (*De Antiq. Eccl. Disc.*, p. 335).

(vi.) *The position of Rome as the one Apostolic See of the West.* S. Irenæus lays great stress upon the Apostolic foundation of the See of Rome as a bulwark against heresy. "Maxima et antiquissima et a duobus Apostolis Petro et Paulo Romæ fundata Ecclesia, eam quam habet ab Apostolis fidem per successiones Episcoporum pervenientem usque ad nos indicantes confundimus omnes eos qui præterquam quod oportet colligunt." (*Adv. Hær.*, iii. 5.)

The equality of S. Peter and S. Paul does not militate against the Primacy of S. Peter. When S. Gregory says that "Paul the Apostle is brother to S. Peter in the first rank of the Apostles" (*Dial.*, cap. ult.), and when S. Ambrose says that "S. Paul was not inferior to S. Peter, although the latter was the foundation of the Church" (*De Spiritu Sancto*, c. 12), Du Pin rightly observes: "Petrum et Paulum in Apostolatu, in potestate, in auctoritate, æquales fuisse, in Primatu non item" (*De Antiq. Eccl. Disc.*, p. 320). He gives his reasons at length, and the idea of the See of the Primate Apostle being finally fixed at the capital of the Roman Empire combined with the other causes we have alleged to fix the Primacy of Christendom in the Roman See. The subsequent developments of the notion of a Supremacy *iure divino*, and an Infallibility which is un-Catholic, must not blind us to the plain fact of the legitimate Primacy of the Roman

See, and its witness to the principle of Primacy in general.[1] A moderate and learned Anglican writes as follows upon the legitimate authority of the Roman See :—

"Though it has been shown that the Bishop of Rome has not by Divine or human right any proper *jurisdiction* over the Universal Church, it would be equally unjust to that See, to the Primitive Church, and to ourselves, to deny or diminish the ancient legitimate privileges of the Chair of S. Peter. While all Bishops are alike successors of the Apostles, it cannot be denied that the Bishops of Metropolitan and Patriarchal Sees have influence and authority in the Church generally, in proportion to the dignity of their Churches : and therefore the Bishop of the elder Rome, being Bishop of the principal Church, and being the first of the Patriarchs, could not fail to have more authority amongst his colleagues, the Catholic Bishops, than any other Prelate. The exalted station in which the Providence of God had placed him, imposed on him a special obligation of exhorting his brethren to the observance of the sacred Canons and of resisting the progress of heresy by formal condemnations. These acts of the Roman Bishop might extend to the whole Church. He might transmit such decrees in faith and morals to all Bishops for their approbation. Such decrees ought to have been received with respect, though no Bishop was bound to approve or act on them, unless they appeared conformable to the doctrine of the Universal Church.

[1] The late Professor Maurice, whose natural bias and temperament would lead him in an opposite direction, yet goes so far as to say that "the Bishop of Rome . . . had a special, most awful, most responsible stewardship entrusted to him, in the discharge of which it is mere arrogance, party spirit, and contempt of history to say he was not often, in the main, faithful" (*Preface to Lectures on the Epistle to the Hebrews*, p. xli.).

It was not unreasonable that the Roman Patriarch should make regulations in discipline for particular Churches, when consulted and requested to do so by those Churches: he might even make such regulations unsolicited, provided it were understood that it was in the way of counsel and admonition, not in that of precept or command. The authority of the Roman See rendered it fitting that in matters of controversy concerning the doctrine or unity of the whole Church, the See of Peter should not be neglected; but that its aid should be sought to re-establish order and peace. In cases of extreme danger or necessity all Catholic Bishops are authorised to dispense even with the laws of Œcumenical Synods. This privilege therefore could not be refused to the Roman Bishop; and the authority of his See would even give his dispensation greater weight than that of other Bishops. Hence would follow the expediency of obtaining that dispensation in some cases, where Bishops desired some authority in addition to their own.

"Whenever the Bishop of Rome was actually in communion with the Universal Church, he would naturally be the centre of unity, because of his authority in the Universal Church, which would lead Churches in every part of the world to communicate with him on many occasions; and thus Churches remote from each other would be united by means of their intercourse with a common centre. But, when the Universal Church is divided, and a great part is not in communion with the Roman See, it ceases to be the centre of unity.

"Such are the privileges naturally flowing from, or connected with, the precedence of the Roman Patriarch in the Universal Church; privileges which were not merely honorary, but which were calculated for the edification, not the subjugation of the Church. In these privileges there was nothing of jurisdiction or coercive power; they arose not from Divine institution, but were founded on reason and on Christian charity. Happy it would have been if this venerable and Apostolical See had not afterwards transgressed its rightful authority, and assumed powers which disturbed the unity and subverted the discipline of the Church." (*The Church of Christ*, by W. Palmer, p. 535.)

Mr. Palmer's wise and cautious words exactly express the true position of a Patriarchal See. Such a centre of unity may be found for the Anglican Communion in the See of Canterbury; and the guarded action of the Lambeth Council of 1897 in providing for "a Council of Advice" to aid the Archbishop of Canterbury to give formal advice, with the full force of moral authority, to any Church or Province of the Anglican Communion that applies to him for an opinion upon any disputed point of faith, discipline, or doctrine, falls well within the limits which Mr. Palmer has laid down in the passage quoted. The Anglican Communion is in no danger of an undue development of the Patriarchal influence of the See of Canterbury. The real danger lies in the direction of the undue autonomy of National and Provincial Churches.

NOTE B.

The Unified Church.

There is a strange contrast between Professor Ramsay's idea of the Imperial unity of the *Ecclesia* and that of Professor Hort. The Cambridge Professor's somewhat startling language leads us away from the idea of the organic unity of the Catholic Church, as a visible polity; whilst the voice from the chair of Aberdeen, speaking amidst surroundings essentially hostile to Catholic theology, is the best answer from an historical standpoint to the minimising speculations of Dr. Hort.

Dr. Hort makes the following statement :—

"Not a word in the Epistle (Ephesians) exhibits the One *Ecclesia* as made up of many *ecclesiæ*. To each local *ecclesia* S. Paul has ascribed a corresponding unity of its own; each is a body of Christ, and a sanctuary of God, but there is no grouping of them into partial wholes, or into one great whole. The members which make up the One *Ecclesia* are not communities, but individual men. . . . It is true that S. Paul anxiously promoted friendly intercourse and sympathy between the scattered *ecclesiæ*, but the unity of the universal *Ecclesia*, as he contemplated it, does not belong to this region; it is a truth of theology and religion, not a fact of what we call ecclesiastical politics. To recognise this is quite consistent with the fullest appreciation of aspirations after an external ecclesiastical unity." (Hort, *The Christian Ecclesia*, p. 168.)

In laying down the truth that the One *Ecclesia* is composed of individual men, namely, of all those that have passed through the entrance-gate of a valid Baptism, the *ianua sacramentorum*, Dr. Hort does not make it plain upon what conditions the other Sacraments are to be obtained. His vagueness as to the relations of the scattered *ecclesiæ* with the One *Ecclesia* leaves the door open to the "freedom of organisation" theory which mars the work of Dr. Hatch. The Anglican Professor's vagueness needs clearing up by the plain historical statement of Professor Ramsay.

"The term *Ecclesia* originally implied that the assembled members constituted a self-governing body like a free Greek city (πόλις). Ancient religious societies were commonly organised on the model of city organisation. The term was adopted in the Septuagint, and came into ordinary use among Grecian Jews. Gradually Paul's idea of 'the unified Church' became definite; and with the true philosophic instinct, he felt the need of a technical term to indicate the idea. *Ecclesia* was the word that forced itself on him. But in the new sense it demanded a new construction; it was no longer the 'Church of the Thessalonians,' but the Church in Corinth, and it was necessarily singular, for there was only one Church. The new usage grew naturally in the mind of a statesman animated with the instinct of administration, and gradually coming to realise the combination of imperial centralisation and local home rule which is involved in the conception of a self-governing unity, the Universal Church, consisting of many parts, widely separated in space. Each of these parts must govern itself in its internal relations, because it is distant from other parts, and yet each is merely a piece carved out of the homogeneous whole, and each finds its justification and perfect ideal in the whole." (Professor Ramsay, *S. Paul the Traveller*, p. 125.)

This passage expresses very clearly the idea of the Catholic Church as a world-wide visible polity. The only criticism upon it that we would venture is that it is not "Paul's idea" in the sense of its being the creation and exclusive product of Pauline statesmanship. The "idea" of the "Unified Church" existed in germ in the Old Testament, and reached its development at Pentecost. It is God's way of bringing the nations to the foot of the Cross of Christ, and binding them together in a visible polity, and heavenly citizenship. It is the virtually unquestioned and unchallenged ideal of the first fifteen centuries of Church life and history. The Protestant Reformation, in a great measure, shattered this ideal amongst the Teutonic races, the majority of whom are practically in a chronic state of religious revolt against the discipline, organisation, and worship of the Catholic Church. The minority who have clung faithfully to primitive ideals find their truest representation in the Anglican Church. But the influence of the majority has, from time to time, pressed heavily upon individual Anglicans, and caused them unconsciously to be biassed in favour of reading into the past facts of Catholic Church organisation, untenable speculations which are advanced in order to make room for the untoward existing developments of the Teutonic ecclesiastical revolt.

Such writers as Dean Stanley and Dr. Hatch, although unlike in dealing with matters of research, are still alike in being forced into a position of anachronism by their vain endeavours to justify the separatist and disintegrating tendencies of the Reformation from the known facts of early Church history. The very fact that Dr. Hatch himself warns us against this kind of anachronism makes his own lapses in this direction the more conspicuous. His theory of the origin of Episcopacy, and his view that "freedom of organisation" is a tenable hypothesis, whereby the polity of Geneva, or the Brownists, is set on an equal level with the divinely ordered polity of the Catholic Church, is more untenable on account of its anachronism than for its manifest disregard of historic proportion. The Presbyterian discipline of Geneva, in its complex order and logical development (if its premises be once granted), is as utterly alien from the tone and temper and discipline

G

of Apostolic days as is the Hildebrandine Papacy with its modern Vatican superstructure. In fact, there is a better historical case to be made out for Papal absolutism than there is for Calvinistic democracy: both alike must shrink from an appeal to Church history. But the Papacy is a distortion of the Primatial principle, which is a part of Church life and order, whereas the polity of Geneva, and the sectarian growths of the Protestant Reformation, are manifestly new departures. If the germs of the polity of Geneva, or the Brownists, had been latent in the Acts of the Apostles, is it possible that fifteen centuries of development would have been necessary to bring them to light? The thing is incredible. The true explanation of the abnormal and un-Catholic developments of the Teutonic ecclesiastical revolt is not far to seek. It was a revolt from the unconstitutional absolutism of mediæval Church government, as well as a recoil from certain doctrinal corruptions and accretions. The true constitutional position of the Episcopate was obscured in the Middle Ages by the Papal despotism which was built up by the Pseudo-Isidorian decretals. Thus the true ideal of the constitutional rule of the Bishop in his Diocese, the Metropolitan in his Province, and the Patriarch in his Patriarchate, as responsible to the whole Church, in General Council assembled, was supplanted by an ecclesiastical feudalism in Western Christendom. The mediæval Bishop in the West became a feudal absolute ruler in his Diocese, subject only to his overlord the Pope, and to the exemptions granted by him. The inherent constitutional rights of the Priesthood and the *Plebs Christiana* became dormant.[1] The revolt of Luther and Calvin swung

---

[1] It is interesting to note that the Counter-Reformation which accompanied and followed the Council of Trent advocated the presence

the pendulum so far back in the opposite direction as to cause men to forsake Apostolic order and succession, and to substitute a ministry of their own devising for the Historic Episcopate with its Divine sanction. The Anglican Church was mercifully preserved from this error, but the Bishops of the Church of England at the Reformation retained the Apostolic succession without any immediate recovery of their true constitutional position. They succeeded to the thrones and civil status of the feudal Bishops, without acknowledging the central authority which the feudal prelate admitted. The Anglican Prelacy of the Elizabethan era was virtually autocephalous and unconstitutional, despite the efforts of Parker and Grindal to exercise a Primatial authority, which was unhappily tainted with Erastianism. The Primacy of Canterbury dwindled to a shadow, save for a brief revival under Laud, which was, from the necessities of the times, unfortunately mingled with an assertion of the Royal Supremacy, which culminated in the judicial murder of the King and the Archbishop by the fiercer spirits of the Puritan Revolution. It is not too much to say that the outburst of that revolt might have been mitigated, or avoided, if the Reformation Bishops had become constitutional rulers of their Dioceses in the Ignatian sense of the term.

The reaction of 1662 did not mend matters much.

of laymen in Synods. Pope Benedict XIV. (*De Synodo Diocesiana*, iii. 9) alludes to the decision of the *Congregatio interpret. Concil.* of April 22, 1598, to introduce well-instructed laymen into Provincial Synods, and the *Cæremoniale Episcoporum* refers to the seats that should be allotted to them. In 1736 Simon Assemani, as Papal Legate, held a Council of the Maronites who had accepted the Latin Obedience. At this Council many laymen of distinction were present, who signed its decrees. (*Vide* n. 5 of the above citation from Pope Benedict, *De Synodo.*)

Even so late as 1860 a thoughtful writer in the *Christian Remembrancer* was constrained to state that "the Primacy of Canterbury is almost, and that of York, entirely a dead letter." If this statement appears too sweeping in the light of present-day facts, it certainly shows that the Bishops of the Church of England have yet much to recover before they fulfil the ideal of the constitutional position of a Bishop in the Primitive Church.

The Bishops of the Anglican Communion out of England itself have, in a great measure, recovered this ideal, although the rank and file of the clergy in England are too insular in their sympathies to recognise the fact. We cannot expect opponents to recognise it, although a writer in the *Contemporary Review* for July 1897, who condemns the Historic Episcopate root and branch, and apparently identifies it with the development of Prelacy in England, has yet a word of praise for the type of the Episcopate developed in America and the Colonies, which he would be graciously pleased to accept if it parted with its distinctive principles. The main difficulty in the way of an English writer, attempting to take a dispassionate view of the organisation of the early Church, is that he has either been nurtured under the shadow of English Prelacy, or is its hereditary opponent. The attack and defence are alike tempted into anachronism. The defender ought boldly to admit that the Episcopate in England must alter its type and methods, whilst he strenuously maintains the historic succession, and Divine sanction, of the Bishops in England, as Bishops of the Catholic Church. Such an assailant as the aforesaid writer in the *Contemporary Review* should be reminded that the anachronism of making S. Ignatius of Antioch a defender of modern Congregationalism of the *City Temple* type is a trifle absurd. The appeal to history is just as treasonable to this sort of Dissenting writer as it was to Cardinal Manning. The germ of Church order is known by its historical results and legitimate developments. We find that the constitutional historic Episcopate of the undivided Church is the sole legitimate development of the Ministry in the Apostolic Age. The Patriarch, Primate, and Metropolitan are the historic factors which touch the exercise of a Bishop's responsibilities to his Diocese from without. His responsibilities to his Diocese from within are conditioned by his constitutional relations with his priests and with the *Plebs Christiana*. All these matters are clearly defined either by direct precept, or plain inference, in the history of the Primitive Church. Outside these limits history forsakes us, and we come into the unhistoric region of new departures and unauthoritative experiments. The Primitive Church knew nothing of Vaticanism, Calvinism, or Congregationalism.

CHAPTER III

THE CONSTITUTIONAL AUTHORITY OF BISHOPS AS DEVELOPED IN THE PERIOD OF THE "ECCLESIA PRESSA" BEFORE THE EDICT OF MILAN, AND THE EVIDENCE FOR THE EXERCISE OF PATRIARCHAL AND METROPOLITICAL RIGHTS BY THE CHIEF SEES OF CHRISTENDOM DURING THE SAME PERIOD

WE have now arrived at a most difficult stage in our inquiry. The period of the "Ecclesia Pressa," and the subsequent bitter ecclesiastical conflicts of the fourth century, which we shall deal with in the next chapter, caused such confusion in Church discipline and order, that the general principles of constitutional government (which we have already traced in the Apostolic and sub-Apostolic ages) became from time to time obscured and overridden by imperious local necessities. Those writers who deny the principle of Primacy, in their fear of yielding to the Vatican ideal of Papal supremacy, can find much evidence in the disordered ecclesiastical procedure which so frequently characterised this period of Church History, to justify their views. On the one side we shall find undue assertions of the legitimate Primacy of Rome, whilst on the other we shall see individual Bishops taking advantage of the pressure of the times to assert their authority in unconstitutional and unlawful methods. We shall also find that the disintegration, caused by persecution and the subsequent strife with heresy, was so great that the Church had to be content with an imperfect system of judicature and discipline until the advent of more peaceful times. During the times of persecution no Œcumenical Council was possible. Local Councils and Synods, often hastily assembled in fear of the civil power, had to take their place. Discipline in like manner had to be locally administered, and free communication between the Primatial Sees and distant Provinces and Dioceses was both dangerous and difficult when persecution was active, and had to be managed without unduly attracting public attention, during the periods of respite. In this way the Metropolitan of the Province, as the President of each local group of Bishops and Dioceses, became, for the time being, the concrete embodiment of Church discipline and authority. As Metropolitan, he presided in his Synod of com-provincial Bishops and decided cases which arose within his Province, and a custom arose of letting matters rest without any appeal from his decision. But the idea of the absolute finality of the decisions of a Metropolitan within his Province being part and parcel of the law and order of the Catholic Church, is a figment in the brain of those controversialists, Gallican and Anglican, who have been driven into an illogical view of the constitution of the Catholic Church, as a whole, and the mutual interdependence of its various parts, by the exigencies of their conflict with the usurped and uncanonical claims of the Roman Patriarch to be the absolute despot of Christendom. The legitimate claims of the Patriarchs of Constantinople, Alexandria, Antioch, and Jerusalem are not to be ruthlessly brushed aside because we resist the illegitimate claims of the Patriarch of Rome.

We must therefore regard the evidence which we may find in the third century for the finality of judgments given by a Metropolitan in his Provincial Synod in the light of the facts and circumstances of the times. The Church was suffering from abnormal pressure, and it is therefore reasonable to regard the position and influence of the Metropolitan at that time as unavoidably abnormal also. We must not be tempted to forge arguments against the Vatican Decrees by allowing that either Bishops or Metropolitans are "autocephalous" lords over God's heritage. We shall find confirmation for this view in the fact that the Patriarchal and Apostolic thrones of Rome, Alexandria, and Antioch exercised a remarkable primacy of *influence* during the Ante-Nicene period. One of the first acts of the Nicene Council was to confirm and stereotype this influence by appealing to its antiquity[1] as part and parcel of the fabric of the Catholic Church.

With regard to the constitutional relation of Bishops to the clergy and laity of their Dioceses, we shall find this period of Church history a time of partial confusion and obscurity. The Ignatian position, whereby the Bishop acted with his Priests as his councillors and assessors, was always the true theory of ecclesiastical procedure. But in practice there were many violations of this true theory of constitutional order. S. Cyprian, as we shall see presently, maintained the true constitutional order. He acknowledged legitimate patriarchal influence, whilst he resisted the undue claims of the Roman Pontiff. Himself a Metropolitan and Primate, he carefully guarded and maintained canonical primatial jurisdiction. He freely accorded to his clergy and laity their constitutional position in the Synods of the Church.

With these prefatory words, we may proceed to examine the historical evidence of the period before us.

[1] τὰ ἀρχαῖα ἔθη κρατείτω. (Conc. Nic., Can. 6.)

The case of the heretic Marcion has been claimed as establishing the principle of an inherent jurisdiction of appeal, extending throughout Christendom, as the legitimate prerogative of the Roman See.[1] But even if we accept the somewhat doubtful story of Epiphanius, which is hard to reconcile with the statements of Tertullian,[2] we cannot develop the Vatican doctrine out of the story of Marcion.

Marcion, son of the Bishop of Sinope, is excommunicated by his father, and goes to Rome, as the political and ecclesiastical centre of the world, to vindicate his position and to push forward the heresy which he had framed by an exaggeration of S. Paul's opposition to Judaism within the Church. The name of S. Paul was linked with that of S. Peter as co-founder of the Roman Church, and Marcion, arriving soon after the death of Pope Hyginus, A.D. 132, appealed to the Roman Presbyters, who were in charge, *sede vacante*, to restore him to communion. This they declined to do, since each Province of the Church is bound to accept the judicial sentence of another Province, or even Diocese, unless it is duly reversed by

---

[1] Bellarmine, Lib. ii., *De Romano Pontifice*.

[2] Tertullian (*De Præse. Hær.* 30) gives a very different view of Marcion from that of Epiphanius, although in c. 57 of the same treatise, spurious additions are made to harmonise his story with that of Epiphanius.

a legitimate course of appeal, such as is provided in the fifth Canon of Nicæa,[1] from the Diocese to the Province. Marcion's case proves only the preëminence of the Roman Church as a religious centre in A.D. 132, and shows that the Presbyters, *sede vacante*, would take no action in restoring him to communion. Even if Marcion had appealed to his Metropolitan and Provincial Synod, and then gone beyond their decision in an appeal to the Patriarch, it is evident (even if so formal a process had been at that date practicable) that Sinope did not fall within the scope of influence of the Roman Patriarch.

We must now briefly touch on the Paschal controversy. S. Polycarp assured Pope Anicetus (A.D. 165) that the Bishops of the province of Ephesus derived their custom of keeping Easter on the day of the Paschal full moon from S. John himself. The Western Church and the rest of the East, except the aforesaid Asiatic Bishops, kept Easter on the Sunday following the Pas-

[1] This Nicene Canon refers to an older canon, which says τοὺς ὑφ' ἑτέρων ἀποβληθέντας ὑφ' ἑτέρων μὴ προσίεσθαι. The same enactment is contained in the thirteenth of the Apostolic Canons, which Bishop Hefele considers to be without doubt Ante-Nicene. The appeal provided in the Nicene Canon from the Bishop to the Metropolitan and Provincial Synod of Bishops shows the constitutional character of the Bishop's office as *iudex ordinarius*, and beyond this lay, even if not at present defined, the appeal to the Patriarch and to an Œcumenical Council.

chal full moon. Pope Soter appears to have required Asiatic Christians living at Rome to keep Easter according to the general rule, and forego their own local custom. This was reasonable and right, and his successor Eleutherus adopted the same policy. But when Pope Victor succeeded him (A.D. 188), a stronger policy was adopted. Victor rightly desired to secure a uniformity in the observance of Easter Day, for which Christendom ultimately had to wait until the final decision of the Nicene Council in A.D. 325. As Primate of Christendom, Victor was the proper person to take the initiative.[1] He accordingly requested the Metropolitans of the various Provinces to summon their Provincial Synods to consider the matter.[2] In so doing he exercised his undoubted rights as the First Patriarch of Christendom. But it is idle to argue about the word used to describe this request. The authority of the "Cathedra Petri" was that of the constitutional Primate of Christendom, and not that of an infallible despot.

---

[1] "He was the first Bishop in the Church, and it was most fitting that he should take the initiative." (Puller, *Primitive Saints and See of Rome*, p. 25.)

[2] Polycrates, Bishop of Ephesus, writing officially to Victor, says: Ἐδυνάμην δὲ τῶν ἐπισκόπων τῶν συμπαρόντων μνημονεῦσαι, οὓς ὑμεῖς ἠξιώσατε μετακληθῆναι ὑπ' ἐμοῦ, καὶ μετεκαλεσάμην. κ.τ.λ. (Euseb., v. 24.) The word ἀξιόω is the equivalent to the Latin *postulare*. Its force need not be minimised to make an unnecessary point against modern Vaticanism.

THE PERIOD OF THE "ECCLESIA PRESSA"

The failure of any Metropolitan and Province to comply with his request was not to be visited with excommunication, but it would carry with it its own punishment in the dangers incurred by a wilful and autonomous isolation from the rest of the Catholic Church. Victor's request was obeyed throughout Christendom wherever Provincial Synods were practicable.[1] In Gaul at this time S. Irenæus of Lyons seems to have been the sole Bishop, and therefore the Synod held there was Diocesan rather than Provincial.[2] The Provincial Synod at Ephesus, under the Metropolitan Polycrates, was the only Synod which resisted the Catholic usage of keeping Easter on a Sunday. Victor seems to have overstepped constitutional limits in dealing with Polycrates.

In communicating to him the decision of the Roman Synod, he appears to have threatened the Asiatic Christians with excommunication in case of non-compliance. Polycrates characteristically replied, "I am not scared by those that terrify us with threats, for they, who are greater than I, have said we ought to obey God rather than men."[3] Then Eusebius tells us that "Victor,

---

[1] See Note A.
[2] See the Abbé Duchesne in the *Transactions of the National Society of Antiquaries of France*, tome i. pp. 387-390.
[3] Οὐ πτύρομαι ἐπὶ τοῖς καταπλησσομένοις. Οἱ γὰρ ἐμοῦ μείζονες εἰρήκασι, 'πειθαρχεῖν δεῖ Θεῷ μᾶλλον ἢ ἀνθρώποις.' (Euseb., v. 24.)

Bishop of the Church of the Romans, forthwith attempts[1] to cut off the Churches of all Asia, together with the neighbouring Churches, as heterodox, from the common unity; and he proscribes them by letters, and proclaims that all the brethren there are utterly separated from communion. But these measures did not please all the Bishops. They exhort him, therefore, to pursue peace and unity and love towards his neighbours. Their written opinions, too, are extant, very severely reproving Victor."[2]

And then S. Irenæus intervened in the con-

---

[1] On the significance of πειρᾶται, the comment of a Roman Catholic writer is significant. "Neque propterea secum pugnare credendus est Eusebius, cum Victorem dicit *conatum* esse Asianos abscindere. Et abscidit enim re verâ Asianos, cum eos a communione sua removit: et *conatus* est *ab Ecclesiæ corpore* segregare, cum cæteris Episcopis ad idem præstandum et litteris et exemplo auctor fuit. At plerique eum potius commonendum censuerunt, ut in proposito non permaneret." (Dom. Constant., *Romanorum Pontif. Ep.* i. 100.) This view is utterly irreconcilable with the modern theory of Vaticanism. For an infallible Pope to be censured by other Bishops for his disciplinary action is nowadays impossible. Note too, the distinction between "communione sua," and "ab Ecclesiæ corpore."

[2] Ἐπὶ τούτοις ὁ μὲν τῆς Ῥωμαίων προεστὼς Βίκτωρ ἀθρόως τῆς Ἀσίας πάσης ἅμα ταῖς ὁμόροις ἐκκλησίαις τὰς παροικίας ἀποτέμνειν, ὡς ἑτεροδοξούσας, τῆς κοινῆς ἑνώσεως πειρᾶται· καὶ στηλιτεύει γε διὰ γραμμάτων, ἀκοινωνήτους πάντας ἄρδην τοὺς ἐκεῖσε ἀνακηρύττων ἀδελφούς. Ἀλλ' οὐ πᾶσί γε τοῖς ἐπισκόποις ταῦτ' ἠρέσκετο. Ἀντιπαρακελεύονται δῆτα αὐτῷ τὰ τῆς εἰρήνης καὶ τῆς πρὸς τοὺς πλησίον ἑνώσεώς τε καὶ ἀγάπης φρονεῖν. Φέρονται δὲ καὶ αἱ τούτων φωναί, πληκτικώτερον καθαπτομένων τοῦ Βίκτορος. (Euseb., v. 24.) Pope Nicholas I. (A.D. 858) does not hesitate to condemn Victor's action as follows:—"Videamus Victorem papam ... pæne a totius Ecclesiæ præsulibus pertinaciæ redargutum." (Coleti, ix. p. 1360.)

troversy, as in absolute agreement with Pope Victor on the main question, but deprecating his attempt to excommunicate the adherents of Polycrates and the Synod of Ephesus. He wrote to Victor bidding him " not to cut off whole Churches of God, which preserve the tradition of an ancient custom " (ὡς μὴ ἀποκόπτοι ὅλας ἐκκλησίας Θεοῦ, ἀρχαίου ἔθους παράδοσιν ἐπιτηρούσας).[1] S. Irenæus also wrote to many other rulers (ἄρχουσιν) of the Church on this question, and preserved the peace of the Church. The whole episode is most instructive, and teaches us what patriarchal rights really were. As Primate of Christendom, it was Victor's duty to take the matter up, and summon the Provincial Synods to deal with it. It was also his duty to carry out the decisions of the Provincial Synods of his own Patriarchate, and to declare that none could be permitted to observe the Quartodeciman practice within the limits of his influence and jurisdiction. He could be the mouthpiece of the various Provincial Synods of his own Patriarchate in declaring that Quartodecimans within its limits would be excommunicated. But he had no authority to excommunicate the Asiatic Quartodecimans. That ultimate authority over the whole Church was never vested in the

---

[1] Euseb., v. 24. Socrates says that S. Irenæus "*stoutly opposed* (γενναίως κατέδραμεν) Victor" in this matter. (Socr., *H. E.*, v. 22, 16.)

Roman See, but in a General Council of the Catholic Church, in which the Primate of Christendom would be the President, just as the Archbishop of Canterbury is *ex officio* President of the Lambeth Conference. The attempt of Victor to usurp the functions of a General Council ended in failure. He attempted to turn his Primacy, which no one disputed, into a Supremacy, which neither S. Irenæus, who agreed with his view, nor Polycrates, who differed from him, would for one moment accept.

The Paschal controversy was ultimately settled in a Catholic and orderly manner by the first Œcumenical Council of Nicæa. The Council, as representing the whole Church, possessed an authority which Victor did not possess, and the Asiatic Christians obeyed its ruling. It is significant that Victor's attempt to excommunicate the Asiatics showed the limitations of his authority. He could lay down the conditions of communion so far as his Patriarchal authority extended, but he could not make communion with the Roman See a condition of Catholic communion. The Asiatics, who rejected the decision of Victor and of the majority, were not excommunicate, as Catholics, because they were out of communion with the Roman See.

It is interesting to note that S. Irenæus, notwithstanding his opposition to Pope Victor's attempt to turn his Primacy into a Supremacy, had at the same time a deep sense of the honour due to the "Cathedra Petri" as the Primatial See of Christendom. In his famous treatise *Against all Heresies*, he appeals to the *consensus* of Catholic tradition from the Apostles, through their successors the Bishops of Christendom, against the novelties of the heretics. He points to the tradition of "that very great and very ancient and universally known Church, which was founded and established at Rome by the two most glorious Apostles, Peter and Paul ; we point, I say, to the tradition which this Church has from the Apostles, and to her faith proclaimed to men, which comes down to our time through the succession of her bishops. . . . *For to this Church, on account of its superior preëminence, it is necessary that every Church should resort—that is to say, the faithful from all sides, and in this Church the tradition from the Apostles has been always preserved by men from all parts."* [1]

It is idle to argue overmuch upon the disputed

---

[1] "Ad hanc enim ecclesiam, propter potentiorem principalitatem, necesse est omnem convenire ecclesiam, hoc est, eos qui sunt undique fideles, in qua semper ab his, qui sunt undique, conservata est ea quæ est ab Apostolis traditio." (S. Iren., *Contra Omnes Hæreses*, iii. 3, 1, 2.) Although we have dealt with this passage in a previous note, its importance is so great that we make no apology for recurring to it with a view to its bearing on the action of S. Irenæus towards Pope Victor.

meaning of the latter portion of this passage. To begin with, we are dealing with a Latin translation of a lost Greek original, and we cannot dissect a translation as if it was the actual language of the writer. It would be hard to make S. Irenæus responsible for the Ultramontane or the Protestant view of the Latin words which represent the Greek original as it came from his pen. A simple and common-sense view of the passage is that it bears powerful witness to the Primacy of Rome, and to the vast services of the "Cathedra Petri" as the chief centre of Catholic unity.

But this strong testimony was written by a man who did not believe that communion with the Roman See was necessary to salvation, and who also did not believe that the Roman Patriarch could excommunicate the Asiatics who differed from him, so as to exclude them from the communion of the Catholic Church. We also trace in the language of S. Irenæus in this passage that the fact that Rome was the Imperial capital, and centre of the world's business, was a contributing cause to the ecclesiastical importance of the Roman See. It was the meeting-place of Christians from all over the world, and thus it was the natural ecclesiastical centre of the Roman Empire, even after the seat of government had been transferred to Constantinople. And, even in the palmiest days of the power of

Constantinople, "Old Rome," as a centre, more than held its own against the glories of "New Rome."

We now turn from the Roman Patriarchate to that of Alexandria, which for the next two centuries stood next to it in point of influence. The ordination of the great scholar Origen by Alexander, Bishop of Jerusalem, was without doubt irregular, and, for private reasons, uncanonical. Demetrius of Alexandria exercised Patriarchal authority over the six civil provinces into which Egypt, Libya, and Pentapolis were divided, which were also ecclesiastical provinces under their own Metropolitans. We use the term "Patriarch" to express the position of "a Primate of Metropolitans," which existed undoubtedly, as we have shown, from the earliest times. We shall see that the actual word "Patriarch" was not applied to the Primates of Rome, Alexandria, and Antioch till the fifth century. But it is convenient to use the word "Patriarch" as a pardonable anachronism, to express the position of the Primates of the great Sees in Ante-Nicene times—a position which the Council of Nicæa subsequently stamped with its œcumenical authority as in accord with the ancient usage of the Catholic Church.

With this explanatory digression, we will proceed to examine the action of Demetrius of Alexandria in the case of Origen. In A.D. 231 Demetrius assembled a Synod of Bishops and priests at Alexandria, to deal with the case of Origen. The priests of Alexandria had certain special prerogatives in electing the successor of S. Mark, the discussion of which forms no part of our present inquiry.[1] We may note, however, that the summoning of priests to this Synod points to the Ignatian ideal of the rights of the priesthood. When Origen had been condemned by this Synod, on account of his opinions, as well as his ordination, Demetrius summoned a second Synod of Bishops only, most probably from a wider circle of his Primatial jurisdiction. The condemnation pronounced by the former Synod was ratified, and the further step taken of deposing Origen from the priesthood. An encyclical letter from Demetrius made these resolutions known to all the ecclesiastical provinces which acknowledged Alexandria as their primatial See.[2] We have here an important instance of Patriarchal authority in Ante-Nicene times. A later writer, in dealing with the Patriarchal position of Alexandria just before the Nicene Council, assumes it as a well-established and time-honoured custom for the Alexandrian "Pope"

---

[1] Gore, *Church and the Ministry*, note B., p. 357.

[2] Hefele, *Hist. Councils*, vol. i. p. 88. Photii, *Bibliothec.*, cod. 118.

[3] S. Athanasius, in his Epistle concerning the Councils of Ariminium and Seleucia (ii. 3) quotes the letter of the Arians "To our

to have Archbishops or Metropolitans under him.[1]

It is instructive to note, even in Ante-Nicene times, how the Patriarchal Sees acted upon and influenced each other.[2] Antioch, as the third See in Christendom, had its special prestige as being founded by S. Peter, and the lustre of its succession was maintained by the great name of S. Ignatius, and subsequently by the theologian S. Theophilus (A.D. 177) and the martyr S. Babylas

---

Blessed Pope and Bishop Alexander." In his retractation Ischyras addresses S. Athanasius as "the Blessed Pope" (S. Ath., *Apol. c. Ari.*, 63). S. Cyprian, as Archbishop of Carthage, is also addressed as "Pope" (*Ep. ap. Cypr.*, 31). It is a title reserved to the leading Primates of Christendom, and was also used as a compliment to eminent Bishops like S. Augustine of Hippo.

[1] ὁ ἀρχιεπίσκοπος Μελήτιος, ὁ κατὰ τὴν Αἴγυπτον, ὑπὸ δὲ χεῖρα Ἀλεξάνδρου . . . (Epiphan., *Hær.*, 69, n. 3). Meletius, the author of the schism, appears to have been the senior Metropolitan next to the Patriarch. Ὁ Μελήτιος τῶν κατὰ τὴν Αἴγυπτον προήκων, καὶ δευτερεύων τῷ Πέτρῳ (the Patriarch) κατὰ τὴν ἀρχιεπισκοπήν. κ.τ.λ. (Epiphan., *Hær.*, 68, n. 1.)

[2] The intercommunication of the Patriarchal Sees was the means of maintaining Church unity. So Du Pin:—"Cæterum quoniam fieri non poterat, ut omnes orbis Ecclesiæ ad se invicem scriberent, et sibi mutuo notæ essent, ac proinde immediate communicarent, idcirco magnæ quædam sedes eligebantur, per quas Ecclesiæ secum invicem communicabant. Sic Ecclesiæ Orientis censebantur communicare cum Occidentalibus, quando communicabant Antiocheno Patriarchæ qui iunctus erat communione cum Romano, cui adhærebant Occidentales. Ita etiam Ægyptii per Alexandrinum cum Romano communicabant et Occidentales omnes cum Orientalibus et Œgyptiis per Romanum." (*De Antiq. Eccl. Disc.*, p. 255.) The previous passage, which quotes the thirty-second Apostolic Canon on "Letters Commendatory," as part of the discipline of intercommunion, is very interesting and noteworthy.

(A.D. 251). But although its influence was widespread throughout the East, it lacked the cohesion of Rome and Alexandria, and was subsequently distracted by heresy and schism. When we examine the case of Novatian, the first Anti-Pope, we shall see that Antioch, as well as the other Primatial and Patriarchal Sees, took part in the settlement of the controversy. Novatian's claim to the Roman See was invalid, and he had carried his original Stoicism into the Church with him in adopting the severe line of refusing all reconciliation to those who had lapsed under persecution. S. Cornelius, the lawful Pope, was, as we shall subsequently see, supported by S. Dionysius of Alexandria, and by S. Cyprian of Carthage. He wrote four letters to Fabius of Antioch, as it was necessary to vindicate his position to the whole of Christendom, and Fabius had been inclined, possibly through ignorance of the facts, to favour the cause of Novatian.[1] S. Dionysius of Alexandria also wrote to the Patriarch of Antioch, and Fabius convoked a Synod to deal with the question. The letter of invitation to this Synod which Dionysius received was signed by Helenus of Tarsus, the chief Metropolitan of the Patriarchate of Antioch,[2] and he notified to S. Cornelius that he

[1] Φαβίῳ ὑποκατακλινομένῳ πως τῷ σχίσματι. (Euseb., vi. 44.)
[2] ἑαυτὸν παρακεκλῆσθαι ὑπό τε Ἑλένου τοῦ ἐν Ταρσῷ τῆς Κιλικίας ἐπισκόπου, καὶ τῶν λοιπῶν τῶν σὺν αὐτῷ (i.e., by the rest of the Metro-

had received this invitation, which also announced the death of Fabius and the succession of Demetrian.

The Synod was duly held at Antioch in A.D. 252,[1] and appears to have had great weight in settling the controversy, although its acts have not come down to us. But the fact of its being held, involving, as it does, the further fact that an Eastern Synod was summoned to discuss the difficulties and troubles of the Patriarch of the West, shows conclusively that the Primate of Christendom was not its monarch, but only first of the great Patriarchs, whose mutual interdependence and intercommunion was the means of cementing and maintaining the unity of the Church. The case of Paulus of Samosata, who became Patriarch of Antioch in A.D. 260, furnishes us with a further instance of the interdependent relations between the Patriarchal Sees. To Antioch we trace the true origin of Arianism,[2] and the way for one heresy concerning our Lord's Person was paved

politans and Bishops of the Patriarchate, who were available). Φιρμιλιανοῦ τε τοῦ ἐν Καππαδοκίᾳ, καὶ τοῦ κατὰ Παλαιστίνην Θεοκτίστου (the Metropolitans of Cappadocia and Palestine), ὡς ἂν ἐπὶ τὴν σύνοδον ἀπαντήσοι τὴν κατὰ 'Αντιόχειαν. κ.τ.λ. (Euseb., vi. 46.)

[1] The idea was to make the Synod as representative as possible. Helenus acted as senior Metropolitan, pending the succession of Demetrian to Fabius.

[2] Dr. Newman traces this very clearly. See *Arians in the Fourth Century*, chap. i., sections 1 and 2, and also Appendix I., *On the Syrian School of Theology*. The rhetorical and sophistical methods of

by another. Paulus denied the Trinity and the Incarnation in terms of such a Humanitarianism as the Semi-Arians of the next century felt bound to condemn.[1] He had the powerful support of Zenobia of Palmyra, and in the splendour of his prelacy and the scandals of his life he anticipated the worst type of mediæval Prince-Bishop. But Christendom could not tolerate a heretic upon its third Apostolic Throne. S. Dionysius of Alexandria[2] was still living, and ruling the Patriarchate of the "Evangelical Throne" of S. Mark.

Despite his age and infirmities, he stirred up the Metropolitans and Bishops of the Patriarchate of Antioch to convoke a solemn Council to sit in judgment upon their erring Patriarch. He was too infirm to attend the Council himself, but he strenuously urged the assembled prelates to do their duty,[3] and he also appealed to Paulus, urging him to reconsider his errors. The

---

the School of Antioch, when applied to the interpretation of Scripture, produced, firstly, Arianism, and then (through Theodore of Mopsuestia) Nestorianism.

[1] The Semi-Arian Synod of Sirinium, known as the Second Sirinian Synod, condemned the heresy of Paulus in A.D. 357.

[2] S. Dionysius is called by Eusebius ὁ μέγας ᾽Αλεξανδρέων ἐπίσκοπος (*H. E.*, vii. Præf.). S. Athanasius calls him τῆς καθολικῆς Ἐκκλησίας διδάσκαλος (S. Ath., *De Sent. Dion.*, 6).

[3] See Theod., *Hær. Fab.*, ii. 8. Euseb., *H. E.*, vii. 27. The letter of S. Dionysius was addressed to the Church at Antioch, and was of a formal character. It was not addressed to Paulus as Patriarch. τὸν ἡγεμόνα τῆς πλάνης οὐδὲ προσρήσεως ἀξιώσας, οὐδὲ πρὸς πρόσωπον γράψα αὐτῷ ἀλλὰ τῇ παροικίᾳ πάσῃ. κ.τ.λ. Euseb., *H. E.*, vii. 30.

Council met at Antioch in A.D. 264, and S. Dionysius died in the following year, before the case was finally settled. Firmilian of Cæsarea, in Cappadocia, as senior Metropolitan, presided at the Council, which was not confined in membership to the Metropolitans and Bishops dependent on Antioch. Their position was most difficult and delicate, owing to the secular support accorded to Paulus by Zenobia, and also to the fact that the Christians were at any moment liable to persecution at the will of the Emperor. Quite apart from his personal abilities, the prelates of Antioch felt that the Cappadocian Primate would be a more weighty president than Helenus of Tarsus, their own senior Metropolitan, who might be accused of prejudice against Paulus. Other eminent prelates, who were outside the jurisdiction of Antioch, were also invited to be present. S. Gregory Thaumaturgus, Archbishop of Neocæsarea, and his brother S. Athenodorus, Nicomas of Iconium, Hymenæus of Jerusalem, and Theotecnus of Cæsarea, the metropolis in those days of Jerusalem itself, were present at the Council.

Eusebius gives countenance to the view that the Council was meant to be of a quasi-œcumenical character,[1] and that all the Bishops of Christendom, so far as was practicable and possible, were invited

---

[1] After stating that S. Dionysius gave his opinion in writing because he was too infirm to attend, Eusebius proceeds: Οἱ δὲ λοιποὶ τῶν

to be present. In this case we have an early precedent for the constitutional usage of the Church, whereby an offending Patriarch is subject to the jurisdiction of an Œcumenical Council. Eusebius tells us of the vast number of priests and deacons who were present at this Council.[1] The deacons had not any right of voting, but they were at all events present as spectators. The partisans of the popular Paulus also attended and stood by their accused Patriarch, whilst Firmilian's logic unmasked his heresy. He took refuge in a simple denial of the charges against him, and the Bishops, overawed doubtless by the secular support which Paulus received from Zenobia, professed themselves satisfied.

Bishop Hefele holds that a second Council was shortly afterwards held, with the same abortive result. Others, with Dr. Neale, deny this, but the matter does not touch our argument.

The final Council, which deposed and excommunicated Paulus, was held in A.D. 269. Firmilian, who had presided at the first Council, died at Tarsus on his journey to this final Council. Helenus of Tarsus presided in his place as Senior Metropolitan

---

ἐκκλησιῶν ποιμένες, ἄλλος ἄλλοθεν, ὡς ἐπὶ λυμεῶνα τῆς Χριστοῦ ποίμνης συνίεσαν, οἱ πάντες ἐπὶ τὴν Ἀντιόχειαν σπεύδοντες. (*H. E.*, vii. 27.)

[1] μυρίους τε ἄλλους οὐκ ἂν ἀπορῆσαί τις, ἅμα πρεσβυτέροις καὶ διακόνοις. κ.τ.λ. (*H. E.*, vii. 28.)

THE PERIOD OF THE "ECCLESIA PRESSA" 123

of the Patriarchate. Malchion, an eminent priest,[1] who had been head of the sophists' Greek school at Antioch, was fitly chosen as the prosecutor of Paulus, whose tenets were enmeshed and confused with dialectical subtleties and sophistries. The Council, after deposing and excommunicating Paulus, elected Domnus to fill the vacant throne of Antioch. The clergy and laity of Antioch were not allowed to take their usual part in this election for fear of the partisans of Paulus and his secular influence. For two years he remained in possession of his episcopal residence, and when Zenobia had been conquered by Aurelian, the Catholics appealed to Aurelian for the possession of the Church property, which Paulus declined to give up.[2]

Aurelian, though a Pagan unversed in the merits of the case, set an example to future ages of that equity in matters of Church property which is all that the Church ought to expect at the hands of the Civil Power. He ordered the building to be given up to those persons who were in com-

[1] Μάλιστα δ' αὐτὸν εὐθύνας ἐπικρυπτόμενον διήλεγξε Μαλχίων. κ.τ.λ. (Euseb., vii. 29.) The part taken by Malchion as the prosecutor of Paulus before the Synod, must not be referred solely to his skill in dialectics. As a priest he had a constitutional right to accuse his Patriarch before the Synod and act as assessor in his trial. When Bishop Colenso was tried by the Metropolitan and Bishops of South Africa, the Dean of Capetown, and Archdeacons Merriman and Badnall were the prosecutors, and addressed the Court, as priests accusing the Bishop of heresy, in accordance with this ancient precedent.

[2] Euseb., *H. E.*, vii. 30. ἐπεὶ ἀντέτεινε καὶ τὴν τῆς ἐκκλησίας κατεῖχεν ἡγεμονίαν, Αὐρηλιανὸν ἔπεισαν ἐξελάσαι τῆς ἐκκλησίας. (Theodoret, *Hæret. Fab.*, xi. 8.)

munion with the Italian Bishops and the Roman Patriarch. Gibbon views his act as a piece of centralising policy meant to enhance the dignity of the Imperial city.[1] But it is safer to regard it as an independent testimony to the commanding position of the Roman See, and its value as a centre of unity. We need not refer in detail to the action of the Fathers at Antioch with regard to the ὁμοούσιον.[2] There are some interesting points, however, in the Encyclical Letter addressed to the Catholic Church by this final Council in the matter of Paulus. Its inscription is worth careful comment. It recounts the heresy and evil life of Paulus, and his excommunication. It further states his deposition, and the appointment by the Council of Domnus as his successor. It is addressed "To Dionysius (of Rome), Maximus (of Alexandria), and to all our fellow ministers throughout the world; the Bishops, Priests, and

---

[1] "He considered the Bishops of Italy as the most impartial and respectable judges amongst the Christians, and as soon as he was informed that they had unanimously approved the sentence of the Council, he acquiesced in their opinion, and (A.D. 274) immediately gave orders that Paul should be compelled to relinquish the temporal possessions belonging to an office, of which, in the judgment of his brethren, he had been regularly deprived. But while we applaud the justice, we should not overlook the policy of Aurelian; who was desirous of restoring and cementing the dependence of the Provinces on the Capital by every means which could bind the interests or prejudices of any part of his subjects." (Gibbon, vol. i. p. 414.)

[2] See Hefele on the Councils, vol. i. p. 123; also S. Ath., *De Synodis*, c. 45. (Newman's Notes in Oxf. Transl.)

THE PERIOD OF THE "ECCLESIA PRESSA"

Deacons, and to the whole Catholic Church under Heaven; Helenus (of Tarsus), and Hymenæus (of Jerusalem), and Theophilus (See unknown), and Theotecnus (of Cæsarea); Maximus (of Bostra), Proculus (See unknown), Nicomas (of Iconium), and Œlianus; Paul and Bolanus, and Protogenes, and Hierax, and Eutychius, and Theodorus, and Malchion, and Lucius (both Priests), and all the rest who are Bishops, Priests, and Deacons, dwelling with us in the neighbouring cities and nations, together with the Churches of God, send greeting to the beloved brethren in the Lord."[1]

We note that the Patriarch of Rome is addressed first, and next the Patriarch of Alexandria.[2] The

---

[1] Διονυσίῳ καὶ Μαξίμῳ καὶ τοῖς κατὰ τὴν οἰκουμένην πᾶσι συλλειτουργοῖς ἡμῶν ἐπισκόποις καὶ πρεσβυτέροις καὶ διακόνοις, καὶ πάσῃ τῇ ὑπὸ τὸν οὐρανὸν καθολικῇ ἐκκλησίᾳ, Ἕλενος καὶ Ὑμέναιος καὶ Θεόφιλος καὶ Θεότεκνος καὶ Μάξιμος, Πρόκλος, Νικόμας, καὶ Αἰλιανός, καὶ Παῦλος καὶ Βώλανος καὶ Πρωτογένης καὶ Ἱέραξ καὶ Εὐτύχιος καὶ Θεόδωρος, καὶ Μαλχίων καὶ Λούκιος, καὶ οἱ λοιποὶ πάντες οἱ σὺν ἡμῖν παροικοῦντες τὰς ἐγγὺς πόλεις καὶ ἔθνη ἐπίσκοποι καὶ πρεσβύτεροι καὶ διάκονοι, καὶ αἱ ἐκκλησίαι τοῦ Θεοῦ, ἀγαπητοῖς ἀδελφοῖς ἐν Κυρίῳ χαίρειν. (Euseb., *H. E.*, vii. 30.) Bossuet holds that, because the decree was addressed to the whole Catholic Church and received by its Patriarchs and Bishops, this Council of Antioch was of œcumenical authority. (Bossuet, Lettre xxii., cited by Trevern, *Discussion Amicale*, t. i. p. 223.)

[2] It is interesting to note that the Roman Dionysius, who was a skilled theologian, wrote to Dionysius of Alexandria, when the latter was accused of Sabellianism, and the Alexandrian Patriarch replied with a defence that satisfied his Roman brother Patriarch and namesake. Baronius sees in this incident the supremacy of the Roman Patriarch. But the incident really does not touch the question. It illustrates the interdependence and intercommunion of the great Patriarchs, and not the supremacy of one over the others. This is plain from the account of the matter given by S. Athanasius (Ep. *De Senten.*

first and second Thrones of Christendom are addressed by the third Throne of Antioch, as represented by its senior Metropolitan and the Prelates gathered by his invitation to a Patriarchal Council of a semi-œcumenical character. The occupants of the first and second Thrones, who were not at the Council, are addressed by name, as the leaders of Christendom, but they alone do not represent the Provinces and Dioceses who were not represented at Antioch. The Bishops, Priests, and Deacons of the Threefold Apostolic Ministry throughout the world (who were unable to take any part in the proceedings at Antioch), are also addressed. And the salutation does not end even with them. The whole Catholic Church, which includes not only Clergy, but the "Plebs Christiana," is addressed also. The Encyclical of the Antiochene Fathers emanates not only from Helenus, the senior Metropolitan, and his brother Metropolitans and Prelates, but from Priests of eminence, like Malchion, and from the Bishops, Priests, and Deacons of the Patriarchate, and neighbouring cities and people, and from the

---

Dionysii, Opp. i. 252). He says that the Roman Patriarch ἐπέστειλε Διονυσίῳ δηλῶσαι, which at first sight looks like an authoritative calling to account, till we remember that ἐπιστέλλω in Euseb. vi. 46 is used of the letters of the Alexandrian Dionysius, and simply means to send a letter or message. The fragments of the reply of Dionysius of Alexandria bear no traces of submission to the jurisdiction or supremacy of the Roman Patriarch.

Churches of God, which includes the laity. The constitutional position of the Priesthood as councillors, and of the Deacons as office-bearers in the Church, who might speak without voting in her Synods, and lastly, of the "Plebs Christiana," whose general concurrence in the proceedings is intimated, is very clearly indicated in the inscription and address of this Antiochene Encyclical.

In conclusion, we may note that just as Antioch dealt with the Roman trouble concerning Novatian the Anti-Pope, so did Rome deal with the Antiochene trouble concerning Paulus. Probably Synods were held at Rome in the matter of Paulus, both under Dionysius and his successor Felix.[1] The judgment of Aurelian in the case of Paulus must surely have involved a meeting of the Bishops of Italy with the Roman Patriarch in order to formally endorse the condemnation of Paulus, pronounced by the Synod of Antioch.

This appears to have taken place under Felix, as Dionysius died before the final condemnation of Paulus by the Roman See and the Bishops

---

[1] "In A.D. 264 the Alexandrian and Roman Dionysii acted together with the Council of Antioch in condemning and degrading Paul of Samosata." (Smith and Wace, *Dict. of Christian Biography*, vol. i., p. 852.) *How* they acted is not clear, for Baronius was misled by the Latin translation of S. Ath., *De Synod.*, 43, in positively attributing to Dionysius of Rome the condemnation of Paulus in a Roman Synod. Baronius (*Ad. Ann.*, 265, n. 10) makes this statement, and is corrected by Hefele (*Hist. of Councils*, vol. i. p. 122, n.).

of Italy. As a Greek scholar and theologian, Dionysius was specially fitted to deal with the sophistries of Paulus, and thus the way was prepared for the final endorsement of the decree of Antioch by Felix, the next Roman Patriarch.

The case of Paulus shows that Rome was *primus inter pares* amongst the Patriarchal Sees, and that its central position gave it a commanding Primatial influence, even in the eyes of the Pagan Emperor Aurelian. But it does not show that the legitimate Primacy of Rome could be distorted into a Vatican supremacy.[1]

We now turn from Antioch to North Africa, the true cradle of Latin Christianity, and to Carthage, its Primatial See. We may remark in passing that if the Roman Church had not been Greek-speaking during the greater part of the Ante-Nicene period, it would have been unfitted to become the practical centre of Christian unity. Greek was the universal language of business and commerce, whilst Latin was the official language of the Empire. The subtleties of theological definitions found more

[1] A learned Roman Catholic theologian remarks of the case of Paulus:—" Porro nec Itali, nec Romanus Episcopus causam Pauli in Oriente iudicatum retractare aggressi sunt ; sed iudicium Orientalium sine ullo examine ratum habuerunt. Hæc autem in isto Pauli iudicio observanda sunt ad propositum pertinentia. Primum ad Synodum vocatur Paulus, non ad Romanum Pontificem. Secundo, a Synodo sine Pontificis Romani consensu et participatione damnatur. Tertio, ab ea damnatus, ad Romanum sedem non provocat." (Du Pin, *De Antiqua Ecclesiæ Disciplina*, p. 157.)

accurate expression in Greek than in Latin, and whilst the Roman Church was Greek speaking, it was in touch with Eastern theology and modes of expression in a manner that ceased when it became more exclusively the centre of Latin Christianity. Although Carthage was not an Apostolic See, or the seat of a Patriarchate, properly so called, the Archbishop of Carthage wielded an influence almost as powerful as that of the Roman Patriarch throughout Latin Christendom. He was in communication with Spain and Gaul, as well as in constant touch with Rome and Italy. S. Cyprian was the most famous of the Primates of Carthage. To him it was given to consolidate the constitution and order of the Catholic Church with a brilliant insight and sagacity founded upon a true loyalty to the Divine order of its being. S. Cyprian has been described as an innovating sacerdotalist, who invented the Catholic Church, as we now see it. But he was conservative to the backbone, and based his methods exclusively upon first principles of the Gospel of Christ. It is very important to examine the views of S. Cyprian upon the special subject with which these pages deal. We need no apology for alluding to S. Cyprian's oft-quoted dictum upon the solidarity of the Episcopate. "Episcopatus unus est, cuius a singulis in solidum pars tenetur." (*De*

Unit. Eccl., Benedictine ed., p. 195.)[1] We may freely translate it as follows: "The Episcopate is one; it is a whole in which each enjoys full possession." Archbishop Benson paraphrases it as follows: "The Apostleship, continued for ever in the Episcopate, is thus universal, yet one; each Bishop's authority perfect and independent, yet not forming with the others a mere agglomerate, but being a full tenure on a totality, like that of a shareholder in a joint-stock property."[2] The illustration of the shareholder is admirable. Individual Bishops cannot act as autocephalic diocesan autocrats, any more than an individual shareholder in a joint-stock property can exercise by himself the joint authority belonging to all. Each individual Bishop's authority to ordain, and confirm, and judge as *iudex ordinarius* is perfect and indepen-

---

[1] S. Cyprian expresses the same truth in his letter to Pope Stephen, in which he states that a heretical Bishop's flock is the care of the universal Episcopate, on the principle that, though the Pastors be many, yet the flock that they feed is one. "Idcirco copiosum corpus est sacerdotum, concordiæ mutuæ glutine atque unitatis vinculo copulatum, ut si quis ex collegio nostro hæresin facere, et gregem Christi lacerare et vastare tentaverit, subveniant cæteri. . . . Nam etsi pastores multi sumus, unum tamen gregem pascimus, et oves universas, quas Christus sanguine suo et passione quæsivit colligere et fovere debemus." (S. Cypr., Ep. 68, *ad Steph.*) Again he writes, "Scire debes episcopum in ecclesia esse, et ecclesiam in episcopo . . . ecclesia quæ catholica una est, scissa non (est) neque divisa. Sed (est) utique connexa et cohærentium sibi invicem sacerdotum glutine copulata." (S. Cypr., Ep. 66, 8.)

[2] S. Cyprian (Smith and Wace, i. p. 745).

dent, just as each shareholder's vote in controlling a joint-stock property is perfect and independent. Any individual action which a shareholder may take with regard to property belonging in common to the whole body, must be limited in its range by the scope entrusted to the individual by the whole body; and further, it must be remembered that the individual is responsible to the whole body for his exercise of the trust committed to him.[1] Therefore the authority of the individual Bishop is, in the first place, limited to his Diocese, which is the sphere of action immediately assigned to him by his Metropolitan and com-provincial Bishops. The Metropolitan and Bishops of a Province, in Provincial Synod assembled, have authority to create new Dioceses, and to subdivide or alter the boundaries of old ones.[2] In his Diocese the Bishop acts as a shareholder of the common Apostleship, and is responsible for his every action, primarily, to his immediate brother-shareholders, the com-provincial Bishops, who, with the Metropolitan or Archbishop, as *primus inter pares*, form the Provincial Synod.

[1] Cardinal Bellarmine, whose ultra-Papal views are well known, was yet constrained by his knowledge of facts to write as follows: "Episcopi sunt ecclesiæ representativi, ut nostri loquuntur, quilibet enim Episcopus gerit personam suæ ecclesiæ particularis, et proinde omnes Episcopi gerunt personam totius Ecclesiæ." (Bellarmine, *De Concil. Auctoritate*, iii. 14.)

[2] See Note B.

But the judgment of a Provincial Synod is not absolutely final. Beyond it lies the appeal to the Patriarch and his Synod, whilst above all lies the appeal to the entire body of the Episcopate in General Council assembled, which, to pursue Archbishop Benson's figure, stands for the general body of the shareholders. The Diocesan Bishop possesses, however, liberty of individual action within certain well-defined limits which do not touch the common heritage of the faith and discipline of the Church. The *ius liturgicum* is an instance. A Bishop can order the details of worship in his Diocese in matters which do not conflict with the common law of Christendom. At the risk of appearing to anticipate in the order of our authorities we may venture to quote S. Augustine's counsel of peaceful common sense in discussing a point of this nature. One Casulanus applied to him with regard to the practice of observing the Saturday as a fast, which was practised in some Churches and not in others. S. Augustine replied that it was within the discretion of the Diocesan Bishop to do as he thought fit in the matter, and that the Bishop's ruling should be adhered to without further scruple.[1]

[1] "Mos eorum mihi sequendus videtur, quibus eorum populorum congregatio regenda commissa est. Quapropter si consilio meo acquiescis ; episcopo tuo in hac re noli resistere, et quod facit ipse, sine ullo scrupulo vel disceptatione sectare." (S. Aug., Ep. 86, *Ad Casulan.*)

To return to S. Cyprian. There is one luminous fact in his view of the Episcopate. The individual Bishop is responsible to the whole Episcopate for what he does, and yet, however that responsibility finds expression, whether it be in his obligations to his Metropolitan, or Patriarch, or to an Œcumenical Council, he is not (to use a modern phrase) the "Assistant Curate" of another Bishop, or Patriarch, however eminent. No Bishop, not even the Primate of Christendom, is "*Episcopus Episcoporum,*" and herein, by anticipation, he condemns the present servile subjection of the Bishops of Latin Christendom to the Roman See. The occasion which caused S. Cyprian to use these words is well known. His controversy with Pope Stephen on the question of the Re-baptism of heretics is familiar ground to every student of Church history. That S. Cyprian was in the wrong as a theologian, and that Pope Stephen was in the right in this controversy, does not touch our present argument. In A.D. 256 S. Cyprian presided over a Council at Carthage, at which seventy-two Bishops were present. The Council endorsed his view, that heretical baptism was invalid, even though the right form and matter were used. S. Cyprian, using due respect to the Primate of Christendom, formally communicated to him the decision of this Council, which, however, he did not consider necessarily exclusive of the opposite view. He wished the matter left open to the judgment of individual Bishops.[1] But Pope Stephen, with a clearer statesmanship, saw that this was impossible. He attempted the policy of Victor in the Paschal controversy, and tried to close the question by threatening to excommunicate the African Bishops. S. Cyprian wrote to Pompeius (Ep. lxxiv.) in indignant terms upon "the harsh obstinacy of our brother Stephen." He owned the Primacy of Rome in the fullest possible way.[2] But he knew nothing of the modern Vatican novelty, that the Pope is "the supreme judge of the faithful, and that the judgment of the Apostolic See cannot be revised by any one, and that no one may pass judgment upon its decisions."[3] S. Cyprian convoked another Council, at which eighty-five Bishops were present (A.D. 256), and in his opening speech he says: "It remains for each of us to deliver our sentiments on this matter, judging no one, nor

---

[1] Qua in re nec nos vim cuiquam facimus, aut legem damus, cum habeat in ecclesiæ administratione voluntatis suæ arbitrium liberum unusquisque præpositus, rationem actus sui Domino redditurus. (S. Cyprian, *Ep. ad Steph.*, ed. Bened., p. 129.) This passage cannot be divorced from its context, and is therefore limited in its application.

[2] S. Augustine says that "without doubt holy Cyprian would have yielded, if the truth of this question had been thoroughly sifted, and declared, and established by a plenary council." (S. Aug., *De Bapt.*, ii. 4.) The Vatican claims were unknown alike to S. Cyprian and S. Augustine. An Œcumenical Council was to their minds the final deciding authority, and not the Roman Patriarch.

[3] Vatican Decrees (*Collect. Lacens.*, vii. 487) confirmed by Pius IX., July 18, 1870.

removing any one, if he be of a different opinion, from the right of communion. For no one of us sets himself up to be a Bishop of Bishops, or by tyrannical terror compels his colleagues to the necessity of obedience, since every Bishop, according to the freedom of his liberty and power, possesses the right of his own opinion, and can no more be judged by another Bishop than he himself can judge another Bishop."[1]

It is interesting to note S. Cyprian's real meaning in this passage. He is not defending the irresponsible autonomy of any individual Bishop, but he is asserting the principle that no single Bishop can be judged by another single Bishop.[2] No single Bishop is "Episcopus Episcoporum" in the sense that he is the sole irresponsible judge of another Bishop. S. Cyprian's words were directed against the claims of Pope Stephen to excommunicate the North African Bishops in a matter which might well be left (in S. Cyprian's opinion) an open question. But S. Cyprian's *dictum* with regard to an "Episcopus Episcoporum" must be read in con-

---

[1] "Superest ut de hac ipsa re singuli quid sentiamus, proferamus; neminem iudicantes, aut a iure communionis aliquem, si diversum senserit, amoventes. Neque enim quisquam nostrum Episcopum se Episcoporum constituit, aut tyrannico terrore ad obsequendi necessitatem collegas suos adigit; quando habeat omnis episcopus pro licentia libertatis et potestatis suæ arbitrium proprium; tanquam iudicari ab alio non possit, quam nec ipse potest iudicare." (Conc. Carth., *ap. S. Cypr.*, ed. Bened., p. 330.)

[2] See *Jurisdiction*, by J. W. Lee. *Union Review* for 1866, p. 363.

junction with his strong assertion of the Primacy of the Roman See, and his firm adhesion to the principle of Primacy generally.

The strong hand of the Primate of Carthage is very manifest in the various Councils over which he presided, and S. Cyprian never meant to advocate either irresponsible episcopal autocracy, or to minimise legitimate Primatial authority by his action towards Pope Stephen. We have already[1] dealt with S. Cyprian's description of Rome as "the principal Church whence sacerdotal unity has taken its rise." There are other passages in which S. Cyprian expresses the same view. As we have already stated, the question at issue between Pope Cornelius and Novatian was really a matter of succession. S. Cyprian wrote to Cornelius after the Council of Carthage (A.D. 251) had sent two Bishops, Caldonius and Fortunatus, to Rome to investigate the claims of Novatian, and stated in his letter that he was satisfied that Cornelius was the true Bishop of Rome, and that the party of Novatian "had refused the bosom and embrace of her who is their root and mother."[2] In a subsequent letter to Cornelius he says, "We who furnish all who sail hence with instructions, lest they should journey with any scandal, know that we have ex-

---

[1] See Note A., Chapter II.
[2] "Radicis et matris sinum atque complexum recusavit." (S. Cyp., *Ep. ad Corn.*, xliii.)

horted them to hold and acknowledge the root and stem of the Catholic Church."[1] It is obviously impossible to suppose that S. Cyprian meant in these two passages to state that the Roman Church was "the root and stem" of the Catholic Church in such a sense as to render communion with the Roman See a necessary condition of Catholic unity or orthodoxy.[2] His own dealings with Pope Stephen render the modern ultramontane view of his words quite inadmissible and impossible;[3] but, on the other hand, it is equally inadmissible to minimise them in such a manner as to say that they contain "no allusion to Rome's position as the original spring of evangelisation in the West, and as the ecclesiastical metropolis of Central and Southern Italy."[4] S. Cyprian did not refuse to recognise Rome as the capital of the world, and it was equally far from his thoughts to minimise the legitimate Primacy of the Roman See, however strenuously he might resist the undue supremacy claimed by Stephen. The safest view of these passages of S. Cyprian is the moderate one which

---

[1] Nos enim singulis navigantibus, ne cum scandalo ullo navigarent, rationem reddentes, scimus nos hortatos esse ut Ecclesiæ Catholicæ radicem et matricem agnoscerent ac tenerent. (*Ep. ad Corn.*, xlv.) Bossuet favours the rendering of "stem" for "matricem." (*Œuvres*, ed. 1816, 411-412.)

[2] See Note C.
[3] See Note D.
[4] Puller, *Primitive Saints and the See of Rome*, p. 341.

avoids either extreme. We may safely conclude that S. Cyprian meant to allude to the unique position of the Roman See,[1] and the lawful Primacy of the Roman Patriarch.

S. Cyprian was too able an organiser not to see the immense services Rome could render to Christendom as a centre of unity. His words express his ideal, and not the ideal of the Vatican Council of 1870. S. Cyprian also carefully maintained the rights of the Priesthood and the Christian Laity. We have already said that the Archbishop of Carthage was a man of commanding influence. The Bishops who owned his Primacy seem to have endorsed his views almost absolutely in the great Synods which he held; but yet he was careful to act constitutionally rather than autocratically. He guarded, as carefully as S. Ignatius, the right of the Priesthood to a consultative voice, and he further maintained the right of the "Plebs Christiana" to assent to what was done in Councils and Synods. The constitutional position of a Bishop involves the fullest admission of the rights of his Priests[2] and of his faithful Laity, as well as the

---

[1] Tertullian, whose influence S. Cyprian owns so definitely, recognised the position of Rome as the one Apostolic See of the West: "percurre ecclesias apostolicas ... si ... Italiæ adiaces, habes Romam, unde nobis quoque auctoritas præsto est." (*De Præscr.* 36.)

[2] S. Cyprian's action shows that the priests have a right to be consulted, with reference to candidates for Ordination, as well as the laity, whose canonical right to object is guarded by the "Si quis."

THE PERIOD OF THE "ECCLESIA PRESSA" 139

rights of his Metropolitan and com-provincial Bishops, his Patriarch and Patriarchal Synod, and the ultimate authority of the whole Episcopate in Œcumenical Council assembled.

As S. Cyprian was accustomed to call Tertullian his "Master," Tertullian's views on the position of the laity are worth quoting in this connection. His views on the Priesthood of the Laity are well known.[1] He also says with regard to Councils held in the second century, that they represented "the whole Christian name."[2] By this he evi-

"In ordinationibus clericis solemus vos ante consulere, et mores ac merita singulorum communi consilio ponderare." (S. Cypr., Ep. 33, *ad Cler.*) In other matters concerning the government of the Church they were consulted. "Ut ea quæ circa ecclesiæ gubernaculum utilitas communis exposcit, tractare simul, et plurimorum consilio examinata limare possemus." (S. Cypr., Ep. 6, *ad Cler.*) Cornelius, as Roman Patriarch, did likewise. "Omni actu ad me perlato, placuit contrahi presbyterium—ut formato consilio, quid circa personam eorum observari deberet, consensu omnium statueretur." (Cornel., Ep. 46, *ad Cypr.*) He summoned a Diocesan Synod of his priests to consult in the matter of restoring Maximus, and other confessors, who had at first sided with Novatian.

[1] "Nonne et laici sacerdotes sumus? Scriptum est, Regnum quoque nos et sacerdotes Deo et Patri suo fecit. "Again, in allusion to our Lord's promise to be present where two or three are gathered together in His name, even if the Threefold Ministry is unavoidably absent, he says that the Church is still there. "Sed ubi tres, ecclesia est, licet laici." (Tertullian, *De Exhortat. Cast.*, vii.)

[2] Certain early Councils, to which Eusebius alludes, were held against Montanism about A.D. 150 (see Hefele, vol. i., p. 80). Apollinaris, Metropolitan of Hierapolis, and twenty-six Bishops held a Provincial Council at Hierapolis in Asia, and condemned Montanus and Maximilla. This is the earliest Provincial Synod on record, and Eusebius (quoting a fragment) says: Τῶν γὰρ κατὰ τὴν 'Ασίαν πιστῶν πολλάκις καὶ πολλαχῇ τῆς 'Ασίας εἰς τοῦτο συνελθόντων, καὶ τοὺς προσφάτους λόγους

dently meant that the Laity expressed their consenting voice to the definitions made by the Bishops, after consultation with the Priests. At the outbreak of the Decian persecution in A.D. 250, S. Cyprian retired from Carthage with the courage of a noble prudence. He guided his Diocese during his retirement by frequent letters. He is asked a question involving discipline, and he replies by declining to settle it on his own unaided judgment. "I am unable to give my reply by myself alone," he says, "since I have resolved from the beginning of my episcopate to do nothing of my own private opinion and your counsel" (he was writing to his priests and deacons) "and without the consent of the laypeople."[1] The same view obtained at Rome. The Roman Clergy wrote to S. Cyprian upon the very important subject of the restoration of the lapsed. "In so important a matter," they

ἐξετασάντων καὶ βεβήλους ἀποφηνάντων, καὶ ἀποδοκιμασάντων τὴν αἵρεσιν, οὕτω δὴ τῆς τε ἐκκλησίας ἐξεώσθησαν καὶ τῆς κοινωνίας εἴρχθησαν. (*Ex Anonym. ap. Euseb.*, v. 16.) We cannot assume that the πιστοί meant Bishops and Clergy *alone*, to the exclusion of the Laity. In like manner Tertullian, writing apparently of larger Councils, evidently includes Bishops, Clergy, and Laity. " Aguntur præterea per Græcias illa certis in locis concilia ex universis ecclesiis, per quæ et altiora quæque in commune tractantur, et ipsa repræsentatio totius nominis Christiani magna veneratione celebratur." (Tert., *De Ieiun.* xiii.)

[1] Solus rescribere nihil potui ; quando a primordio Episcopatus mei statuerim nihil sine consilio vestro, et sine consensu plebis, mea privatim sententia gerere. (S. Cypr., Ep. xiv.)

write, "the same thing approves itself to us which you have already dealt with, namely, that the peace of the Church must be deferred (*i.e.* the restoration of the lapsed); and that then, a communication of counsels having been made with the Bishops, Priests, Deacons, Confessors, and Laymen in good standing, the case of the lapsed be dealt with."[1] S. Cyprian, writing to Antonianus, quotes this reply of the Roman Clergy, which lays an additional stress on the concord which existed between Rome and Carthage upon the subject of the "Plebs Christiana." "And this also I wrote very fully to Rome, to the Clergy who were still acting without a Bishop, and to the Confessors, Maximus the Presbyter, and the rest who were then shut up in prison, but are now in the Church, joined to Cornelius. You may know that I wrote thus from their reply. For in their letter they have put the matter thus."[2] And then he quotes the

---

[1] Quanquam nobis in tam ingenti negotio placeat, quod et tu ipse tractasti prius: Ecclesiæ pacem sustinendam, deinde, sic collatione consiliorum cum Episcopis, Presbyteris, Diaconis, Confessoribus, pariter ac stantibus laicis facta, lapsorum tractare rationem. (Ep. xxx., *Cypriano Papæ Presbyteri et Diaconi Romæ consistentes.*) The Roman See was then vacant after the death of Pope Fabian.

[2] "Quod etiam Romam ad Clerum tunc adhuc sine Episcopo agentem, et ad Confessores, Maximum presbyterum, et cæteros in custodia constitutos, nunc in Ecclesia cum Cornelio iunctos, plenissime scripsi. Quod me scripsisse de eorum rescriptis poteris noscere. Nam in epistola sua ita posuerunt." Then follow the quoted words. (S. Cypr., Ep. lv., *ad Antonian.*) It is interesting to note that the senior Clergy of a diocese have authority to administer its affairs *sede vacante.*

passage about referring the case of the lapsed to the Clergy and laymen in good standing. The right of the laity to assent in the election of Bishops is plain and manifest. We shall deal with this point subsequently. Although doubts have been thrown on the right of laymen to attend Synods, we must admit this much from the evidence which has been adduced.

(i.) The *assent* of the whole body of the faithful is necessary to the decisions in matters of Faith, Doctrine, and Discipline, enacted by the Bishops with the counsel of the Clergy.

(ii.) This assent must find expression in some definite way. No better way can be suggested than the presence of certain representative laity in Provincial and Diocesan Synods, who shall have an *assenting* vote, which involves no right of initiative in matters on which the Bishops have, *iure divino*, a *votum decisivum*, after consulting with the Clergy.[1]

The Roman Clergy acted thus in the case of Marcion, as well as in their correspondence with S. Cyprian. This power afterwards was concentrated in the hands of the Arch-priest or Dean, and the Cathedral Chapter; or in the Vicar-General and Chapter.

[1] We may briefly sum up the various indications of this presence of the laity in Synods. At the Council of Carthage on Baptism (A.D. 256), S. Cyprian presided over eighty-seven Bishops, very many Priests and Deacons, and *maxima pars plebis*. (S. Cypr., *Opp.*, ed. Balus, p. 329.) In the Council of Elvira (A.D. 305) the Decrees were issued by the Bishops *alone*, twenty-four Priests *sat*, as representing the *consultative* voice, the Deacons and Laity who were present had to *stand*. (Bruns., *Biblioth. Eccl.*, vol. i. pt. ii. p. 1.) In Spain the presence of the laity was usual. The Council of Tarragona (A.D. 516) *ordered* the

THE PERIOD OF THE "ECCLESIA PRESSA" 143

We must now deal with S. Cyprian's view of his own office as Primate. He referred back to the Diocesan Bishop a case of discipline, which primarily belonged to Diocesan authority, and declined to deal with it in the first instance as Primate. The complaint of Bishop Rogatianus was laid before S. Cyprian and a Synod of Bishops. S. Cyprian wrote in reply as follows: "I and my colleagues who were present with me were deeply and grievously distressed, dearest brother, on reading your letter in which you complained of your deacon, that forgetful of your sacerdotal rank, and unmindful of his own office and ministry, he had provoked you by his insults and injuries. And you indeed have acted worthily, and with your accustomed humility towards us, in rather complaining of him to us; although you have power, according to the inherent right belonging to your episcopate and the authority of your throne, whereby you might at once obtain legal satis-

---

presence of the laity. (*Hardouin*, ii. 1053.) The fourth Council of Toledo ordered that "After the entrance and seating of all the Bishops those Presbyters are called *quos causa probaverit introire*. After these enter such approved Deacons as the rule permits to be present. *Deinde ingrediantur et Laici, qui electione concilio interesse meruerunt*." (Mansi., *Conc.* i. p. 10.) Elected laity thus had a distinct place in the Spanish Councils. In the Council of Orange in A.D. 529, laymen signed the decrees with the formula *consentiens subscripsi*. This is unusual. The Bishops were accustomed to sign *definiens subscripsi*, and the Priests Deacons, and laymen simply *subscripsi* (Hefele, vol. i. p. 25). (Cf. *Field on the Church*, chap. xxix. p. 646.)

faction upon him; being assured that all we your colleagues would be well pleased with whatsoever steps you might take with regard to your insolent deacon, in accordance with your sacerdotal power."[1]

In accordance with this clear definition of rights, the Bishop, as *iudex ordinarius* in his Diocese, cannot delegate his authority to his Metropolitan, or Primate. He must, in the first instance, exercise it himself as of inherent right. For the manner of his exercising it he is responsible to the Collective Episcopate, through his Metropolitan and com-provincial Bishops, in the first instance; through his Patriarch and Patriarchal Synod, in the second instance; and, finally, to an Œcumenical Council. We do not, of course, claim that this matured method of applying the authority of the Collective Episcopate to the case of a single Bishop was accurately defined in S. Cyprian's day,[2]

---

[1] Graviter et dolenter commoti sumus ego, et collegæ mei, qui præsentes aderant, frater carissime, lectis litteris tuis, quibus de diacono tuo conquestus es, quod immemor sacerdotalis loci tui, et officii ac ministerii sui oblitus contumeliis et iniuriis suis te exacerbaverit. Et tu quidem honorifice circa nos et pro solita tua humilitate fecisti, ut malles de eo nobis conqueri, cum pro episcopatus vigore et cathedræ auctoritate haberes potestatem, qua possis de illo statim vindicari; certus quod collegæ tui omnes gratum haberemus, quodcunque circa diaconum tuum contumeliosum sacerdotali potestate fecisses. (S. Cypr., Ep. lxv.)

[2] S. Cyprian, in the passage above quoted, makes it plain that, whilst he and his colleagues had such confidence in Rogatianus that they would be "well pleased" with his action against his offending

but it can be fairly deduced as the ideal of constitutional Church authority in Ante-Nicene times. We now touch upon the earliest Canon Law which deals with the constitutional authority of Bishops. The arguments as to the date and authority of the Apostolic Canons are too complex and lengthy for these pages.[1] We may safely conclude that some of them embody the precepts and authority of the Apostolic and sub-Apostolic age, whilst others are of later date. We have already alluded to Bishop Beveridge's conclusion that these Canons are Ante-Nicene. "Beveridge considered this collection to be a repertory of ancient Canons given by Synods in the second and third centuries. In opposition . . . Daillé regarded it as the work of a forger who lived in the fifth and sixth centuries, but Beveridge refuted him so convincingly, that from that time his opinion, with some few modifications, has been that of all the learned." (Hefele, *Councils*, vol. i. p. 452.)[2]

deacon, the reverse was also possible. Rogatianus was responsible to the Metropolitan and Bishops of his Province in the first instance, and then to the Primatial Council of the Archbishop of Carthage.

[1] The modern Roman view of these Canons is as follows: "Canones illi non sunt opus genuinum apostolorum, nec ab omni nævo immunes; merito tamen reputantur insigne monumentum disciplinæ Ecclesiæ per priora sæcula." (Icard., *Prælect. Iuris Can.*, 1862.)

[2] Bunsen concludes that in these Canons "we find ourselves unmistakably in the midst of the life of the Church of the second and third centuries." (*Christianity and Mankind*, vol. ii. p. 405.)

K

Von Drey, on the other hand, while claiming to refute the conclusions of Beveridge, is yet obliged to admit that certain of the Apostolic Canons are Ante-Nicene. The Canon concerning Metropolitans and Primates is certainly Ante-Nicene, for it reflects accurately the historic position of Primates in the second and third centuries. It is numbered 35 in the collection of Dionysius Exiguus, who translated a collection of Canons from Greek into Latin in about A.D. 500. He prefaces his collection with fifty Canons, which in his preface he calls " Canones qui dicuntur Apostolorum."[1] In the Latin it runs as follows : " Episcopos gentium singularum scire convenit, quis inter eos primus habeatur, quem velut caput existiment, et nihil amplius præter eius conscientiam gerant quam illa sola singuli, quæ parochiæ propriæ et villis, quæ sub ea sunt, competunt. Sed nec ille præter omnium conscientiam faciat aliquid. Sic

---

[1] Dionysius compiled a second collection, in which he omitted the Apostolic Canons in deference to the decree of Pope Hormisdas, who declared them apocryphal, about A.D. 514. A previous decree of Gelasius, according to Gratian, had taken the same view, but Archbishop Hincmar of Rheims expressly states that Gelasius was silent on the subject of these Canons. The 46th Canon declared that all baptism by heretics was invalid, and this in itself would militate against their reception in Rome and the West. But notwithstanding this, they were gradually received in the West, and partly incorporated by Gratian in the *Corpus Iuris Canonici*. Besides which, when Humbert, the Legate of Pope Leo IX., condemned certain apocryphal writings in 1054, he accepted the fifty Apostolic Canons.

etiam unanimitas erit, et glorificabitur Deus per Christum in Spiritu Sancto."

About fifty years after Dionysius Exiguus, Joannes Scholasticus, who was made Patriarch of Constantinople in A.D. 565, published a Greek Collection of Canons, in which the Apostolic Canons were increased in number to 85. The Greek text used by Dionysius differs in details, and in the numbering of the Canons, from the text used by Joannes Scholasticus; but the 85 Canons of his edition were subsequently accepted by the second Canon of the Synod in Trullo (A.D. 792), which the Eastern Church accepts as Œcumenical. Thus, whilst we may reckon the 50 Canons accepted in the West as practically Ante-Nicene, it is not safe so to reckon the additional 35 Canons of the Eastern recension. Bishop Beveridge holds that the Apostolic Canons were expressly confirmed by Canon i. of the Council of Chalcedon.[1] But Canon Bright is doubtful,[2] and the text appears to refer expressly to Canons enacted in known Synods. Bishop Hefele, however, shows that the Council of Chalcedon appealed to the authority of the 29th, 31st, and 32nd of the Apostolical Canons.[3] Pro-

---

[1] Τοὺς παρὰ τῶν ἁγίων πατέρων καθ' ἑκάστην σύνοδον ἄχρι τοῦ νῦν ἐκτεθέντας κανόνας, κρατεῖν ἐδικαιώσαμεν. (Conc. Chal., i.)
[2] *Notes on the Canons of the First Four General Councils*, p. 125.
[3] Hefele, vol. ii. p. 68.

bably the Council of Chalcedon sanctioned such of the Apostolical Canons as had been re-enacted by subsequent Synods. This bears on Canon xxxv. with which we are now dealing, as it was re-enacted by the 9th Canon of the Synod of Antioch in A.D. 341. The Greek of the 35th Apostolical Canon is as follows: Τοὺς ἐπισκόπους ἑκάστου ἔθνους εἰδέναι χρὴ τὸν ἐν αὐτοῖς πρῶτον, καὶ ἡγεῖσθαι αὐτὸν ὡς κεφαλήν, καὶ μηδέν τι πράττειν περιττὸν ἄνευ τῆς ἐκείνου γνώμης ἐκεῖνα δὲ μόνα πράττειν ἕκαστον, ὅσα τῇ αὐτοῦ παροικίᾳ ἐπιβάλλει καὶ ταῖς ὑπ' αὐτὴν χώραις· ἀλλὰ μηδὲ ἐκεῖνος ἄνευ τῆς πάντων γνώμης ποιείτω τι· οὕτω γὰρ ὁμόνοια ἔσται καὶ δοξασθήσεται ὁ Θεὸς διὰ Κυρίου ἐν Ἁγίῳ Πνεύματι. A careful comparison of the Latin and Greek text will give us the following translation: "The Bishops of every nation ought to know who is the first amongst them, and to esteem him as their Head, and not to do anything extraordinary[1] without his judgment, but for every one to manage only the affairs of his own Paroikia (*i.e.* Diocese), and the places which are within its jurisdiction. But let not him (*i.e.* the Primate) do anything without the judgment of all, for it is by acting thus that there will be unanimity, and God will be glorified through our Lord in the Holy Spirit." It would be difficult to suggest

---

[1] *i.e.* "beyond their ordinary jurisdiction."

clearer words than those used in this Canon to express the constitutional relation subsisting between Diocesan Bishops and their Primates. We use the word "Primate" advisedly, for the leading principle of this Canon applies not only to Metropolitans and the Bishops of their Provinces, but is capable of a wider and more extended application. The Bishops of the Church of *each nation*, in which there may be several Metropolitans and Ecclesiastical Provinces, are to recognise the Primacy of the first in rank of their Metropolitans.[1] The position of the Archbishop of Carthage, as a Primate of Metropolitans, and the principle of Primacy, as vested in the great Patriarchal Sees, is distinctly recognised in this Canon. The position [2] which has been attri-

[1] Bishop Beveridge, writing on this Canon, takes the same view as is expressed in the text. "Præsertim cum is simpliciter Primus *suæ gentis* Episcopus hic dicatur, non Metropolita, non Archiepiscopus, non Exarchus, non Patriarcha, quæ nomina postmodum in usum ecclesiasticum recepta sunt, nonnulla quidem eorum Concilii Nicæni tempore, vel paulo ante, alia vix ante quartam universalem Synodum a Chalcedone celebratam. Verum de nominibus istis non opus est hic disputemus, cum rem ipsam ab ipsis Apostolorum temporibus obtinuisse pro comperto certoque habeamus, ut unus scilicet in unaquaque gente Episcopus, et quidem is qui Metropoli eiusdem præest, Primatum quendam supra cæteros et prærogativum haberet." (*Cod. Canon. Eccl. Prim.*, ii. 5, p. 73).

[2] The South African Church in 1876 took a step somewhat in advance of the unwritten common consent of the Catholic Bishops in communion with the See of Canterbury. The Provincial Synod of that year expressed its desire (by a formal resolution) "that the relation of His Grace the Lord Archbishop of Canterbury to the other Bishops of the Anglican Communion be that of Primate among Arch-

buted by common consent to the Archbishop of Canterbury by the Catholic Bishops in communion with that great and venerable See, is equally covered by this Canon, although the centrifugal tendencies of Teutonic Christianity have as yet hindered its Canonical delimitation. The 38th Apostolic Canon is also worth quoting, since it applies the principles laid down in Canon xxxv. to regular Synodical action. " Bis in anno episcoporum concilia celebrentur, ut inter se invicem dogmata pietatis explorent, et emergentes ecclesiasticas contentiones amoveant ; semel quidem quarta septimana Pentecostes, secundo vero duodecimo die mensis Hyperberetæi (id est iuxta Romanos quarto idus Octobris)." Δεύτερον τοῦ ἔτους σύνοδος γινέσθω τῶν ἐπισκόπων καὶ ἀνακρινέτωσαν ἀλλήλους τὰ δόγματα τῆς εὐσεβείας καὶ τὰς ἐμπιπτούσας ἐκκλησιαστικὰς ἀντιλογίας διαλυέτωσαν· ἅπαξ μὲν τῇ τετάρτῃ ἑβδομάδι τῆς Πεντηκοστῆς, δεύτερον δὲ Ὑπερβερεταίου δωδεκάτῃ. " Let a Synod of Bishops be held twice a year, and let them examine in counsel with one another the dogmatic decrees of Religion (*i.e.* matters pertaining to faith, discipline, and worship), and let them set at rest

bishops, Primates, Metropolitans and Bishops, under due Canonical limitations, and that these Canonical limitations be defined; and further, that the Bishops of this Province be respectfully requested at the next meeting of the Pan-Anglican Synod, to take such measures as shall lead to the desired result." Time and patience will be needed to ensure this result.

such ecclesiastical controversies as may arise—once (meeting) on the fourth week of Pentecost, and for the second time on the twelfth day of the month Hyperberetæus" (the last month of the Kalendar according to the Macedonian year (Heb. *Tizri*), and in the Roman Kalendar the fourth day before the Ides of October).

This Canon orders the regular convocation of Provincial Synods of Bishops. The Bishops, as is plain from the wording of this Canon, form the complete Synod of the Province *quâ votum decisivum*, although the Canon must not be construed apart from other enactments which provide for the *votum consultativum* of the Priesthood and the assent of the laity. The rule here made for holding Provincial Synods twice a year was repeated in the 5th Canon of Nicæa, and also in the 20th Canon of the Council of Antioch. The sole final responsibility of decision rests with the Episcopate of the Catholic Church, and such finality as appears to be allowed (by the wording of certain Canons) to the decrees of Provincial Synods is always conditioned by this fact.

It will be convenient at this stage to quote the 74th Apostolic Canon, which deals with the trial of Bishops. Parts of this Canon are certainly ancient,[1] but in dealing with it here we are not

---

[1] Hefele, vol. i. p. 487.

unmindful of the considerations we have previously alleged with regard to the 35 supplementary Greek Canons. "Episcopum ab hominibus christianis et fide dignis de crimine accusatum in ius vocent episcopi. Si vocationi paruerit, responderitque, fueritque convictus, poena decernatur ; si vero vocatus haud paruerit, missis ad eum duobus episcopis iterum vocetur ; si ne sic quidem paruerit, duo rursus ad eum missi tertio vocent episcopi. Si hanc quoque missionem aspernatus non venerit, pronunciet contra eum synodus quæ videbuntur, ne ex iudicii detrectatione lucrum facere videatur." Ἐπίσκοπον κατηγορηθέντα ἐπί τινι παρὰ ἀξιοπίστων ἀνθρώπων, καλεῖσθαι αὐτὸν ἀναγκαῖον ὑπὸ τῶν ἐπισκόπων· κἂν μὲν ἀπαντήσῃ καὶ ὁμολογήσῃ ἢ ἐλεγχθείη, ὁρίζεσθαι τὸ ἐπιτίμιον· εἰ δὲ καλούμενος μὴ ὑπακούσοι, καλείσθω καὶ δεύτερον, ἀποστελλομένων ἐπ' αὐτὸν δύο ἐπισκόπων· ἐὰν δὲ καὶ οὕτω καταφρονήσας μὴ ἀπαντήσῃ, ἡ σύνοδος ἀποφαινέσθω κατ' αὐτοῦ τὰ δοκοῦντα, ὅπως μὴ δόξῃ κερδαίνειν φυγοδικῶν. "If a Bishop be accused of any crime by credible and faithful persons, it is necessary that he be cited to appear by the Bishops (*i.e.* of his Province); and if he appears and confesses his error, and yet is condemned, let his punishment be determined. But if when he is cited he does not obey, let him be cited a second time by two Bishops sent to him. But if even then he despises them and will not come, let the Synod pass what sentence they please against him, so that he may not appear to gain advantage by avoiding their judgment."

The trial of a Bishop by his com-provincial Bishops, under the presidency of the Metropolitan, was the universal rule in Ante-Nicene times. It is obviously in accord with the solidarity of the Episcopate as a whole, and it marks clearly the constitutional responsibility of each Bishop. The tendency of Church order was not to encourage appeals from the Provincial Synod, but an appeal to the Patriarch and his Synod was obviously a condition of justice, before appealing to the collective Episcopate, as represented in an Œcumenical Council.

The Apostolic Constitutions, like the Apostolic Canons, may be treated, on the whole, as belonging to the Ante-Nicene period. We find there some glimpses at Church life and order which bear upon our subject. We need not enter into detail upon the careful examination of the life and character of persons about to be ordained to the office and work of a Bishop,[1] or upon the directions given as to his treatment of persons falsely accused, guilty, or penitent.[2] As Ordinary, the Bishop sat as judge in his Diocesan Court to hear ecclesiastical causes, and also civil disputes between individual Chris-

---

[1] *Const. Apostol.*, Lib. ii., secs. 1 and 2.   [2] Ibid., sec. 3.

tians, to avoid lawsuits before the ordinary civil courts,[1] which were forbidden until the Empire became Christian.[2] The Bishop had to sit as judge on Mondays, so as to give time for cases to be settled before the next Lord's Day. The Priests and the Deacons were present when the Bishop held his Court.[3] The Priests were his Assessors and Councillors, both in Court and in Synod, as the Senate and Council of the Diocese (σύμβουλοι τοῦ Ἐπισκόπου, συνέδριον καὶ βουλὴ τῆς Ἐκκλησίας, *Const. Apostol.*, ii. 28). The 40th Apostolic Canon keeps the Priests and Deacons from usurping undue power, and specifies that the cure of souls in the whole of his Diocese belongs rightfully to the Bishop. "Presbyteri et diaconi præter episcopum nihil agere pertinent, nam Domini populus ipsi commissus est, et pro animabus eorum hic redditurus est rationem." Οἱ πρεσβύτεροι καὶ οἱ διάκονοι ἄνευ γνώμης τοῦ

---

[1] *Const. Apostol.*, ii. 6; which takes the Pauline precept (1 Cor. vi.) as binding upon Christians, and enjoins that disputes between Christians must not come before heathen tribunals.

[2] Even then the Imperial laws permitted civil cases to be heard in the Bishop's Courts, where both parties consented to abide by his arbitration. "Si qui ex consensu apud sacræ legis Antistitem litigare voluerint, non vetabuntur. Sed experientur illius in civili duntaxat negotio, more arbitri sponte residentis iudicium." (*Cod. Iustin.*, I. iv. 7.) Bishops and Clergy were forbidden by subsequent Canon Law to judge in criminal cases, where matters of life and death were frequently involved in the issue. "Habeant licentiam iudicandi, *exceptis criminalibus negotiis*." (Concil. Tarracon., A.D. 516, Canon 4.)

[3] *Const. Apostol.*, ii. 47.

ἐπισκόπου μηδὲν ἐπιτελείτωσαν· αὐτὸς γάρ ἐστιν ὁ πεπιστευμένος τὸν λαὸν τοῦ Κυρίου, καὶ τὸν ὑπὲρ τῶν ψυχῶν αὐτῶν λόγον ἀπαιτηθησόμενος. "Let not the Priests and Deacons do anything without the judgment of the Bishop, for it is he who is entrusted with the people of the Lord, and will be required to give an account of their souls." This Canon clearly implies the Bishop's constitutional power of veto upon a resolution arrived at by his Diocesan Synod. He exercises this power by virtue of his Episcopal Office, and he is responsible, first, to his Metropolitan, and comprovincial Bishops, and then to the collective Episcopate, for its due and lawful exercise. The Apostolical Constitutions speak of the laity as a "royal priesthood, a holy nation, a peculiar people," who nevertheless must reverence the Bishops, as the Aaronic High Priests, the Priests, as the Priests of the Old Covenant, and the Deacons, as the Levites. The Bishop presides over his Diocese "as one honoured with the authority of God," which he has to exercise in ruling his Clergy and Laity, who can "do nothing without the Bishop."[1] The 8th Book gives particulars of the election and consecration of Bishops, which appears to belong to the Post-Nicene age. The Laity have their voice in the election, which is

[1] *Const. Apostol.*, ii. 25, 26, 27.

certainly a primitive right. "And silence being made, let one of the principal Bishops, together with two others, stand near the Altar, the rest of the Bishops and Presbyters praying silently, and the Deacons holding the Divine Gospels open upon the head of him that is to be ordained, and say unto God thus," &c.[1] The 1st Apostolic Canon is clear on the number of consecrators required. "Episcopus a duobus aut tribus episcopis ordinetur." Ἐπίσκοπος χειροτονείσθω ὑπὸ ἐπισκόπων δύο ἢ τριῶν. "A Bishop must be consecrated by two or three Bishops." The subsequent course of Canon Law tended to increase the number of consecrators required. It touches our subject because the idea which underlay the requirement for more Bishops than one, as consecrators, was the solidarity of the Episcopate, as a whole, as well as the precaution of maintaining the Apostolic Succession by a threefold strand.[2] This is manifest from the Apostolical Constitutions, which illustrate

[1] Καὶ σιωπῆς γενομένης, εἷς τῶν πρώτων Ἐπισκόπων ἅμα καὶ δυσὶν ἑτέροις πλησίον τοῦ Θυσιαστηρίου ἑστώς, τῶν λοιπῶν Ἐπισκόπων καὶ Πρεσβυτέρων σιωπῇ προσευχομένων, τῶν δὲ διακόνων τὰ Θεῖα Εὐαγγέλια ἐπὶ τῆς τοῦ χειροτονουμένου κεφαλῆς ἀνεπτυγμένα κατεχόντων, λεγέτω. κ.τ.λ. (*Const. Apostol.*, viii. 4.)

[2] The dispensations now given by the Popes to permit Bishops to be consecrated by a single Bishop are contrary to ancient Canon Law. This practice is a fresh instance of the theory of modern Rome on the Episcopate. The Latin Episcopate has lost its solidarity, and each Bishop is "curate" to the Pope, and is consecrated at his will; so that the plurality of consecrators does not any longer imply the consent of com-provincial Bishops.

the meaning of the Canon, by prescribing that "if any one be ordained by one Bishop, let him be deprived, both himself and he who ordained him. But if there be a *necessity* that he have *only one* to ordain him, because more Bishops cannot come together, as in time of persecution, or for such like causes, let him bring *the suffrage of permission* from more Bishops."[1] This means that if the Metropolitan and com-provincial Bishops are hindered by persecution from being personally present, they must send their assent and permission for the consecration to take place, as an urgent necessity. Their permission implies their assent to the admission of the priest elected into the Episcopate in its corporate capacity.

The following passage is also worth quoting, as bearing upon the Bishop's office : "A Bishop blesses but does not receive the Blessing. He lays on hands, ordains, offers, receives the Blessing from Bishops, but by no means from Priests. A Bishop deprives any cleric who deserves deprivation, excepting a Bishop ; for of himself he has not the power to do that."[2]

In closing this chapter, we may fairly claim that the constitutional powers of the Episcopate are clearly borne out by the evidence which has been adduced.

[1] *Const. Apostol.*, viii. 27.   [2] Ibid., 28.

NOTE A.

The Provincial Synods on the Paschal Question.

Bishop Beveridge says of these Synods, as touching the principle of Primacy: "Primo itaque aliqualem nonnullorum supra alios Episcoporum primatum videre licet e Synodis illis, quæ de Paschali festivitate secundo labente sæculo celebratæ sunt.

"Enimvero Synodo in Palestina de ista controversia habitæ præsidebant Theophilus Cæsariensis, et Narcissus Hierosolymitanus; Romanæ Victor Romanus;[1] Ponticæ Palma Amastridis Episcopus, et Gallicanæ Irenæus Lugdunensis. . . . Nulla autem causa dici potest, cur magnarum harum urbium (*i.e.* Rome, Alexandria, and Antioch) et Metropoleon Episcopi, aliis prætermissis, tanta cum laude toties commemorarentur, nisi quod illi primi erant, in sua quisque ecclesia, Episcopi. . . . Hinc itaque constat, quare Polycrates omnibus Asiæ Episcopis præesset, nimirum quoniam ille Metropoleos erat Episcopus, atque ideo totius Provinciæ Primas. . . . Quod igitur antiquo hoc Canone (35th Apostolic Canon) definitum est, Episcopi Asiani religiose admodum tunc temporis observabant. Nam Primum, sive Primatem suum agnoscebant, eumque ut caput existimabant. Quod liquido demonstrat hunc Canonem istis diebus, secundo labente sæculo, obtinuisse, atque ideo horum supra alios Episcopos primatum non novitium esse, sed longe ante ipsam Nicænam Synodum introductum, et ab ipsis Ecclesiæ primordiis institutum."
(*Cod. Can. Eccl. Prim.*, II. v.)

---

[1] The Roman Patriarch Victor would preside over a Synod of his sub-urbicarian Dioceses, which were under his immediate jurisdiction as Metropolitan.

NOTE B.

On the Formation and Sub-Division of Dioceses.

Every Bishop had authority to sub-divide his own Diocese with the consent of his Metropolitan and the Provincial Synod. S. Augustine in this way sub-divided his Diocese of Hippo by the erection of a new See at Fussala. "Quod ab Hippone memoratum castellum millibus quadraginta seiungitur, cum in eis regendis, et eorum reliquiis licet exiguis colligendis — me viderem latius quam oportebat extendi, nec adhibendæ sufficerem diligentiæ, quam certissima ratione adhiberi debere cernebam, episcopum ibi ordinandum constituendumque curavi." (S. Aug., Ep. 261, *ad Cælestin.*) But a Diocese could not be sub-divided without the consent of its Bishop.[1] The 5th Canon of the second Council of Carthage (A.D. 397) is explicit on this point: "Si accidente tempore, crescente fide, Dei populus multiplicatus desideravit proprium habere rectorem, eius videlicet voluntate, in cuius potestate est diœcesis constituta, habeat episcopum."

Ferrandus (A.D. 533) gives the process of sub-dividing a

---

[1] The same reasoning applies to the sub-division of a cure of souls within a Diocese. A Priest is instituted to a certain cure of souls, defined by territorial limits, and now called a Parish. His Diocesan Bishop gives him Mission by instituting him to this Parish, which forms a part of the Bishop's own cure of souls, as a part of his Diocese. But the Bishop cannot deprive him without just cause, or judicial process, of his cure of souls. Therefore it follows that the Bishop cannot deprive him of any portion of his cure of souls by forcibly sub-dividing his Parish *mero motu*. It must be proved that a Priest is committing a wilful obstruction in refusing his consent to a sub-division of his Parish before it can be forcibly subdivided, and such refusal must be dealt with by the Bishop as *index ordinarius*.

Diocese at greater length. The consent of the Bishop was necessary in the case of sub-dividing his Diocese, but the further consent of a plenary Council and of the Primate was also required. "Ut episcopus non ordinetur in diœcesi, quæ episcopum nunquam habuit, nisi cum voluntate episcopi ad quem ipsa diœcesis pertinet, ex concilio tamen plenario, et primatis auctoritate." (*African Code, Canon* 98: Ferrandus, *Breviar. Canonum*, c. 13.) This was the rule in Latin Christendom till the time of Gregory V. (A.D. 996), when the Papal consent was demanded as a right, which had grown out of what may be termed "the missionary jurisdiction" of the Pope in establishing the episcopate in countries newly converted from heathenism. *Primacy* in directing missions, such as S. Gregory the Great exercised in sending S. Augustine to England in A.D. 597, and founding the See of Canterbury, is a more accurate term than "missionary jurisdiction," although this latter phrase expresses pretty accurately the position which S. Boniface ascribed to the Pope, as Patriarch of the West. In the East the Emperors in this matter acted as "King-Priests," and sub-divided Dioceses, or created new ones, *proprio motu*, without the consent of the Bishop, the Metropolitan, the Provincial Synod, or the Patriarch.

The same rules, and consents of Primate, Provincial Synod, and Bishops concerned, applied in the case of the union of two Sees, or the removal of the Bishop's See from one city to another. The Council of Lugo (A.D. 569) erected a new Metropolitan See at Lugo, with several Suffragan Sees, on a complaint being made that the Dioceses of Gallæcia (in Spain) were unwieldy, and that the Bishops could not work them efficiently.

NOTE C.

Communion with the Roman See not essential to Catholic Communion.

If there is one fact in early Church history that stands out with luminous clearness, side by side with the fact of the Roman Primacy, it is that the Catholic Church never held that communion with the Roman See was essential in such a manner as to involve the modern Roman teaching that communion with the Roman See is necessary to communion with the Catholic Church, so that persons out of communion with Rome are *ipso facto* out of communion with the Catholic Church. It is as well to prove this point from the words of an eminent Roman Catholic theologian, who held the current theology of his communion on the subject of the Roman Primacy.

"Sed ut ad propositum redeamus, cum Ecclesia Romana propter primatum centrum sit unitatis, eiusque Antistes cæterorum omnium caput constitutus sit, ut schismatis tolleretur occasio, haud dubium quin magnum ac certissimum sit argumentum, eos esse de Ecclesia qui ipsi tanquam capiti adhæreant, et cum eo communione iungantur. E contra vero magnum esse schismatis præiudicium, si quis ab eius communione sit alienus. Quod tamen intelligendum est de Pontifice legitime electo, et sedente in Cathedra Petri, et clavibus sibi a Deo datis, ut par est, utente. Nam si quis Ecclesiam Romanam invaderet, et illegitime ordinaretur, non esset cum isto communio habenda. Similiter si Pontifex in hæresim incideret, et a Concilio deponeretur, iam non esset schismaticus is qui ab eo discederet. Ac demum si Pontifices Romani sine causa excommunicationem ferrent, totaque Ecclesia iudicaret excommunicationem temere latam, tunc ab ipsis excommunicati pro schismaticis habendi non essent, modo animum retinerent servandæ cum Romano Pontifice unitatis, et ad recuperandam eius communionem totis viribus allaborarent. Sic nemo Asiaticos licet a Victore excommunicatos dixerit fuisse schismaticos, et ab Ecclesia extorres. Nemo Cyprianum et Africanos Antistites, nec non Firmilianum et Orientales, licet a communione Stephani pulsos, ab Ecclesia alienos fuisse pronuntiabit: quin e contra Augustinus sæpe sæpius probat Africanos dici non potuisse schismaticos, et moderationem Cypriani nunquam non commendat. Quis affirmaverit Meletium, Cyrillum et alios Orientales ab ipso stantes schismaticos fuisse, quia cum Ecclesia Romana non communicabant, aut quis e contra non fateatur Paulinum et eius socios in periculum schismatis venire, licet cum Ecclesia Romana communione iuncti fuerint? Quis audeat dicere Athanasium et alios fuisse schismaticos, Arianos vero in Ecclesia eo quod Liberius hos ad communionem suam admisisset, illos ab ea repulisset? Nemo etiam Atticum Constantinopolitanum, et omnes Orientis Patriarchas, pro schismaticis et excommunicatis unquam habuit, licet a communione Romanæ Ecclesiæ divisi aliquamdiu fuerint." (Du Pin, *De Antiq. Eccl. Disc.*, p. 257.)

Contrast the teaching of Du Pin with the following words of Cardinal Wiseman: "According to the doctrine of the ancient Fathers, it is easy at once to ascertain who are the Church Catholic and who are in a state of schism, by simply discovering who are in communion with the See of Rome, and who are not" (*Dublin Review*, vol. vii. p. 163). It is curious to note that both these theologians lived and died in the Roman Communion, and the fact that their teaching is flatly contradictory is a significant comment upon the unity of teaching which is supposed to mark the superiority of the Post-Tridentine Latin Obedience over the rest of Catholic Christendom. It is not as if Du Pin and Wiseman differed upon a minor detail. They differed upon a point of paramount importance, in which Du Pin represented the faith of Christian antiquity, and Wiseman the modern fashion of doctrine current in the Rome of to-day.

NOTE D.

S. Cyprian and the Modern Papal Theory.

There are three clear instances of S. Cyprian's action which show that he knew nothing of the claims of the Roman Patriarch to be the infallible autocrat of Christendom. In his 54th Epistle to Cornelius he warns the Roman Church against receiving a schismatical Bishop named Fortunatus, who had been consecrated as opposition Bishop of Carthage by Privatus, an excommunicated heretical Bishop. Fortunatus was playing the same part at Carthage as Novatian had played at Rome. S. Cyprian writes to vindicate his position as lawful Primate of Carthage, just as Cornelius had written against Novatian to vindicate his own position as Patriarch of Rome. He states that Fortunatus and his ally Felicissimus have been judged and condemned in Africa, and that the sentence against them has already been pronounced by himself and his Synod of Bishops. S. Cyprian's position at Carthage was quasi-patriarchal, and the offenders condemned by him had no right to appeal against his sentence to the judgment of another Patriarch; or, to use his words, "count the authority of the African Bishops inferior" (nisi si paucis desperatis et perditis minor videtur esse auctoritas Episcoporum in Africa constitutorum, qui iam de illis iudicaverunt, &c.).

In S. Cyprian's 67th Epistle to Stephen of Rome, he deals with the case of Marcianus, Bishop of Arles, who had joined the Novatian schism. Faustinus, Bishop of Lyons, and other Bishops of Gaul, had applied to Stephen of Rome for aid in their difficulty. There was a twofold reason for their application. Stephen was Primate of Christendom, and, in addition to this fact, the schism of the Anti-pope Novatian specially concerned the Roman See, as S. Cyprian remarks in his letter to Stephen ("Verum servandus erat honor antecessorum Lucii et Cornelii"). The Bishops of Gaul had also written of their trouble to S. Cyprian, as the second Primate of Latin Christendom, whose Primacy of influence extended far beyond his immediate jurisdiction. S. Gregory of Nyssa said that S. Cyprian "presided not only over the Church of Carthage and over Africa . . . but also over all the countries of the West, and over nearly all the regions of the East and the South and the North."[1] Making every allowance for S. Gregory's rhetoric, S. Cyprian's position was such that it was natural for the Bishops of Gaul to tell him of the action they had taken. It appears that Marcianus had not been deposed by a Provincial Synod. Possibly there was no Metropolitan in Gaul at the time, and for this reason the appeal was made to Stephen to deal with the matter directly. S. Cyprian wrote to Stephen urging him to prompt action, since there was no doubt about the facts of the case, which were patent from the admission of Marcianus himself. We note here that, although this case is a remarkable instance of

[1] S. Greg. Nyss., *Orat.* xxiv. 12.

Ante-Nicene Patriarchal action, S. Cyprian does not urge Stephen to act because he was the ecclesiastical autocrat of Christendom, with plenary jurisdiction to try and depose every Bishop. The language of S. Cyprian points in the other direction. Stephen is urged to act on the principle, "*multi Pastores sumus, unum tamen gregem pascimus.*" Novatianism was condemned by the whole Catholic Church. Marcianus is not to be allowed to act in opposition to the collective Episcopate, "*quasi ipse iudicaverit de Collegio Episcoporum, quando sit ab universis sacerdotibus iudicatus.*"

S. Cyprian's view seems to be that Stephen had to carry out the decision of the "College of Bishops" against the Novatians, and that this was his duty as Primate of Christendom. Novatianism had been condemned at Rome, Alexandria, Antioch, and Carthage. A Bishop who boasted that he was a Novatian must be deposed by every Patriarch and Metropolitan as *ipso facto* in heresy and schism.

In the case of Marcianus of Arles we see S. Cyprian invoking the exercise of the legitimate Primacy of the Roman See. But when we come to his letter (Ep. 57) written in the name of his Primatial Council of African Bishops, "*ad clerum et plebes in Hispania consistentes,*" concerning the case of Basilides and Martialis, we find him boldly and clearly pointing out the error of the Roman Patriarch in dealing with the matter. During the Decian persecution, Basilides and Martialis, who were both Spanish Bishops, had become *libellatici*. Basilides confessed his lapse and resigned his See, and Martialis was deposed and excommunicated by the Bishops of the Province. Sabinus was duly elected and consecrated to succeed Basilides, and Felix to succeed Martialis. Basilides went to

Rome and got Stephen to admit him to communion and furnish him with "Letters of Communion," armed with which he returned to Spain and tried to procure restoration to his See. Martialis adopted a similar course, although its details are not equally clear. The position of the lawful occupants of the Sees when the deposed Bishops reappeared on the scene was paralleled in our own days by the position of Bishop Macrorie in Natal, when his deposed and excommunicated predecessor, Dr. Colenso, came back from England, armed with State authority, to call himself Bishop of Natal. Of course the Spanish case was really the worse, for no one in South Africa paid much regard to Dr. Colenso's claims except a handful of Erastian Protestants, and Basilides returned armed with "Letters of Communion" from the Primate of Christendom. S. Cyprian told the Spanish clergy and laity to hold their ground against the consequences of Stephen's action. Stephen had been deceived, said S. Cyprian, and his deception of the Roman Patriarch only made the sins of Basilides more flagrant. "Hoc eo pertinet, ut Basilidis non tam abolita sint quam cumulata delicta, ut ad superiora eius peccata etiam fallaciæ et circumventionis crimen accesserit." Some canonists have thought that S. Cyprian's exhortation to the Spaniards to maintain the decision of their Provincial Synod, and to disregard Stephen's rehabilitation of Basilides, is an argument in favour of the finality of the decisions of Provincial Synods. But unfortunately for this theory, S. Cyprian tells the Spaniards to stand firm because of a decree of the collective Episcopate on the subject of the lapsed, which was decreed by Stephen's penultimate predecessor Cornelius, in agreement with the African Bishops, "and with all the Bishops appointed throughout the whole world."

S. CYPRIAN AND MODERN PAPAL THEORY 167

By this decree the lapsed were admitted to repentance, but deposed from ecclesiastical office.

S. Cyprian does not hint that Stephen consciously or wilfully departed from this ruling.

Basilides deceived him into believing that he had *not* lapsed. S. Cyprian viewed the Roman Patriarch as he would any other Patriarch. His errors of judgment were not to be allowed to injure the Church, and were to be corrected accordingly.[1]

[1] S. Augustine held the same view. The errors of the Roman Patriarch, or any other Patriarch or Primate, could not commit the whole Catholic Church. " Prorsus qualescunque fuerunt Marcellinus, Marcellus, Silvester, Melchiades, Mensurius, Cæcilianus, atque alii, quibus obiiciunt pro sua dissensione quod volunt, nihil præiudiciat Ecclesiæ Catholicæ toto terrarum orbe diffusæ: nullo modo eorum innocentia coronamur, nullo modo eorum iniquitate damnamur." (S. Aug., *De Unico Baptismo*, cap. xvi.)

CHAPTER IV

THE CONSTITUTIONAL AUTHORITY OF BISHOPS AND THE RIGHTS OF PATRIARCHS AND METROPOLITANS AS FINALLY DEVELOPED BETWEEN THE EDICT OF MILAN (A.D. 313) AND THE COUNCIL OF CHALCEDON (A.D. 451).

WE have now arrived at the closing stage of our inquiry. We have traced the constitutional authority of Bishops from the Apostolic age, through the sub-Apostolic period, as manifested in the writings of S. Clement of Rome and S. Ignatius of Antioch, and through the developments of the second and third centuries to the mighty change wrought by the Edict of Milan, which resulted in the alliance of the Church with the Empire, and the consequent admission of the world within its borders. We have already traced the fundamental idea of the Episcopate as a great corporation in which each Bishop is an individual shareholder. We have seen how the powers of the individual Bishop are conditioned on the one hand by the principle of Primacy, whereby his veto upon the acts of his Diocesan Synod, and his general administration of his Diocese, is liable to review by the Synod of his Metropolitan and com-provincial Bishops, and, on the other hand, by the consultative voice of his Clergy and the assent of his Laity. We have also traced, from the Primacy of S. Peter onwards, the idea of the grouping of Metropolitans and their Provinces into Patriarchates, and the legitimate Primacy of the Roman Patriarch which was due to the greatness of the Imperial city, and the Apostolic foundation of the "Cathedra Petri." We have observed also the strict limitations of this Roman Primacy, as evidenced by the Paschal Controversy, and the attitude of S. Cyprian to the Roman See, by which it is evident that the Roman Patriarch was *primus inter pares*, and that the great Patriarchates of Rome, Alexandria, and Antioch were mutually interdependent as centres of Catholic unity, so that their intercommunion and fellowship was the means of maintaining the visible intercommunion and unity of the Catholic Church as a whole.

In the period of Church history which we are now about to examine the undreamt of possibility of a Christian Cæsar was realised, and the whole life of the Church was affected thereby in a manner which would have seemed incredible to the great men of the Ante-Nicene period. Constantine was possessed by the old Imperial idea that impelled the Flavian Emperors to persecute the Church.

Unity of religion was to be the bond to cement the Imperial unity. The unity of the Church had stood face to face in battle array with the Imperial unity for nearly three hundred years. The end of the Diocletian persecution was ignominious failure. The utmost efforts of the persecutors had failed to uproot the ordered unity of the Church. The Empire could but anticipate Julian's "Vicisti, O Galilæe," and make the best terms for itself with the conquering Church. The world-wide unity of the Church was to be knit by Imperial statecraft to the unity of the Empire, and Constantine intended, with the aid of the Church, to carry out the Flavian policy of a single State religion. The official Paganism of the Flavian State religion was wide enough to embrace various Provincial cults in a Roman Pantheon. Here was the weakness of its accommodating toleration. It looked like strength to the eye of the Imperial statesman. But it fell before the mighty and uncompromising unity of the Catholic Church.

The problem before Constantine was a difficult matter of statecraft. The unity of the Church, which he sought to ally with the unity of the Empire, was, to his eyes, an unaccommodating and impossible ideal. But he did his best to deal with it. The subsequent result of the alliance between the Church and the Empire was the destruction of the visible and corporate unity of the Church, and the ultimate fall of the Empire. One of the first consequences of this alliance was the enormous increase in the power of the Roman Patriarch, which eventually caused the divisions of Catholic Christendom. In saying this we do not mean to undervalue the immense services rendered to Christianity by the Papacy in the form it took between the age of Gregory the Great and the age of Hildebrand. The Papacy, during this period, formed part of God's great scheme for governing the world. But the fact remains that the Papal monarchy divided Christendom, and the further fact remains that the alliance between the Church and the Empire virtually created the Papal monarchy.

"On the establishment of Christianity as the religion, if not of the Empire, of the Emperor, the Bishop of Rome rises at once to the rank of a great accredited functionary. . . . The Bishop is the first Christian in the first city of the world, and that city is legally Christian. The Supreme Pontificate of heathenism might still linger from ancient usage among the numerous titles of the Emperor; but so long as Constantine was in Rome, the Bishop of Rome, the head of the Emperor's religion, became in public estimation the equal, in authority and influence immeasurably the superior, to all of sacerdotal rank. The schisms and factions of Christianity now became affairs of state. As long as Rome is the Imperial residence, an appeal to the Emperor is an appeal to the Bishop of Rome. The Bishop of Rome sits by the Imperial authority at the head of a Synod of Italian prelates to judge the disputes with the African Donatists."[1]

It is impossible to endorse the details of Dean Milman's statement of the position. But it furnishes a graphic illustration of the main facts of the situation.

In tracing our historical inquiry upon the constitutional authority of Bishops during what has been termed "the Council Period" of Church history, we must never forget the influence of the Empire upon the Church. It enhanced the greatness of the Roman Patriarch in the first instance. The founding of the Christian Imperial city of Constantinople not only gave to the Church the Patriarchate of "New Rome," which gradually dominated Eastern Christendom, but it further enhanced the dignity of the Roman Patriarch by leaving him in virtual possession of "Old Rome," by the withdrawal of the seat of Empire to Constantinople. During this period of Church

---

[1] Milman, *Latin Christianity*, vol. i. p. 71. It is true that Constantine told the Donatists that they ought not to have appealed to him in this matter, but to have submitted to the judgment of the Church.

history we shall see perpetually the untoward influence of the State upon the Church. It is not too much to say that "the whole world" would never have "groaned to find itself Arian," if it had not been for what Dean Milman calls "the fierce and busy heterodoxy of Constantius, when sole Emperor."

If it had not been for State interference, Arius would have been dealt with as readily by the Church as his Antiochene forerunner, Paulus of Samosata. The relations between Church and State found their ideal in the action of the Pagan Emperor Aurelian, who expelled Paulus from the temporalities of his See (without concerning himself with the religious merits of the case), when he had been satisfied by the Roman Patriarch and his Synod that Paulus was not technically a Christian, in such a sense that he had the right to use and occupy property dedicated exclusively to Christian uses. *O si sic omnia!* has been the cry of all thoughtful Christians, who have realised the evils wrought to the Church by the action of the State from the days of Constantine to the days of the Tudors and Stuarts in England, where the words of the great Charter, *ut Ecclesia Anglicana libera sit*, have been emptied of all meaning by a succession of Churchmen too submissive to assert the rights of the Church, and statesmen who, in the fulness of their knowledge or ignorance, deliberately suppressed them. But to return to our immediate subject. We have to remember that the Edict of Milan alone made it possible for the Church to assemble her universal Episcopate in an Œcumenical Council. We have also to remember with thankfulness that the Providence of God, and the Covenanted Presence of our Lord, as King in His Church, did not permit any undue interference on the part of the State in the undisputed Œcumenical Councils that defined the Catholic Faith concerning the Incarnation and the Person of our Lord. But these great Councils, and others of almost equal importance, dealt with questions of discipline and order quite as fully as they dealt with doctrine.

We must investigate their Canons in the light of what has already been established in the previous chapters, and we shall find that the same principles which governed the Church in Ante-Nicene times continued to govern it after its alliance with the State.

We must first deal with certain Councils held at the beginning of the fourth century before the Nicene Council. The Council of Elvira (A.D. 306) laid down afresh an important principle of ecclesiastical order in its 53rd Canon. "Placuit cunctis ut ab eo episcopo quis recipiat communionem a quo abstentus in crimine aliquo quis fuerit, quod si alius episcopus præsumpserit eum admittere, illo adhuc minime faciente vel consentiente a quo fuerit communione privatus, sciat se huiusmodi causas inter fratres esse cum status sui periculo præstaturum." "It is agreed by all that a person must be restored to communion by that same Bishop by whom he was deprived of it for the commission of some crime ; but if another Bishop shall have presumed to receive him, whilst the Bishop by whom he was deprived of communion has not as yet restored him, or consented to his restoration, let him know that he must answer judicially before his brethren for actions of this kind, with the danger of being deprived of his office."

We see in this Canon that, although all Bishops share in the common Episcopate, the very equality of their rights must prevent their subversion of each other's discipline. An offence of this kind, committed by one Bishop against another, is so serious that the offending Bishop is tried by his brethren, with the penalty of deprivation as the sentence fitting his offence if he is proved guilty. The principle of the trial of a Bishop by his peers is first carried out in his being summoned to answer for his offence before the Synod of his Province, whilst, as we shall see later on, an appeal from the Provincial

Synod to higher authority was open to him. Canon 58 of Elvira is interesting on account of its reference to the position of Primates in Spain. "Placuit ubique et maxime in eo loco, in quo prima cathedra constituta est episcopatus, ut interrogentur hi qui communicatorias litteras tradunt an omnia recte habeant suo testimonio comprobata." "It is agreed that everywhere, and especially in that place in which the Primatial Chair of the Episcopate is constituted, those who present letters of recommendation should be asked whether they could on their own testimony affirm that all things were in sound order" (*i.e.* in the Dioceses which they came from). The last clause of this Canon is somewhat obscure. Hefele thinks that it refers to the duty of the Primate to inquire of persons who brought "letters of commendation"[1] to him concerning the state of the Church in the Dioceses whence they came. But on the whole, as the direction in the title of the Canon is that these persons *de fide interrogentur*, it seems more likely that the inquiries of the Primate would be directed to the circumstances of the persons themselves, and that the Canon directs him to satisfy himself as to the regularity of the documents they presented, and also as to the faith and orthodoxy of the persons them-

---

[1] These "Epistolæ communicatoriæ" were the religious *passports* of the age. They were issued with the greatest care and formality. See *Dict. Christian Antiquities*, vol. i. p. 408.

selves. The principle of Primacy is clearly involved in this Canon. It has been thought probable that at this date the African rule of a movable Primacy under the senior Bishop, irrespective of his See, obtained also in Spain. This is the more probable because the Bishop of Acci[1] presided at the Council of Elvira, and his See never became a Metropolis. He was Primate, as Senior Bishop. But when Constantine the Great divided Spain into seven civil Provinces, the Church formed the Provinces of Tarragona, Carthagena (afterwards Toledo), Boetica, Lusitania, and Gallecia (afterwards divided in the Provinces of Braga and Lugo).

We have already mentioned the Donatist schism. Such issues of it as touch the matters we are specially investigating can be briefly noted here. The Donatists, like the Novatians, professed that their party *alone* constituted the whole Catholic Church, and the occasion of their schism was a question of discipline. They professed, like the Novatians, to be stricter than the Church in dealing with the lapsed, or with those who had made such concessions to the persecutors during the Diocletian persecution as the *Traditores* did. Mensurius, the

---

[1] Acci was a Diocese afterwards included in the Province of Toledo. The rule of a movable Primacy under the Bishop senior by Consecration subsists at this day in the Church of the United States of America. A movable and elective Primacy obtains also in the Churches of Scotland, Canada, and New Zealand. It has very great and practical disadvantages.

Primate of Carthage, was accused of being virtually a *Traditor*, because he is said to have deceived the persecutors by delivering up secular books instead of the sacred ones. His real offence, however, was his discouragement of fanatical martyrdom, in which his Archdeacon, Cæcilian, supported him. After the death of Mensurius, Cæcilian was elected to the Primatial See, and consecrated by Felix of Aptunga, one of the suffragans of Carthage. The party afterwards known as Donatist, brought Secundus, Primate of Numidia, to Carthage, where he held a Synod of the Bishops of Numidia, and after condemning Cæcilian, as having been consecrated by a *Traditor*,[1] consecrated Majorinus as Bishop in his place. The schism spread, and after the death of Majorinus gained great strength under Donatus the Great, who succeeded him as schismatical Primate of Carthage. The subsequent steps taken by Constantine, and the Synods of Rome and Arles, which resulted in disproving that Felix was

[1] The accusation of Bishop Felix of Aptunga was conducted unfairly by the Donatist party. They employed hired witnesses to prove their accusation. When he was acquitted by the Council of Arles, it was decreed by Canon 13 that paid witnesses should not be employed in ecclesiastical trials of this nature. (Multi sunt qui contra ecclesiasticam regulam pugnare videntur, et per testes redemptos putant se ad accusationem admitti debere; hi omnino non admittantur.) The same principle applies to all disciplinary ecclesiastical trials, and Archbishop Benson was mindful of it in his judgment in the case of the Bishop of Lincoln, who was accused on the evidence of witnesses paid by the Church Association. The Archbishop said, "*It is not decent for religious persons to hire witnesses to intrude on the worship of others for purposes of espial.*"

a *Traditor*, and confirmed the position of Cæcilian as Primate, do not concern the course of this inquiry. There is, however, one point that is worthy of our notice. The Donatists complained that the Primate of Numidia and his suffragans had not been consulted with regard to the election of Cæcilian. But since the Primate of Carthage was virtually the Patriarch of the whole Latin Church of Africa,[1] the Primate of Numidia and his suffragans had a consultative voice in his appointment, and there was some ground for the Donatist view.[2] They further claimed that the Primate of Numidia had the right to consecrate the Archbishop of Carthage; but here, as S. Augustine afterwards pointed out, they were in the wrong.

Writing in the name of the whole African Episcopate, after a conference held at Carthage in A.D. 411, he reminds the Donatists that the Primate of

[1] The first Canon of the Council of Hippo (A.D. 393) says that all Provinces of the African Church shall be guided by the Church of Carthage as to the date for keeping Easter; and by the fourth Canon of the same Council the Primate of Carthage had the right of decision if disputes arose in the election of Primate for the other African Provinces. The seventh Canon of the second Council of Carthage (A.D. 397) confirms the Patriarchal privileges of the Primate of that See with regard to the appointment and consecration of the African Bishops. He also presided over the General African Synod, to which the various Provincial Synods sent deputies.

[2] The subsequent Council of Sardica must have enshrined an old custom in its seventh Canon, where it is laid down that at the appointment of a Metropolitan the Bishops of the neighbouring Provinces are summoned. χρὴ δὲ καὶ μετακαλεῖσθαι καὶ τοὺς ἀπὸ τῆς πλησιοχώρου ἐπαρχίας ἐπισκόπους πρὸς τὴν κατάστασιν τοῦ τῆς μητροπόλεως ἐπισκόπου.

Numidia had no inherent right to consecrate the Archbishop of Carthage, because the Roman Patriarch was not consecrated by the Primate nearest to him in rank, but by the Bishop of Ostia, who was close at hand.[1] The Patriarchal position of the Archbishop of Carthage is worthy of note as presenting a close parallel to the true position of the Archbishop of Canterbury. The Archbishop of Carthage fulfilled the rights and duties of a Patriarch over the homogeneous Provinces which formed the widespread and vigorous Latin Church of Africa, although he was not a Patriarch *eo nomine*. The like duties and functions are gradually being assigned to the Archbishop of Canterbury, although not a Patriarch *eo nomine*, for we cannot lay too much stress on the phrase *alterius orbis Papa*, although it implies a living fact in the present day far more than it did when it was first used of S. Anselm at the Council of Bari (A.D. 1098). Neither this courteous phrase, nor the subsequent precedence accorded to Canterbury as the second See of the Western Patriarchate, measures the true greatness of the See of Canterbury in our own times, when the English Primate, who in S. Anselm's day was at most the Primate of the British Isles, has now become the first Prelate of a world-wide Anglo-Saxon Christendom. To-day the General

---

[1] S. Aug., *Breviculus collat. cum Donatistis.*, cap. 16, n. 29.

DEVELOPMENT AFTER EDICT OF MILAN 181

Councils at Carthage, which represented the various Provinces of the African Church, are paralleled by the Lambeth Synods (or Conferences, if a dry legal exactitude is to be observed), which carry an incalculable moral weight of authority throughout the Churches and Provinces which own the Chair of S. Augustine as their Primatial See.

We now turn for a brief space to the Synod of Arles in A.D. 314, which was really a General Council of the Western Patriarchate. The presence of three British Bishops at its deliberations forms a well-known historical landmark in British Christianity. But neither this fact, nor the effect of this great Council upon the Donatist schism, directly concerns us at present. The Roman Patriarch Sylvester did not preside, nor did the two priests, who were his Legates, preside in his stead. The Bishop of the city where the Council was held, Marinus of Arles, was President by direction of the Emperor Constantine.[1] The decrees of the Council were forwarded to Sylvester, whose predecessor, Miltiades, had previously condemned Donatism in a Synod held at Rome in A.D. 313 at the Emperor's request.

The Roman Patriarch, who was Patriarch over the greater Provinces (*maiores diœceses*),[2] is asked,

[1] So the Ballerini admit virtually (*cf.* Ballerini, *Obss. in dissert. v. Quesnell.*, ii. 5. 4).
[2] As holding a special Primacy in the West, and also as Patriarch of

as Primate of Christendom, to promulgate the decisions concerning Donatism, and the disciplinary Canons enacted at Arles under the formulary "*Placuit ergo, præsente Spiritu Sancto et angelis eius.*" But although the Council is Western alone, and not Œcumenical, it does not address Sylvester as the autocratic ruler of Christendom, whose utterances cannot be judged by a Council, and whose authority is above the authority of a Council. On the contrary, the Council of Arles informs Sylvester of its Decrees without any idea that they need his ratification or final approval. The wording of the preamble of the document sent to Sylvester is plain enough. "Domino sanctissimo fratri Silvestro Marinus, vel coetus Episcoporum, qui adunati fuerunt in oppido Arelatensi. Quid decrevimus communi consilio caritati tuæ significamus, ut omnes sciant quid in futurum observare debeant." "To our most holy Lord and Brother Sylvester, Marinus, or rather the assembly of Bishops, who were united together at Arles. What we have decreed by taking counsel in common we announce to your Grace, so that all may know what they ought to observe in future." The office of Sylvester is the traditional function of the Primate of Christendom, from the

the sub-urbicarian Churches, the Roman Patriarch is appealed to by a Western Synod, in the character of their immediate ecclesiastical superior. The word "diœcesis" is here used in an unusual meaning.

days of S. Clement of Rome. His duty is to promulgate the decrees εἰς τὰς ἔξω πόλεις (Hermas, *Vis.* ii. 4), and to make them known officially throughout Christendom. The fact that Sylvester had not been present personally at the Council is alluded to with regret by the Fathers of Arles, and had he been present personally he would have presided, as Patriarch of the West. The first Canon of Arles is addressed personally to the Roman Patriarch, and requests him to send letters to all the Churches to fix the time for observing Easter after the Roman computation ("et iuxta consuetudinem literas ad omnes tu dirigas"). The 17th Canon forbids a Bishop to obstruct the work of another Bishop, "Ut nullus Episcopus alium episcopum inculcet;" for to do so would be an invasion of the common rights of the Episcopate as a whole, because the mission of each Bishop is primarily to his own Diocese. But though a Bishop is thus forbidden to intrude in the Diocese of another Bishop, due courtesy is to be shown by the Diocesan Bishop to a Bishop visiting his Diocese. The 19th Canon says, "De episcopis peregrinis qui in urbem solent venire, placuit iis locum dare ut offerant." Concerning Bishops from other dioceses "who may have occasion to come into a (cathedral) city, it is agreed that provision should be made for them to offer the Holy Sacrifice." This sacred courtesy, as shown by one Bishop to a visiting Bishop, was always regarded as the bond of Catholic unity.

In the 20th Canon we find the careful precautions taken to secure the validity of Episcopal Consecrations. "De his qui usurpant sibi quod soli debeant episcopos ordinare, placuit ut nullus hoc sibi præsumat nisi assumptis secum aliis septem episcopis. Si tamen non potuerit septem, infra tres non audeat ordinare." "Concerning those who assert for themselves the right of consecrating Bishops by themselves alone, it is agreed that no one should venture to take this upon himself unless with the aid of seven other Bishops. If, however, he cannot procure seven, he must not venture to consecrate with a less number than three."

This Canon represents an advance upon the number required by the Apostolic Constitutions, because the altered circumstances of the Church, after the Edict of Milan, made it possible to command the presence of a greater number of Bishops, since persecution had ceased. The idea of requiring a larger number of co-consecrators was to emphasise the inherent solidarity of the Episcopate.[1]

[1] The Roman Church in modern times has been influenced by the Scholastic theory of the Episcopate as being only a superior department of the Priesthood, and exercising its functions as an inferior

The Council of Arles was a *concilium plenarium* of the West, and when the death of Maximin in A.D. 313 gave liberty to Eastern Christendom, a General Council of the East was held at Ancyra, shortly after Easter, A.D. 314, under the presidency of Vitalis, Patriarch of Antioch, which was the Primatial See of the East, previous to its displacement by Constantinople.

The Primacy of Antioch in a purely Eastern Council, which did not include the Patriarchate of Alexandria, was as natural as the Primacy of Rome in a General Council of the West, and beyond this fact there is little that touches our subject in the Canons of Ancyra, save the 13th Canon, which has the first mention of *Chorepiscopi*, or rural Suffragan Bishops, who were forbidden to ordain without the permission of the Bishop of the Diocese, and Canon 18th, which deals with the case of Bishops elected, but subsequently not accepted by the Diocese to which they had been appointed. Εἴ τινες ἐπίσκοποι κατασταθέντες καὶ μὴ δεχθέντες ὑπὸ τῆς παροικίας ἐκείνης, εἰς ἣν ὠνομάσθησαν, ἑτέραις βούλοιντο παροικίαις ἐπιέναι καὶ βιάζεσθαι τοὺς καθεστῶτας καὶ στάσεις κινεῖν κατ' αὐτῶν, τούτους ἀφορίζεσθαι· ἐὰν μέντοι βούλοιντο εἰς τὸ πρεσβυ-

---

order of the ministry in subjection to the sole monarchy of the Pope. Consequently little is made of Episcopal Consecrations, and we know of modern instances of Consecrations performed by a single Bishop in violation of ancient Canon Law.

τέριον καθέζεσθαι, ἔνθα ἦσαν πρότερον πρεσβύτεροι, μὴ ἀποβάλλεσθαι αὐτοὺς τῆς τιμῆς· ἐὰν δὲ διαστασιάζωσι πρὸς τοὺς καθεστῶτας ἐκεῖ ἐπισκόπους, ἀφαιρεῖσθαι αὐτοὺς καὶ τὴν τιμὴν τοῦ πρεσβυτερίου καὶ γίνεσθαι αὐτοὺς ἐκκηρύκτους. "If Bishops, when elected, but not accepted by the Diocese for which they are nominated, introduce themselves into other Dioceses, and stir up strife against the Bishops who are there instituted, they must be excommunicated. But if they (who are elected and not accepted) wish to live as Priests in those places where they have hitherto served as Priests, they need not lose that dignity. But if they shall stir up discord against the Bishop of that place, they shall be deprived of their Priesthood, and be shut out of the Church."

Cases occasionally arose out of a disputed Episcopal election in which the rightful occupant of a See was forced for the sake of the peace of the Church to stand aside, and continue to serve as a Priest, even though he had been consecrated to the office of a Bishop. The Canon enjoins in such a case the quiet acquiescence of the Bishop who has been so injuriously treated, as the best solution of the difficulty, and further demands his acquiescence, on the pain of ecclesiastical censure. The exact circumstances contemplated by this Canon arose in the Church of New Zealand when Bishop

Jenner was consecrated the first Bishop of Dunedin in 1866. The then Primate of New Zealand had taken all the regular steps to procure his consecration by the Archbishop of Canterbury, but subsequently factious opposition to Bishop Jenner developed in the Diocese of Dunedin, and it became impossible for him to maintain his ground. The General Synod of New Zealand in 1871 took the unprecedented step of declining to recognise Bishop Jenner's original appointment, and declared that he had no status as first Bishop of Dunedin. This action was taken in defiance of the judgment of the Archbishop of Canterbury, who stated that Bishop Jenner had "an equitable claim to be considered Bishop of Dunedin." The New Zealand Primate and Bishops, not content with this assertion of Provincial autonomy, proceeded to consecrate a Bishop for the See of Dunedin. When their proceedings were laid before the Archbishop of Canterbury and the English Bishops they accepted the Bishop thus consecrated as "second Bishop of Dunedin," Bishop Jenner having by this time sent in his resignation to the Archbishop of Canterbury. The New Zealand Primate and Bishops then took further and most dangerous autonomous action. The Primate wrote to the whole Anglican Church stating that the Archbishop of Canterbury and the English Bishops "had exercised an authority over the New Zealand Church, which was certainly not given them by that Church, nor ever sanctioned by the Catholic Church in her undivided state."

This uncanonical and erroneous position showed that the Church of New Zealand had adopted views of Provincial autonomy and the finality of Provincial action that were without due precedent.

Bishop Jenner laboured henceforward as a Priest in England, and fulfilled loyally the conditions of the Canon of Ancyra which we have quoted.

Our digression to a modern ecclesiastical dispute is by no means foreign to the purpose of this treatise. We do not write to elucidate antiquarian points of Canon Law in the interest of students. Our whole investigation is meant to show that the principles of Church order and Canon Law, which applied in the first centuries, are equally applicable and necessary of application in the present day. The condition of the Anglican Communion as a whole imperatively demands the wise centralisation of a living Primacy or Patriarchate to prevent it from drifting asunder. The assertion of undue Provincial autonomy on the part of the Church of New Zealand is a valuable object-lesson which tends to redeem these pages from the charge that they are merely concerned with the past. The principles of Primatial authority and the constitutional position of the Episcopate need vindicating just as much against the uncanonical and autonomous action of a Province as against the undue autocracy of an individual Bishop. The practical application of these root-principles is more clearly discerned from one such modern instance as we have quoted, than from many examples drawn from primitive times. The ordinary reader imperceptibly forgets that the Church and her laws in every age are to us the *Kingdom* of our Living King, and the *rules* whereby the organisation of that Kingdom are shaped and guided. However strongly we may hold this truth in theory, we are apt in practice to forget to measure the Catholic Church in our own times by primitive standards. We view the Primitive Church through the vista of the intervening centuries until it becomes unreal to us, and we idealise it overmuch. The Church of our own days is so close to us that we fail to discern the bulwarks of our Zion, as we walk round about her. We idealise so little that we are in danger of failing to discern the true standards of Church polity and order.

About the year A.D. 316, another Eastern Council was held at Neocæsarea in Cappadocia, which was also under the presidency of Vitalis, Patriarch of Antioch. Its Decrees do not touch our subject directly. Its 13th Canon debars country priests from offering the Holy Sacrifice in the Cathedral, when the Bishop and Cathedral Clergy are present. They may only do so, on invitation, if the Bishop and the Cathedral Clergy are absent. This rule was found necessary for the sake of preserving the special rights of the Bishop and his Chapter, and to maintain the principle that each priest's right of officiating was limited to his own cure of souls. The 14th Canon, however, allowed this right to the Chorepiscopi,[1] on account of their special position.

We now come to the consideration of the First General Council of Nicæa in A.D. 325. Our inquiry does not touch upon the Arian controversy, which was the immediate cause of its convocation. We shall confine our attention to those points in which its convocation and enactments elucidate the principle of Primacy, and the constitutional authority of Bishops. The first questions before us are the authority by which it was convoked, and the presidency under which it was held.

We have previously seen that the policy of Constantine was the policy of the Flavian Emperors in a Christian dress. The unity of the Empire demanded unity in the religion of the Empire. Constantine, by his subsequent conduct, showed that he did not understand the vital nature of the

[1] See Note A.

issues raised by Arius at Alexandria. All he wanted was religious peace and unity. He sent the venerable Bishop Hosius of Cordova to Alexandria to settle the matter, but his mission was futile. Hosius was the Emperor's chief adviser in ecclesiastical affairs, and he is credited with suggesting an Œcumenical Council as the best method of re-establishing the faith and peace of the Church.[1] Such an assembly of Bishops would have been well-nigh impossible without the consent and co-operation of the Emperor. Travelling was costly and difficult, and the Emperor not only placed the Government public conveyances and transport animals at the disposal of the Bishops, but he entertained them during their stay at Nicæa as the guests of the State.[2] The Emperor summoned the Council *ex sententia sacerdotum*,[3] as Rufinus observes, and whilst Hosius and Eusebius would figure as the Emperor's chief advisers, doubtless they consulted the leading Patriarchs, and amongst them the aged Roman Patriarch Sylvester. There is nothing to be gained by strong assertions that the Roman Patriarch was utterly ignored in the summoning of the Nicene Council, and that his Legates had no place of influence in that august assembly. The attempted

---

[1] Sulpitius Severus says, "Nicæna synodus auctore illo (Hosio) confecta habeatur." (*Hist.*, ii. 55.)

[2] Euseb., *Vita. Const.*, iii. 6 and 9.

[3] Ruf., i. 1.

proof of negations of this kind is an indirect service to modern Ultramontane theories. The defenders of the Vatican Decrees can, with some show of justice, assert that Anti-Papal controversialists of this type are afraid to face the facts and probabilities of early Church history, and the real truth lies midway between the unbalanced statements of Bellarmine and his modern successors, and the equally unbalanced statements of certain Protestant (and we may add Anglican) controversialists on the other side. It is well known that (to use Bishop Hefele's words) "the first eight Œcumenical Synods were convoked by the Emperors, all later ones by the Popes."[1] Without admitting Bishop Hefele's computation of the number of Œcumenical Councils, we can yet admire the candour with which he refutes the views which Bellarmine based upon the Pseudo-Isidorian Decretals.

Bellarmine's contention that the summoning of all Œcumenical Councils was vested in the Pope[2] is as unconvincing as the bald assertion on the other side, that the Pope had nothing whatever to do with the summoning of the Nicene Council, because there is no direct historical evidence that he was consulted.[3] What we have already proved with regard to the position of the Roman Patriarch

---

[1] Hefele, *Hist. of Councils*, Introd. p. 8.
[2] Bellarmine, *Disputat.*, I. i. 12.
[3] Puller, *Primitive Saints and the See of Rome*, p. 143.

as Primate of Christendom, cannot be pushed aside to suit controversialists who meet the false and exaggerated claims of modern Vaticanism by arguments which are touched with the spirit of exaggeration. Let us for a moment try to forget the schism between East and West,—the Hildebrandine Papacy and its Vatican outcome,—the Reformation and its Babel of discordant religionisms. Let us, by an effort of calmly balanced thought imagine a Free Œcumenical Council of a reunited Christendom, with the great Patriarchates restored to their purity of faith and power of influence.

Who would preside at such a Council?

The Patriarch of New Rome would give the answer of ancient precedent and tradition in the name of the unchanging East. The Patriarch of Old Rome, and none other, would have the traditional right to preside as *Primus inter pares* of the Great Patriarchs of the Church. This being so, let us return to the Nicene Council with an open mind, and examine the historical probabilities of its convocation and presidency. The second Œcumenical Council affords no illustrative argument, because it became œcumenical by its subsequent general reception throughout Christendom. Although the Emperor Theodosius summoned the Third General Council of Ephesus, we see from the letter of Pope Celestine that he concurred with the summoning of the Council,[1] and Pope Leo the Great asked the Emperor Theodosius II. to convoke an Œcumenical Council, which ultimately resulted in the summoning of the Fourth Œcumenical Council of Chalcedon.[2] It is, therefore, historically probable that when Constantine "consulted the Clergy" before summoning the Nicene Council, he, or his advisers, consulted the Roman Patriarch. The matter of Arius directly concerned the Patriarch of Alexandria, and he must have been consulted. The prominence of the Patriarch of Antioch in the Council itself leads us to think that he also was consulted, because men who think it their due to be consulted, and are not, are apt to keep in the background, like Achilles in his tent. It is thus highly improbable, to say the least of it, that the Patriarch of the Imperial city, which was still the sole capital of the Empire, the first of Primates, who was throned *in cathedra Petri*, should be the only great Patriarch who was not consulted with regard to the summoning of the Nicene Council. The same line of argument applies to the Presidency of the Council itself. We have already seen that the Roman Patriarch would

---

[1] Mansi, vol. iv. p. 1291.

[2] It is true that Leo first asked for a Council at Rome, and that he demurred to holding it at Chalcedon. Yet he wrote that it was held "ex præcepto Christianorum principum et ex consensu apostolicæ sedis." (S. Leo, *Ep.* 114.)

naturally preside at an Œcumenical Council, by virtue of his position as Primate of Christendom. But in the exigencies of controversy with the modern Roman claims, writers are found who vehemently deny that Hosius, the President of the Nicene Council, and the two Roman legates who signed the decrees of the Council next in order to him, represented in any way Sylvester's position as President by virtue of his See. The position which the Ultramontanes assert with regard to Hosius may be legally untenable.

The evidence of the fifth-century writer Gelasius may be weak, and his categorical assertion that Hosius was the representative of Sylvester at the Nicene Council may be incapable of satisfactory historical proof;[1] but it is at all events within the bounds of historic probability that Hosius, as a Western Prelate, did represent the Roman Patriarch as President of the Nicene Council. It is in consonance with the principles of Primatial rank and authority that he should have done so, even if the actual facts of the case cannot be correctly ascertained. And to admit that Hosius may have presided, as the representative of the Primate of Christendom, is no concession of any implied superiority of the Pope to a General Council, or to the un-Catholic modern claims of the Vatican

---

[1] Gelasius, *Volumen Actorum Conc. Nic.*, ii. 5.

Decrees. The admission that Hosius presided as the representative of the Pope makes against the claims of Vaticanism. For Hosius did not pose as the delegate of an infallible Ruler of Christendom, nor did he put forth any claims of the Roman See to universal jurisdiction. The question of the exact position of Hosius must perforce be left open. It is not pleasant to think of a Spanish Bishop being thrust by the sole authority of Constantine into a position of superiority to the Patriarchs of Alexandria and Antioch, who were both present at the first Œcumenical Council.

The Patriarch of Alexandria was the virtual prosecutor of Arius, so that he could not preside. The theory that Eustathius of Antioch presided is based upon the fact that one of his successors in the Patriarchate spoke of him as "first of the Nicene Fathers."[1] It is more in accordance with the true spiritual independence of the Church to hold that Hosius was not thrust into the Presidency by the *sic volo sic iubeo* of Constantine, but that he presided by virtue of some ecclesiastical commission from the Primate-Patriarch of the Catholic Church. But some minds are perverse enough to prefer the idea of a President appointed by the Emperor to that of a President appointed by ecclesiastical authority.

---

[1] So also the Chronicle of Nicephorus; *vide* Tillemont, *Mémoires*, vi. 272 b.

The fact that Constantine appointed Marinus to preside at Arles is minimised by the further facts that the Council of Arles was not œcumenical, and that its decisions were sent to the Roman Patriarch for the purpose of official promulgation. We incline to the view that Hosius, and the two Roman priests Vitus and Vincentius, formed a sort of joint delegation as representing the Roman Patriarch. Eusebius speaks of the Presidents of the Council in the plural number.[1] It is at least as likely that he alluded to some such joint delegation as we have suggested, as that he meant to imply that several Presidents took turns in presiding over the Council. And then we have to consider the order of the signatures to the Nicene Decrees. In every copy we find that Hosius signs first, and next to him the two Roman priests. Then followed the signature of the Patriarch of Alexandria, who ranked next to the Roman Patriarch. Then followed the Metropolitans and Bishops of his Patriarchate, and then the other signatures grouped into Provinces, each Bishop signing after his own Patriarch or Metropolitan. We may, on the whole, safely conclude that the convocation and presidency of the first Œcumenical Council bear, in their special circumstances, a distinct witness to the Primatial rights

---

[1] After Constantine's opening discourse to the Council, "he made way for the Presidents" ($\pi\alpha\rho\epsilon\delta\iota\delta o\upsilon\ \tau\grave{o}\nu\ \lambda\acute{o}\gamma o\nu\ \tau o\hat{\iota}s\ \tau\hat{\eta}s\ \sigma\upsilon\nu\acute{o}\delta o\upsilon\ \pi\rho o\acute{\epsilon}\delta\rho o\iota s$). Euseb., *Vita Const.*, I. 3. 13.

and precedence of the great Sees of Christendom.[1] All that is preserved to us of the proceedings of the Nicene Council is the Creed, the twenty genuine Canons, and the Synodal Decree.[2] The exhaustive arguments of Bishop Hefele in proof of the twenty Canons of the earliest Greek authorities, and also of the ancient Latin collection (the *Prisca*), and the subsequent one by Dionysius Exiguus, are absolutely conclusive in demonstrating that they are the only genuine ones.[3] The fourth Nicene Canon deals definitely with the appointment of Bishops, and the confirmation of Bishops-elect by the Metropolitan and his com-provincial Bishops. Ἐπίσκοπον προσήκει μάλιστα μὲν ὑπὸ πάντων τῶν ἐν τῇ ἐπαρχίᾳ καθίστασθαι· εἰ δὲ δυσχερὲς εἴη τὸ τοιοῦτο, ἢ διὰ κατεπείγουσαν ἀνάγκην ἢ διὰ μῆκος ὁδοῦ, ἐξάπαντος τρεῖς ἐπὶ τὸ αὐτὸ συναγομένους συμ-

---

[1] No special or formal ratification of the decrees of an Œcumenical Council is required from any external authority, and certainly the Roman Patriarch never had the power of ratifying the decrees of Councils over which he did not preside in person. Bossuet says of the Nicene decree against Arius: "Facto patrum decreto, adeo res transacta putabatur, ut nulla mora interposita, *nullo expectato Sedis Apostolicæ speciali decreto,* omnes ubique terrarum Episcopi, Christiani omnes, atque ipse Imperator, ipsi etiam Ariani, tanquam Divino iudicio cederent." (*Defensio*, iii. 7. 7.) Bossuet is defending the Gallican position that a General Council was of superior authority to the Pope. The temporary submission of the Arians at Nicæa to the Decree adds point to his argument that the Decree became immediately effectual.

[2] The Synodal Decree is given in full by Socrates. (*Eccl. Hist.*, i. 9.)

[3] *History of Councils*, vol. i. p. 356.

ψήφων γενομένων καὶ τῶν ἀπόντων καὶ συντιθεμένων διὰ γραμμάτων, τότε τὴν χειροτονίαν ποιεῖσθαι· τὸ δὲ κῦρος τῶν γινομένων δίδοσθαι καθ' ἑκάστην ἐπαρχίαν τῷ μητροπολίτῃ.

"The Bishop (elect of a diocese) must be appointed by all the Bishops of the Province; but if this be impossible, either on account of pressing necessity or on account of the length of journeying, three of them at the least shall meet at the same place and perform the consecration by imposition of hands, with the permission of those absent signified in writing; but the confirmation of what has been done belongs to the Metropolitan in each Province."

This Canon shows us, first of all, the Cyprianic principle of the solidarity of the Episcopate, and the interdependence of each Bishop of a Province with the universal Episcopate, as shown primarily by his relations with the Bishops of his own Province, as common shareholders of joint privileges and duties. Next it points out clearly the principle of Primacy by its assertion of the κῦρος of the Metropolitan. It will be noticed that this Canon does not prescribe the method whereby a Diocesan Bishop is elected. It deals with his appointment and consecration subsequent to his election. It describes the confirmation and consecration of a Bishop-elect. The process of election was as follows. The κατάστασις or appointment, which included consecration, rested with the Apostles and their successors. The initial steps in the process of filling up the vacant See rested with the Metropolitan, who had also the final power of ratifying the proceedings (κῦρος). The "choice" or election (συνευδόκησις) rested with the Clergy. The "testimony" to the character of the person elected by the Clergy rested with the Laity (μαρτύριον). The Laity could not be expected to pronounce on the orthodoxy or the ecclesiastical fitness of the person elected. Their withholding of their μαρτύριον, which practically gave them a veto on the election, could only be based on grounds of conduct or past action on the part of the person elected which would lead them to consider him unfit to bear rule. We have already seen that S. Peter to some extent anticipated the after-usage of Metropolitans in dealing with a vacant See in the steps that he took with regard to the vacancy in the College of Apostles which was filled by the election of S. Matthias. In the appointment of the seven Deacons in Acts vi. 2, 3, the μαρτύριον was given by the Plebs Christiana, and the κατάστασις was reserved to the Apostles. The ἐλλόγιμοι ἄνδρες, or men of Apostolic rank, in S. Clement's Epistle to the Corinthians, appointed the Presbyter-Bishops, with the consent of the whole

Church (συνευδοκησάσης τῆς 'Εκκλησίας πάσης).[1] S. Cyprian is equally plain on this point. The appointment of Cornelius is in order because he was elected by the Clergy, with the assent of the Laity, and with the consent of the Bishops of the Province, which made his appointment and consecration valid.[2] Eusebius tells us that when Fabian was elected to the See of Rome in A.D. 236, the whole Laity cried out that he was worthy to be Bishop.[3] To anticipate the historical order of our testimony, we may add that Nectarius was appointed Patriarch of Constantinople in A.D. 381, κοινῇ ψήφῳ τῆς συνόδου, which was that Patriarchal Council of the East which was afterwards acknowledged as the second Œcumenical Council. The Laity also had their voice, and the appointment of S. Chrysostom in

---

[1] S. Clem. Rom., *Ad Cor.*, c. 44.

[2] "Cornelius factus est episcopus de Dei et Christi Eius iudicio, de clericorum poene omnium testimonio, de plebis quæ tunc affuit suffragio et de sacerdotum antiquorum et bonorum virorum collegio." (S. Cypr., *Ep.* lv.) Again he says: "Episcopo Cornelio in Catholica Ecclesia de Dei iudicio de cleri et plebis suffragio ordinato." (*Ib. Ep.* lxviii.) In another place he explains the position of the laity to be "ut plebe præsente vel detegantur malorum crimina vel bonorum merita prædicentur" (*Ib. Ep.* lxvii.); so that his use of "suffragium" for the laity means their μαρτύριον.

[3] Τὸν πάντα λαὸν ... ἄξιον ἐπιβοῆσαι τῶν ἀδελφῶν ἁπάντων χειροτονίας ἕνεκεν τῆς τοῦ μέλλοντος διαδέχεσθαι τὴν ἐπισκοπὴν ἐπὶ τῆς 'Εκκλησίας συγκεκροτημένων. (Euseb. vi. 29.) The Council of Laodicea (A.D. 365) had to restrain tumultuous partisanship amongst the laity in general, which provoked disorder, and their assent was gradually restricted to representative men of eminence who could act for the laity generally without tumult.

A.D. 397 was made ψηφίσματι κοινῷ ὁμοῦ πάντων κλήρου τέ φημι καὶ λαοῦ, so that even in the appointment of a Patriarch the Clergy had a consultative voice, and the Laity the right of assent. The well-known dictum of Pope Celestine (A.D. 422) passed into a recognised maxim of ecclesiastical law: " Let no Bishop be given to those unwilling to receive him. The consent and desire of the Clergy, the People, and of the Episcopal Order is necessary."[1] Pope Leo the Great took the same line.[2]

The κατάστασις included Confirmation and Consecration. Confirmation implied the consent of the Co-episcopate, primarily expressed by the Bishops of the Provinces and then ratified by the Metropolitan and Patriarch. Confirmation conferred *jurisdiction* upon the Bishop-elect, and Consecration conferred *Order*, whereby the person consecrated received the *potestas ordinis*, and the gift of the Holy Ghost for the office and work of a Bishop in the Church of God.

[1] " Nullus invitis detur Episcopus. Cleri, plebis, et ordinis consensus et desiderium requiratur." (S. Cœlest., *Ep.* ii. 5.)

[2] "Cum de summi sacerdotis electione tractabitur, ille omnibus præponatur, quem cleri *plebisque* consensus concorditer postularit ; ita ut si in aliam forte personam partium se vota diviserint, metropolitani iudicio is alteri præferatur, qui maioribus et studiis iuvatur et meritis: tantum ut nullus invitis et non petentibus ordinetur, ne plebs invita Episcopum non aptatum aut contemnat aut oderit." (*Ep.* 84, *ad Anastas.*, c. 15). S. Augustine takes the same line : " In ordinandis sacerdotibus et clericis consensum maiorum Christianorum et consuetudinem Ecclesiæ sequendum esse arbitrabatur." (Possid., *Vita S. Aug.*, cap. 21.)

Objections could be heard at the Court of Confirmation, and a Bishop-elect could be rejected at this stage.[1] We may anticipate once more with regard to the means which had to be taken to obviate tumultuous assemblages of the Laity at Episcopal elections. The election in a popular assemblage (ὄχλοις) was forbidden by the 13th Canon of the Council of Laodicea (A.D. 363), but this prohibition, as Van Espen[2] shows, does not affect the right of the Laity to give their *testimonium* and assent in an Episcopal election. Tumult was avoided by a certain system of representation of the popular *testimonium* by leading laymen. This seems to be implied by S. Leo the Great's reference to the decision of men of honourable rank in the election of a Bishop.[3] The fifth Nicene Canon is one of the most important which bears upon our present investigation. It sets forth at once the solidarity of the Episcopate as a whole,

---

[1] The Greek Pontificals speak of the Bishop to be consecrated as ὑποψήφιος (elect) and ἐστερεωμένος (confirmed).

The Court of Confirmation has become a lifeless form in the Established Church of England. In the unestablished and free Churches of the Anglican Communion it is a living reality. The Church of the Province of South Africa approaches most closely to the primitive model in the procedure it has adopted in Canon IV. for the Confirmation of a Bishop-elect.

[2] Van Espen, *Commentarius in Canones*, p. 161 seq.

[3] "Vota civium, testimonia populorum, *honoratorum arbitrium*" (which apparently voiced the testimony and wishes of the laity) "electio clericorum." (S. Leo., Ep. lxxxix.)

and the constitutional authority of the individual Bishop. We must quote it in full :—

Περὶ τῶν ἀκοινωνήτων γενομένων, εἴτε τῶν ἐν τῷ κλήρῳ εἴτε ἐν λαϊκῷ τάγματι, ὑπὸ τῶν καθ' ἑκάστην ἐπαρχίαν ἐπισκόπων κρατείτω ἡ γνώμη κατὰ τὸν κανόνα τὸν διαγορεύοντα, τοὺς ὑφ' ἑτέρων ἀποβληθέντας ὑφ' ἑτέρων μὴ προσίεσθαι. Ἐξεταζέσθω δέ, μὴ μικροψυχίᾳ ἢ φιλονεικίᾳ ἤ τινι τοιαύτῃ ἀηδίᾳ τοῦ ἐπισκόπου ἀποσυνάγωγοι γεγένηνται. ἵνα οὖν τοῦτο τὴν πρέπουσαν ἐξέτασιν λαμβάνῃ, καλῶς ἔχειν ἔδοξεν, ἑκάστου ἐνιαυτοῦ καθ' ἑκάστην ἐπαρχίαν δὶς τοῦ ἔτους συνόδους γίνεσθαι, ἵνα κοινῇ πάντων τῶν ἐπισκόπων τῆς ἐπαρχίας ἐπὶ τὸ αὐτὸ συναγομένων, τὰ τοιαῦτα ζητήματα ἐξετάζοιντο, καὶ οὕτως οἱ ὁμολογουμένως προσκεκρουκότες τῷ ἐπισκόπῳ κατὰ λόγον ἀκοινώνητοι παρὰ πᾶσιν εἶναι δόξωσι, μέχρις ἂν τῷ κοινῷ τῶν ἐπισκόπων δόξῃ τὴν φιλανθρωποτέραν ὑπὲρ αὐτῶν ἐκθέσθαι ψῆφον· αἱ δὲ σύνοδοι γινέσθωσαν, μία μὲν πρὸ τῆς τεσσαρακοστῆς, ἵνα πάσης μικροψυχίας ἀναιρουμένης τὸ δῶρον[1] καθαρὸν προσφέρηται τῷ Θεῷ, δευτέρα δὲ περὶ τὸν τοῦ μετοπώρου καιρόν.

"Respecting those who, whether of the clergy or in the laic rank, have been excommunicated by the Bishops in every Province, let the sentence hold good according to the rule which prescribes that those who are excommunicated by some be not

---

[1] The offering of the Gift means the offering of the Holy Eucharist in its sacrificial aspect.

received by others. But let it be inquired whether their exclusion proceed from any petty jealousy or party feeling, or any such frowardness in the Bishop. Accordingly, that this may receive due examination, it seems good that twice every year Synods be held in each Province, that such questions may be examined before a public assembly of all the Bishops of the Province; and so they who have confessedly offended the Bishop may be reasonably held excommunicate in the sight of all, until the Episcopal Body think fit to pronounce a more indulgent sentence respecting them. Let one of the Synods be held before Lent, that all petty jealousy being got rid of, the Gift may be purely offered to God, and the second about autumn."

The first clause in this Canon refers to the 12th of the Apostolic Canons, which prohibited the reception of persons excommunicated who present themselves without Letters of Commendation. The Canon runs as follows: Εἴ τις κληρικὸς ἢ λαϊκὸς ἀφωρισμένος, ἤτοι ἄδεκτος, ἀπελθὼν ἐν ἑτέρᾳ πόλει δεχθῇ ἄνευ γραμμάτων συστατικῶν, ἀφοριζέσθω καὶ ὁ δεξάμενος καὶ ὁ δεχθείς. "If any cleric or layman who has been excommunicated, or who is under suspension, departs to another city, and is received without letters of commendation, both the recipient and the person who receives him must be excommunicated." The slight obscurity in the wording of this Canon is explained by its latter clause, which we have not quoted, which prescribes a different penalty for the two classes of offenders, the suspended and the excommunicate. The point of the enactments is the same. The Episcopate is one, and the sentence of one Bishop must be received by the universal Episcopate, with one important qualification, namely, the right of appeal against the sentence of any individual Bishop.[1] This appeal is the great bulwark against all unconstitutional exercise of Episcopal authority. The wording of the Nicene Canon assumes the possibility of Episcopal injustice or "unpleasantness" ($ἀηδία$). For this reason the aggrieved cleric or layman, who considered himself unjustly sentenced by his Bishop, could appeal from his own Diocesan to the Universal Episcopate, as represented primarily by the Provincial Synod of his Province.[2]

---

[1] It may be asked, with reference to this Canon, how the case of a Bishop should be dealt with who relaxes the discipline of his Diocese, and refuses to excommunicate those who ought to be excommunicated. The principle of the solidarity of the Episcopate governs the case. The Bishop in question can be cited for trial before his Metropolitan and com-provincial Bishops for neglecting his duty as administrator of the Divine Law and discipline of the Church. As Du Pin observes, his Metropolitan or Patriarch cannot deal with the case directly, "nisi forte gravis esset eius negligentia aut conniventia, tunc etiam moneri eum oportebat a Metropolitano, et si pertinaciter recusaret noxios punire, tum illi tum Episcopus ipse deferendi erant ad Synodum Provinciæ ibique iudicandi." (*De Ant. Eccl. Disc.*, p. 251.)

[2] The finality of the judgment of a Provincial Synod is often asserted. Du Pin, in commenting upon this Canon, says : "Hoc in Canone iudicium omne definitivum Episcopis Provinciæ committitur sine ullo

The Metropolitan and his com-provincial Bishops form the Provincial Synod for all practical purposes, for they alone have in it the *votum decisivum*.[1] Clergy and Laity could be present for purposes of *consultation* and *assent* when the Provincial Synod dealt with matters of discipline and doctrine; but there is no evidence that they were present when the Provincial Synod sat as a Court of Appeal. It is true that the Encyclical of the Council of Antioch,

recursu aut provocatione." (*De Ant. Eccl. Disc.*, p. 98.) If he means by this that no appeal can lie which involves a re-examining of the proven *facts* of a case, he is correct; but if he means that the Bishops of a single province have such final authority in matters of faith and doctrine that their judgment is equivalent to that of the Universal Episcopate, he is in error. The solidarity of the Episcopate can be just as much jeopardised by the autonomous action of a single province as it is by the autonomous action of a single Bishop. He says again: " Firma autem manebat Synodi Provinciæ sententia nec poterat ab alio rescindi, *cum præsertim non agebatur de fide*. Nam cum de illa erat quæstio quia res communis in periculum veniebat, cæteræ Ecclesiæ poterant inquirere causam propter quam aliquis eiectus foret, et si comperissent doctrinam orthodoxam a Synodo Provinciæ alicuius esse proscriptam, et propterea tantum aliquem esse damnatum quod eam doceret, tunc poterant hominis istius aut potius eius doctrinæ patrocinium suscipere, quæ res sæpe sæpius magnas in Ecclesia turbas excitavit, ob varias de dogmate aliquo Episcoporum et Ecclesiarum opiniones. Cæterum isto in casu nullum aliud remedium præsentius est inventum quam ut ex pluribus orbis partibus Episcopi in unum convenientes sententiam ferrent: quo sancto qui Synodi universalis et liberæ iudicio non obtemperabant, merito ab Ecclesiæ communione separati et schismatici habebantur." (*Ib.* p. 249.)

In this latter passage Du Pin concedes the whole point at issue. But although an Œcumenical Council is the ultimate Court of Appeal, we shall show that the Patriarch and his Council formed an intermediate stage, as standing between an Œcumenical Council and the decision of a Provincial Synod.

[1] See the 38th Apostolic Canon in the previous chapter.

which condemned Paulus, is addressed to the whole Church, and speaks in the name of the Clergy, as well as the Laity, who assented to what was done, but the trial of a Patriarch covered a wider area than an ordinary Provincial Tribunal of Appeal, whose decisions could be carried for review to a Patriarchal or Œcumenical Council.

This Canon has at its root that solidarity of the Episcopate, whereof each Bishop is a shareholder. No Bishop stands alone, or is exempt from the jurisdiction of the Universal Episcopate, to which he is responsible for all his actions. If the Roman Patriarch, as Primate of Christendom, is *ex officio* the President of the Universal Episcopate in Œcumenical Council assembled, if it is his duty to promulgate its decisions *urbi et orbi*, and to be its spokesman and mouthpiece, he is none the less responsible to it than any other Bishop. The principle underlying this Canon is the true justification of the Council of Constance,[1] and of the Gallican theologians who held that an Œcumenical Council could judge the Pope.[2] The Canon also

---

[1] The decree of the Council of Constance (A.D. 1418) is as follows :—
"Definivit Concilium generale universam repræsentans Ecclesiam, potestatem suam immediate habere a Christo cui quilibet cuiuscunque status vel dignitatis, *etiamsi Papalis* existat, obedire tenetur in his quæ pertinent ad fidem et extirpationem schismatis et reformationem Ecclesiæ generalem in capite et in membris." (Conc. Constant., Sess. 4 and 5.)

[2] So Archbishop P. de Marca and Du Pin, who gives a long list of Canonists and Theologians who upheld this view on p. 422 of his treatise *De Antiqua Ecclesiæ Disciplina.*

applies to every exercise of coercive episcopal authority, for the greater includes the less. The sentence of excommunication is the heaviest penalty that a Bishop can inflict, and if this is a matter of appeal, such exercises of authority as the Episcopal veto upon the act of a Diocesan Synod are likewise liable to review. We may state broadly that in every case where a Bishop acts as representing his order his ruling is liable to an appeal. As President of his Synod he represents his order. If a vote by orders is taken, he acts as the sole representative of his order; but he cannot, when acting thus alone, commit the universal Episcopate, or even its immediate representatives in his case (his Primate and com-provincial Bishops), to the endorsement of his action as final, without their assent and co-operation. It follows, therefore, that a Bishop's veto upon any act of his Synod is suspensory and not final, until it has been endorsed by the Episcopate. For this cause an appeal to the Primate and Bishops of the Province from a Bishop's veto in Synod is just as lawful as an appeal from any other exercise of his authority as Diocesan and Ordinary.

The sixth Nicene Canon is of deep interest. It refers to the three great Patriarchates of Rome, Alexandria, and Antioch, and to the lesser Primacies such as Carthage in the West, and

Ephesus, Cæsarea in Cappadocia, and Heraclea in Thrace. It begins with an allusion to ancient usage and custom, which is of itself evidence that the Primacy of the great Sees was rooted in the history of the Catholic Church from the Apostolic age :—

Τὰ ἀρχαῖα ἔθη κρατείτω τὰ ἐν Αἰγύπτῳ καὶ Λιβύῃ καὶ Πενταπόλει, ὥστε τὸν Ἀλεξανδρείας ἐπίσκοπον πάντων τούτων ἔχειν τὴν ἐξουσίαν, ἐπειδὴ καὶ τῷ ἐν τῇ Ῥώμῃ ἐπισκόπῳ τοῦτο σύνηθές ἐστιν· ὁμοίως δὲ καὶ κατὰ Ἀντιόχειαν καὶ ἐν ταῖς ἄλλαις ἐπαρχίαις τὰ πρεσβεῖα σώζεσθαι ταῖς ἐκκλησίαις· καθόλου δὲ πρόδηλον ἐκεῖνο, ὅτι εἴ τις χωρὶς γνώμης τοῦ μητροπολίτου γένοιτο ἐπίσκοπος τὸν τοιοῦτον ἡ μεγάλη σύνοδος ὥρισε μὴ δεῖν εἶναι ἐπίσκοπον· ἐὰν μέντοι τῇ κοινῇ πάντων ψήφῳ, εὐλόγῳ οὔσῃ καὶ κατὰ κανόνα ἐκκλησιαστικόν, δύο ἢ τρεῖς δι' οἰκείαν φιλονεικίαν ἀντιλέγωσι, κρατείτω ἡ τῶν πλειόνων ψῆφος.

"Let the ancient customs prevail which exist in Egypt, Libya, and Pentapolis, so that the Bishop of Alexandria should have jurisdiction over all these Provinces, since this is customary also for the Bishop of Rome. In like manner also at Antioch, and in the other Provinces, let the Primatial privileges[1] of the Churches be preserved. This also is clearly manifest, that if any one be made a Bishop

---

[1] πρεσβεῖα, rights of the eldest; cf. πρεσβεῖα λαβεῖν, to take the rights of the eldest son. (Demosthenes, 955, 11.)

without the consent of the Metropolitan, the Great Synod ordains that such an one ought not to remain Bishop. But if two or three, through their own party feeling, contradict the common vote of all, when it is reasonable and according to the ecclesiastical Canon, let the vote of the majority prevail."

The first point to note in this Canon is the antiquity of the principle of Primacy. Its opening sentence is in itself a strong argument in favour of the principles advocated in these pages.

In the next place we have the witness of the Nicene Council to the ancient privileges of the three Patriarchal Sees of Rome, Alexandria, and Antioch. The authority of the Alexandrian "Pope," as we have already seen, was that of a Primate of Metropolitans. Meletius of Lycopolis had caused a schism against Alexander, the Patriarch of Alexandria, and the Council determined to reassert the ancient prerogatives of his See. The Patriarch of Alexandria not only consecrated the Metropolitans of his subject Provinces,[1] but also their suffragans, which was a privilege unknown elsewhere.

We have now to consider the bearing of this

---

[1] Dioscorus of Alexandria was cited to appear at the Great Synod of Ephesus (*the Latrocinium*) in A.D. 449, and to bring with him ten subordinate Metropolitans. "Imperator dirigens sacram Dioscoro in Alexandriam præcepit, ut cum decem Metropolitanis Episcopis, quos voluisset, veniret Ephesum." (*Liberat. Breviar.*, c. 12.)

Canon upon the privileges of the Roman See.[1] An ancient Latin version of this Canon began with the words, "Quod Ecclesia Romana semper habuit Primatum," which were quoted at Chalcedon by the Roman Legate Paschasinus, and was confronted immediately by the true Greek version. We need not impute bad faith to Paschasinus, and the words which state "that the Roman Church always had the Primacy," were an irrelevant addition, as expressing a fact which no one had ever seriously disputed. The position of the Roman Patriarch, as holding "a Primacy of honour" over the whole Catholic Church, is taken for granted in this Canon, which solely concerns itself with Patriarchal and Primatial jurisdiction. The jurisdiction of Alexandria is territorially defined, and this Patriarchal jurisdiction is paralleled with the customary Patriarchal jurisdiction of Rome. The Roman Patriarch was (i.) Primate of Christendom with a Primacy of honour, influence, and initiative, whose scope we have already in some measure defined. But he was also (ii.) a Patriarch with a defined jurisdiction,

[1] Cardinal Bellarmine's interpretation of this Canon is a strange instance of that perversion of history which is necessary in the interests of Ultramontanism. The Roman Bishop was accustomed to *allow* the Patriarch of Alexandria to govern in his name. "Quia Romanus Episcopus ante omnem conciliorum definitionem consuerit permittere Episcopo Alexandrino regimen Ægypti, Libyæ et Pentapolis; sive consuerit per Alexandrinum Episcopum illas Provincias gubernare." (*De Rom. Pont.*, ii. 13.)

and with an undefined authority over the whole West. He was also (iii.) Metropolitan of his Province, and (iv.) Bishop of his Diocese.

The question of the exact Metropolitical and Patriarchal jurisdiction of the Roman See has been much disputed.[1] The most probable opinion is that he was Metropolitan of the territory of the *Præfectus Urbis*, which extended within one hundred miles of Rome, and Patriarch of the ten Provinces governed by the *Vicarius Urbis*, with jurisdiction

[1] Benedict XIV., in commenting on the version given of this Canon by Rufinus, *Et ut apud Alexandriam et in urbe Roma vetusta consuetudo servetur, ut vel ille Ægypti vel hic suburbicarium ecclesiarum sollicitudinem gerat* (*Hist. Eccl.*, i. 6), takes the view of Schelstrate, that "the Sub-urbicarian Churches" meant the Provinces under the Roman Pontiff *qua* Patriarch. He is naturally inclined to widen the area of these Provinces to the whole West. (*De Synod. Diœces.*, ii. 2.) But Fleury (*Hist. Eccl.*, liv. 41), and Thomassin (*Vet. et Nov. Eccl. Disc.*, i. 8), and the Jesuit Sirmond (*Censur. Coniectur.*, i. 4) hold that the Patriarchal rights of Rome were confined to the ten Provinces of Tuscia, Umbria, Valeria, Picenum, Latium, Samnium, Apulia, Calabria, Lucania, Bruttium, with the islands of Sicily, Sardinia, and Corsica. These were the Provinces governed by the *Vicarius Urbis*, and contained 240 Dioceses, of which 110 (in the territory of the *Præfectus Urbis*) owned the Roman Pontiff as their *Metropolitan*, and the remainder were subject to him as *Patriarch* through their own Metropolitans. (See Dr. Cave, *Ancient Church Government*, p. 256.) The privilege of a Patriarch was to consecrate his Metropolitans. The Archbishop of Carthage and the Spanish and Gallican Primates were not consecrated by the Roman Patriarch. (De Marca, v. 4.) Nor was the Archbishop of Milan, who was consecrated by the Bishop of Aquileia. (*Ib.*, vi. 4.) There is no real ground for Schelstrate's view that the *maiores diœceses* of the Council of Arles referred to the whole of the West. The fact that the Roman Patriarch afterwards became Patriarch of the whole West, by the aid of the Civil Power (*e.g.*, Gratian's decree), is *nihil ad rem* in interpreting this Canon.

over their Metropolitans, and undefined Primatial authority over the whole West as occupying its sole Apostolic See. This Primatial authority in the West was exercised with greater influence, because of the close ties which bound the West to Rome as its centre. The Primate of Christendom found that his Primacy of influence grew more rapidly in the West than in the East, especially in the latter days, when the Patriarch of New Rome became a serious rival. But notwithstanding the witness of this Nicene Canon to the Roman Patriarchate, we cannot help noting that it would have been very differently worded if the Vatican claims had been admitted by the Nicene Fathers. It is impossible to reconcile the wording of this Canon with the modern idea that the Pope is the divinely appointed Ruler of the whole Catholic Church, the Infallible Doctor of Christendom, and the source of all episcopal jurisdiction.

The Canon proceeds to secure the Patriarchal rights of Antioch, which were at that time exercised over the Metropolitans of Cæsarea in Palestine, and of Syria, Phœnicia, Arabia, Euphratensis, Osrhoene, Mesopotamia, Cilicia, and Isauria, which were all included in the great civil "Diocese" of the Roman Empire which was called "Oriens."[1] The third Throne in Christendom, which still was

---

[1] Dr. Neale, *Introd. Eastern Church*, i. 125.

honoured as the first *Cathedra Petri*,[1] had the same privileges as the Patriarchal Sees of Rome and Alexandria. The Patriarch of Antioch consecrated the Metropolitans of his Patriarchate, and the Metropolitans, with his permission, consecrated their com-provincial Bishops. The abnormal use of Alexandria in this matter has already been alluded to. It probably arose from the fact that the "Pope" of Alexandria was originally Metropolitan of the single Province, which afterwards came to be subdivided into other Provinces with their own Metropolitans.[2] In addition to the three great Patriarchates, this Canon preserves the prerogatives of the lesser Primacies already mentioned.

[1] S. Jerome considers that the Patriarchal rights of Antioch were established by the sixth Nicene Canon. "Ni fallor, hoc ibi decernitur, ut Palestinæ metropolis Cæsarea sit, *et totius Orientis Antiochia*." (S. Jerome, Ep. 61, *ad Pammochum*.) So also Innocent I. of Rome, writing to Alexander, Patriarch of Antioch (Ep. 18), says, "The Council of Nicæa has not established the Church of Antioch over a Province, but over a 'Diœcesis' (Patriarchate). As, then, in virtue of his exclusive authority, the Bishop of Antioch ordains Metropolitans, it is not allowed that other Bishops should hold ordinations without his knowledge and consent" (*non sine permissu conscientiaque tua sinas Episcopos procreari*). The Festival of the "*Cathedra Petri*" at Antioch was celebrated in the fourth century, if not earlier. It was adopted by S. Jerome in his Martyrology, and used by S. Ambrose at Milan. The commemoration of the "*Cathedra Petri*" at Rome was first inserted in the Breviary by Paul IV. in 1557.

[2] Synesius, the Metropolitan of Ptolemais, which was within the Alexandrian Patriarchate, writes to his Patriarch Theophilus concerning the election of a Bishop who had been confirmed by him as Metropolitan, and duly elected. Consecration was now the one thing lacking. ἑνὸς ἔτι δεῖ . . . τοῦ μέν τοι, τῆς ἱερᾶς σου χειρός. (Synes., Ep. 76, *ad Theoph.*)

Du Pin[1] and others think that special reference is here made to the three Primatial Sees of Ephesus for Proconsular Asia, Cæsarea in Cappadocia for Pontus, and Heraclea (afterwards Constantinople) for Thrace. This view does not of course exclude the application of the Canon to other Primatial Sees in furtherance of a general principle. These three principal Primacies differed from the Patriarchal Sees in the matter of consecrating their Metropolitans.

This right did not belong to them.[2] In the case of Carthage the Archbishop confirmed the election of his subordinate Metropolitans, who were appointed by seniority of consecration, and not by virtue of their occupying a fixed Metropolitical See. These movable African Primacies were obviously inconvenient in some ways, and the Synod of Hippo in A.D. 393 ordered that each *episcopus primæ sedis*

---

[1] Du Pin, *De Antiqua Ecclesiæ Disciplina*, p. 37, *et seq.*

[2] One of the spurious Nicene Canons of the Arabic version (published by Tunianus) refers to the conversion of Ethiopia and the rights of its Primate or "Catholicus." S. Frumentius converted these Ethiopians when S. Athanasius was Patriarch of Alexandria, and the supposition of the Canon that a regularly organised Episcopate existed in Ethiopia is an additional testimony to its post-Nicene date. Yet it is worth quoting, because it gives evidence of the inherent difference between a Patriarch and a Primate. The "Catholicus," "non tamen ius habeat constituendi archiepiscopos, ut habet Patriarcha." (*Pseudo-Nicene Arabic Canon*, 36.) The South African Church observes this principle in Canon V., which directs that the Archbishop of Capetown and Metropolitan of South Africa shall be consecrated by the Archbishop of Canterbury as Primate of the Anglican Communion.

should report from time to time to the Archbishop of Carthage, and take instructions from him, besides attending the annual General Council of the African Church.¹

The last part of the sixth Nicene Canon appears at first sight to be a mere repetition of the assertion of the κῦρος of the Metropolitan. But it is not so. The Canon deals with the rights of Patriarchs and Primates (Exarchs). We cannot, with Valesius, accept the theory that this last clause refers to Patriarchs, under the name of "Metropolitan," and that it really means that they had the right of confirming all Episcopal elections. It is rather intended to preserve the rights of the Metropolitan against the Patriarch, and to declare that the Patriarch cannot consecrate a Bishop for a Province without the consent of the Metropolitan and a majority of the Bishops of that Province. This assertion of metropolitical rights is just and necessary, for the Metropolitan is not the mere suffragan of the Patriarch, and the

---

¹ See Marca (*De Primatibus*, p. 10, *seq.*) and Van Espen (*Comm. in Canon.*, p. 357). Hefele goes so far as to say that Carthage was "the Patriarchal See of Africa" (vol. ii. p. 397, n.). With regard to the Sees of Ephesus, Cæsarea, and Heraclea we may describe their Primates as superior Metropolitans who, although they had subordinate Metropolitans, were not Patriarchs, but had the title of "Exarch," which may be defined as describing "a lesser Patriarch." After Heraclea was merged into Constantinople the Primates of Ephesus and Cæsarea signed at Chalcedon as "Exarchs."

Patriarch cannot pass over and ignore his canonical rights.[1]

The seventh Nicene Canon need not detain us long. It is concerned with the precedence of the Bishop of Ælia, the name of the new city built by the Emperor Hadrian, early in the second century, upon the devastated site of Jerusalem. The Mother Diocese of Christendom lost its historical continuity and ecclesiastical precedence. The Bishop of Ælia was a suffragan of the Metropolitan of Cæsarea. But the associations of the Holy City were gradually revived. At the Provincial Synod held on the Paschal Controversy, at the request of Victor of Rome, Eusebius tells us that Theophilus of Cæsarea and Narcissus of Jerusalem were presidents.[2] Hymenæus of Jerusalem signed the

---

[1] Once more we refer to a modern instance. We have borne our witness in these pages to the necessity of a Canterbury Patriarchate as a living centre for the Anglican Communion. But when the present Archbishop of Sydney (Dr. Saumarez Smith) was consecrated as Primate of Australia by the Archbishop of Canterbury the ordinary oath taken by the Suffragan Bishops of the Province of Canterbury was administered to him, notwithstanding the fact that the Colonial Clergy Act of 1874 made provision for its omission. Colonial Archbishops and Metropolitans might well take a Declaration of allegiance to the Primatial See of the Anglican Communion, but to cause a Colonial Primate to take a Suffragan's oath to Canterbury is a distinct infringment of metropolitical rights. A worse encroachment took place in 1870, when Bishop Wilkinson was consecrated to Zululand, which is a See within the Province of South Africa. Instead of taking his Suffragan's oath to the South African Metropolitan, he was compelled to take it to the Archbishop of York, who is himself subordinate to Canterbury.

[2] Φέρεται δ' εἰσέτι νῦν τῶν κατὰ Παλαιστίνην τηνικάδε συγκεκροτημένων γραφή, ὧν προὐτέτακτο Θεόφιλος τῆς ἐν Καισαρείᾳ παροικίας ἐπίσκοπος, καὶ Νάρκισσος τῆς ἐν Ἱεροσολύμοις. (Euseb., *H. E.*, v. 23.)

Synodal letter of the Council of Antioch in A.D. 269, *before* the Metropolitan of Cæsarea. It is evident that a special precedence was assigned to the Bishop of Jerusalem, which the Nicene Council desired to confirm (τῇ μητροπόλει σωζομένου τοῦ οἰκείου ἀξιώματος) without trenching upon the metropolitical rights of one of its most distinguished members, Eusebius of Cæsarea, the historian and scholar. De Marca held the theory that this Canon was intended to give the Bishop of Jerusalem a precedency of honour (τὴν ἀκολουθίαν τῆς τιμῆς) next to Antioch, without withdrawing him from the jurisdiction of Cæsarea. But if this view cannot be literally established, we find Maximus of Jerusalem convoking a Synod in Palestine in favour of S. Athanasius, soon after the Nicene Council, and thus practically acting in independence of Cæsarea.[1] The discovery of the Holy Sepulchre and of the True Cross by the Empress Helena naturally gave a great impulse to the revival of the lost glories of the Mother See of Christendom. At the Council of Ephesus (A.D. 431), Juvenal of Jerusalem took a prominent place, and when he attempted to establish his superiority to Cæsarea by false documents (a strange anticipation of the Pseudo-Isidorian Decretals), S. Cyril of Alexandria notified this fraud to Leo the Great,

[1] Socr., ii. 24.

who denounced Juvenal's evil conduct in terms of unmeasured censure. It is distinctly unfortunate that none of his successors in the Roman See found opportunity to denounce the equally "commentitia scripta" of the Pseudo-Isidore.[1]

But notwithstanding the evil conduct of Juvenal, and its condemnation by Rome and Alexandria, the Council of Chalcedon (A.D. 451) raised Jerusalem to Patriarchal rank, with jurisdiction over the three Provinces of Palestine—a step which not only took away the metropolitical rights of Cæsarea, but diminished the Patriarchate of Antioch by subsidising its jurisdiction. We have anticipated the course of events in dealing with the Patriarchate of Jerusalem. But the whole story bears so directly on our subject that it is best dealt with as a whole. The See of Ælia becomes the Patriarchate of Jerusalem after a long ecclesiastical strife. What is the process? The Roman Patriarch does not rule the Catholic Church and issue a decree deciding the question by his plenary authority. As first of the great Patriarchs and Primate of Christendom he condemns the conduct of Juvenal at the request

---

[1] "Sicut etiam in Ephesina Synodo, quæ impium Nestorium cum dogmate suo perculit, Iuvenalis episcopus ad obtinendum Palestinæ Provinciæ principatum credidit se posse sufficere, et insolentes ausus per commentitia scripta firmare. Quod sanctæ memoriæ Cyrillus Alexandrinus merito perhorrescens, scriptis suis mihi, quid prædicta cupiditas ausa sit, indicavit et sollicita prece multum poposcit, ut nulla illicitis conatibus præberetur assensio." (S. Leo, Ep. 62, *ad Maximum*.)

of S. Cyril of Alexandria. But the whole matter belonged to a higher authority than that of the Primate-Patriarch. The Patriarchs could, and did, exchange views upon the matter, but it needed an Œcumenical Council to settle it. The seventh Canon of Nicæa decided the claims of Jerusalem in a certain way. The Roman Patriarch and the other Patriarchs were bound to uphold this Canon, pending the decision of a future Council. When the Council of Chalcedon reversed the Nicene decree, their action was accepted without question. Before passing on to consider the Canons of other Councils, there are several points in the Nicene Canons which indirectly elucidate our subject. The 15th Canon forbids the translation of Bishops, Priests, and Deacons from one sphere to another. Διὰ τὸν πολὺν τάραχον καὶ τὰς στάσεις τὰς γινομένας ἔδοξε παντάπασι περιαιρεθῆναι τὴν συνήθειαν, τὴν παρὰ τὸν κανόνα εὑρεθεῖσαν ἔν τισι μέρεσιν, ὥστε ἀπὸ πόλεως εἰς πόλιν μὴ μεταβαίνειν μήτε ἐπίσκοπον μήτε πρεσβύτερον μήτε διάκονον. εἰ δέ τις μετὰ τὸν τῆς ἁγίας καὶ μεγάλης συνόδου ὅρον τοιούτῳ τινὶ ἐπιχειρήσειεν, ἢ ἐπιδοίη ἑαυτὸν πράγματι τοιούτῳ, ἀκυρωθήσεται ἐξάπαντος τὸ κατασκεύασμα, καὶ ἀποκατασταθήσεται τῇ ἐκκλησίᾳ, ᾗ ὁ ἐπίσκοπος ἢ ὁ πρεσβύτερος ἐχειροτονήθη. " By reason of the frequent disturbance and factions which have taken place, we ordain the total abrogation of the usage which has been established in some countries contrary to the Canon, so that no Bishop, Priest, or Deacon should remove from one city to another. But if any one should venture, even after this ordinance of the Holy and Great Synod, to act contrary to this present rule, or should lend himself to such a thing, the proceeding shall be absolutely annulled, and he shall be restored to the Church to which he had been ordained Bishop or Priest."

The Canon forbidding unauthorised Translations which is here alluded to is the 14th Apostolic Canon, which forbids *personal* and *private* action on the part of the person translated, so as to exclude self-seeking and ambition. No Translation is permitted—εἰ μή τις εὔλογος αἰτία ᾖ τοῦτο βιαζομένη αὐτὸν ποιεῖν, ὡς πλέον τι κέρδος δυναμένου αὐτοῦ τοῖς ἐκεῖσε λόγῳ εὐσεβείας συμβάλλεσθαι καὶ τοῦτο δὲ οὐκ ἀφ' ἑαυτοῦ, ἀλλὰ κρίσει πολλῶν ἐπισκόπων καὶ παρακλήσει μεγίστῃ—" except there be some reasonable cause which compels this step to be taken; such as the fact that some greater advantage to the cause of religion amongst the people of the other diocese would be the result. And even in this case the Bishop himself must not decide the matter, but the decision must come from many Bishops as the result of a very strong demand for the Translation."

Hefele reckons this Canon as Ante-Nicene, and gives reasons for refuting the opposite hypothesis of Drey.[1] It explains the Nicene Canon very clearly, and shows what the Nicene Fathers really meant to forbid. Bishops, Priests, and Deacons, in the threefold order of the Apostolic Ministry, are the organs of the Body of Christ. For this reason the personal element with regard to their defined spheres of action must as far as possible be eliminated. Their "mission" to exercise their functions within certain defined territorial limits is from above. It comes with the permission and authority of the whole Body of Christ, as expressed by the Universal Episcopate and its representatives. The Diocesan Bishop commissions his Priests and Deacons. He is himself commissioned and given spiritual jurisdiction by his Metropolitan and com-provincial Bishops, as representing the Universal Episcopate. It is obvious that every condition of Mission and Jurisdiction rests upon the principle "permissu superiorum."

For a Bishop to *send himself* from one Diocese to another, or for a Priest or Deacon to act, in his

---

[1] Hefele, vol. i. p. 464. Beveridge also proves this 14th Apostolic Canon to be Ante-Nicene. He quotes Eusebius (*De Vita Const.*, iii. 61) as refusing Translation for himself, because he desired to abide by τὸν Ἀποστολικὸν κανόνα, as well as κανόνα τῆς ἐκκλησίας, by which he alluded to the 15th Nicene Canon, which Eusebius had helped to frame. (Beveridge, *Cod. Can.*, vol. i. pp. 70–71.)

lesser sphere, in a similar way, is a total subversion of Catholic order. The ancient Canons forbidding translations were intended to safeguard this true principle of Catholic order and discipline. They must be construed together as a whole. They are as follows: Apostolic Canon (xiv.), Nicene (xv.), Antioch (xxi.), Sardica (i.), Carthage III. (xxxvii.), Carthage IV. (xxvii.).

The Nicene and Antiochene Canons, which forbid Translations absolutely, must be construed with the qualifications of the other Canons, which explain the permissions given in exceptional cases. The 27th Canon of the Fourth Council of Carthage (A.D. 398) follows the line of the 14th Apostolic Canon in laying down that "if the good of the Church demand it, the Translation of a Bishop must take place at the Synod upon the written request of Clergy and people. Other clerics only need (for their removal) the permission of their Bishops."

The stringent wording of the Nicene Canon must be construed by its reference to the permission granted by the 14th Apostolic Canon. It is directed against ambitious Clergy who sought Translation in a spirit absolutely contrary to the permission of the Apostolic Canon. This is plain from its opening allusion to the faction caused by such conduct, and the best commentary upon this Nicene Canon is supplied by the fact that, for good and sufficient reasons, the Nicene Council translated Eustathius, Bishop of Berœa, to the Patriarchal Throne of Antioch.[1] It is a pity that an able historian of our own day should (after stating that certain Canons were set aside "by definite enactment or by tacit consent") dogmatically assert that "this was done, as we know, in the case of the 15th Canon of the first Nicene Council. . . . It has practically been a dead letter from the first, simply because it did not express the mind of the Church."[2] If the writer in question had examined the previous and subsequent Canon Law upon the whole question of Translations, it is possible that he would not have jumped to so hasty a conclusion in dealing with the 15th Canon of Nicæa.

It remains but to touch incidentally upon the idea of a mystical marriage between the Bishop and his Diocese, and a Priest and his charge. Too much has been made of this simile.[3] To compare

---

[1] Socrates (I. 13), and Sozomen (I. 2), who says: "The Bishops assembled at Nicæa were so sensible of the purity of the life and doctrines of Eustathius, that they adjudged him worthy to fill the Apostolic Throne. He was then Bishop of Berœa; they therefore translated him to Antioch."

[2] Professor Collins, *The Nature and Force of the Canon Law*, p. 15.

[3] S. Athanasius uses this simile, and quotes it as the *obiter dictum* of an Egyptian Council (*Apol.* ii.), so also S. Jerome (Epist. *ad Ocean.*, lxxxiii.).

P

the relation of a Bishop to his See to the Sacrament of Holy Marriage, as contracted between two persons, proves too much; because, for the reasons we have already adduced, that relation is not indissoluble. The simile could only be applied in a limited way to persons seeking Translations for their own ends, and to please themselves; since marriage is not a union dependent upon the caprice or will of the contracting parties when it has once taken place. The safest reasons against Translation are those given by Pope Damasus, who forbade it when done "*per ambitionem,*" and Pope Gelasius, who condemned it when done "*nullis existentibus causis.*" The 16th Nicene Canon further illustrates this point in compelling clerics to return to their Dioceses and charges, who have sought Translation "with levity and without having the fear of God before their eyes" (ῥιψοκινδύνως μήτε τὸν φόβον τοῦ Θεοῦ πρὸ ὀφθαλμῶν ἔχοντες). It also condemns a kindred abuse. Sometimes a Bishop ventured "to steal a cleric belonging to the Diocese of another Bishop" (ὑφαρπάσαι τὸν τῷ ἑτέρῳ διαφέροντα), and ordain him for his own Diocese. In this case the ordination is absolutely invalid (ἄκυρος),[1]

---

[1] At this date the subsequent distinction between sacramental and canonical invalidity had not been accurately defined. To use a modern instance, the ordinations of the Cumminsite sect in America are *sacramentally* invalid, although Dr. Cummins was a lawful Bishop previous to his deposition. The ordinations of Dr. Colenso, after his deposition, were *canonically* invalid, and those ordained by him could be recon-

thus showing that the ministration of the Sacraments is part of the corporate life and joint responsibility of the Church, in such a way that the caprice of an individual cannot use a sacramental rite as a sort of mechanical formula to further his own private ends. Validity depends not only upon the intention of doing *quod facit Ecclesia*, but also, in certain cases, of doing *quod vult Ecclesia*.[1] It is manifest that this Canon bears distinct witness to the solidarity of the Episcopate and its constitutional order. The relation of Bishops to their Priests has already been made plain in these pages.

The 18th Nicene Canon deals with the question of Deacons, who, at an early date, acquired great power and influence in the Church. They were permitted to assist in a very prominent way in the celebration of the Divine Mysteries.[2] But the

---

ciled to the Church without reordination, as they were ordained according to the English Ordinal, which was not the case with the Cumminsites.

[1] The maxim *fieri quod non debuit factum valet* may be applied in cases where the distinct will of the Church has not been manifested. It is possible, however, to consider ἄκυρος as meaning "invalid," in the sense that no ministerial acts of a person so ordained would be valid, so that the Sacrament of Order would be in suspense in such a case.

[2] Deacons presented the offerings to the Bishop at the Altar. οἱ διάκονοι προσαγέτωσαν τὰ δῶρα τῷ ἐπισκόπῳ πρὸς τὸ θυσιαστήριον. (*Const. Apost.*, viii. 12.) They read the Gospel. "Evangelium Christi quasi diaconus lectitabas." (S. Jerome, *Ep. ad Sabin.*). In the West the Deacon held the Chalice for the Priest at Mass, but he did not share in its consecration, notwithstanding the reference of Pseudo-Ambrose: "Consors diaconus erat consecrationis." (Bona, *Rer. Lit.*, i. 25.) He in like manner held the Paten for the Solemn Fraction. (Migne,

Nicene rule forbade a very flagrant abuse on the part of Deacons. In some places they administered the Holy Eucharist to Priests,[1] and ventured to communicate before Bishops. The Nicene Canon gave a very valid reason against this first abuse: "Since neither the Canon nor custom permit that those who have *not* the power to offer can give the Body of Christ to those who have the power to offer." ὅπερ οὔτε ὁ κανὼν οὔτε ἡ συνήθεια παρέδωκε, τοὺς ἐξουσίαν μὴ ἔχοντας προσφέρειν τοῖς προσφέρουσι διδόναι τὸ σῶμα τοῦ Χριστοῦ.[2] The second abuse arose in the case of a Bishop who was present without being himself the celebrant. In such a case the Bishop receives the Holy Eucharist immediately after the celebrant. The regulations of this Canon show the great care and

Patrol., 147.) But in times of persecution, in the absence of a Priest, some Deacons ventured to consecrate (*offerre*). This abuse was promptly checked by the Council of Arles. "De diaconibus quos cognovimus multis locis offerre, placuit minime fieri debere." (Canon xv.) The Deacon administered the Chalice to the people. (*Ap. Const.*, viii. 13.) But he did not administer in both kinds unless ordered to do so by a Priest (*Slat. Eccl. Antiq.* (A.D. 505), Can. 38), and Canon xv. of second Council of Arles (A.D. 443), which said that "if a Priest is present, the Deacon must not administer the Body of Christ, under penalty of deposition."

[1] This abuse is not unknown in modern times. The writer once saw at a Diocesan Synod a Deacon administer the Chalice to a great number of Priests at a Celebration held in connection with the Synod. The error made was subsequently pointed out, and steps were taken to prevent its recurrence. The rule holds good whether a Priest is present in choir or in the congregation, and it ought never to be violated on any pretext.

[2] See Note B.

forethought with which the Primitive Church guarded the due prerogatives of both Bishops and Priests.

After the Nicene Council, the main issues of the Arian controversy centred round the person of S. Athanasius, who was consecrated Patriarch of Alexandria on June 8th, A.D. 328. We need not here touch upon the details of the conflict, but we may note, as bearing upon our subject, the relations of S. Athanasius with S. Julius of Rome. After the second exile of S. Athanasius, he arrived at Rome in A.D. 340. His opponents had previously held a Synod at Antioch early in that year, and after unlawfully deposing him, schismatically intruded the Arian Gregory into his See. This Synod must be carefully distinguished from the Synod of Antioch *in Encæniis* in A.D. 341.[1]

The enemies of S. Athanasius of the Eusebian party had previously sent an embassy to Pope Julius in A.D. 339 to ask him, as Roman Patriarch, to signify his acknowledgment of Pistus, their spurious Patriarch of Alexandria, by the usual *Epistolæ communicatoriæ*, whereby intercommunion between Patriarchates and between other Sees was formally maintained. S. Julius refused, and S. Athanasius sent envoys to Rome to represent his

[1] Socrates and Sozomen have both fallen into this confusion. (Socrat. ii. 9, 11, and Sozom. iii. 6.) Bishop Hefele points out their error (vol. ii. p. 51), and so does Canon Bright. (*Orations of S. Ath. against the Arians*, p. xl.)

case. Then came an Encyclical Letter from the Patriarchal Synod of Alexandria in favour of S. Athanasius addressed " to all Bishops, and to Julius, Bishop of Rome." Pistus was afterwards given up by the Eusebians, and, as we have already seen, Gregory took his place as schismatic Patriarch of Alexandria. The Eusebian Synod of Antioch who appointed him wrote to S. Julius, when they found that he did not favour their cause, and immediately attacked his position as Primate of Christendom.[1] They urged that the decision of the Council of Tyre against S. Athanasius was final. Their view was that the decision of a local Council was not liable to review by the collective Episcopate or by an Œcumenical Council. They

[1] The Eusebians, in dealing with S. Athanasius from Antioch, the *third* See in Christendom, are subsequently reminded by Pope Julius that the affairs of Alexandria, the *second* See in rank and precedency, must first be referred to Rome as the Primatial See in Christendom, in accordance with ecclesiastical custom, as a token of the interdependence of the great Patriarchates on each other. This is shown by the correspondence between Dionysius of Rome and Dionysius of Alexandria when the latter was accused of Sabellianism. S. Julius appears to go a little beyond this limit when he asks the Eusebians, "Why nothing was said to us concerning the Church of the Alexandrians in particular? Are you ignorant that the custom has been for word to be written to us first, and then for a just sentence to proceed from this place?" (*i.e.* Rome). (S. Julius in S. Ath., *Apol. c. Arian.*, 35.) In later times S. Leo the Great rests the Primacy of Rome over Alexandria on the relations of S. Mark to S. Peter, and says, "The spirit of the Master and the disciple flowed from the same source of grace, nor could he who was ordained hand anything else than that which he received of his ordainer." (S. Leo, Ep. ix., ed. Migne, liv.)

abused S. Cyprian's maxim concerning the inherent equality of all Bishops, and said that the Roman Patriarch could claim no special rights because of the importance of the city over which he was Bishop. They denied the Primacy of Rome, because S. Julius defended the cause of S. Athanasius.

In the autumn of A.D. 341 S. Julius held a Synod at Rome, which defended S. Athanasius against the false charges of his enemies, and in the name of this Synod, S. Julius replied to the Eusebians at Antioch. He stated that the Nicene Council had agreed that the decisions of one Council could be re-examined by another. He did not apparently allude to any of the twenty genuine Canons, but to some resolution which has not been preserved in an authentic and genuine form. He cleverly disposes of their plea for the equality of all Bishops, by reminding them that if they were consistent in their belief, they would not seek for translation to more important Sees. The Eusebians complained that the Pope alone wrote to them. S. Julius replies, "Although I alone wrote, yet the sentiments that I expressed were not those of myself alone, but of all the Bishops throughout Italy and in these parts."[1] S. Julius wrote as Patriarch of the West, as well as Primate of Christendom, and he

---

[1] Letter of Pope Julius to the Eusebians at Antioch. (Ap. S. Ath., *Apol. c. Arian.*, 26.)

is careful to associate with himself the authority of the Bishops of Italy and the West. "Word should have been written *to us all* concerning the matter" (*i.e.* the charges against S. Athanasius), "so that a just sentence might proceed *from all;*"[1] says S. Julius in the same Epistle. Here we see that S. Julius considers that the universal Episcopate should try the case of a Patriarch.[2] There is no assumption on his part that the Roman Patriarch represented the universal Episcopate in his own person. Even this letter, in which the personal pronoun is so freely used, emanates from his Council as well as himself.[3] The relations of Pope Julius to the Church generally with regard to the Athanasian controversy may be accurately summed up as expressing the legitimate Primacy of Rome.

The Council of Antioch *in Encæniis* in A.D. 341, was held on the occasion of the Dedication of the

---

[1] Ibid., c. 35.

[2] In the preceding sentence of his letter, S. Julius had said that accusations should be conducted "according to the Canon of the Church." His meaning is plain. He alludes to the authority of the universal Episcopate. Both Socrates and Sozomen have fallen into a strange error in commenting upon these words of S. Julius. Socrates says that S. Julius alluded to "the ecclesiastical canon commanding that the Churches ought not to make canons beside the will of the Bishop of Rome." (*Hist.*, ii. 17.) Sozomen goes further when he says that "it was a sacerdotal law to declare invalid whatever was transacted beside the will of the Bishop of the Romans." (*Hist.*, iii. 10.) The words of S. Julius cannot by any possibility be stretched to fit the interpretation thus put upon them.

[3] Its closing words are: "Thus wrote the Council of Rome by Julius, Bishop of Rome." (S. Ath., *Apol. c. Ar.*, 36.)

"Golden" Church at Antioch, and contains some Canons that bear upon the principle of Primacy. Although the Council was attended by the Eusebian party as well as the Catholics, the conclusions at which it arrived, as expressed in its 25 Canons, have always been regarded as orthodox, mainly because its Canons, in most instances, were in accord with previous enactments, and thus became incorporated into that general body of Canon Law, whose authority was confirmed by the 1st Canon of the Œcumenical Council of Chalcedon.[1] The 1st Canon of Antioch reiterates the Nicene decision on the Paschal controversy, the 3rd is virtually a reproduction of the 16th Nicene Canon against irregular removals and Translations. The 4th Canon is directed against contumacy. It enacts that if a Bishop, Priest, or Deacon be deposed from office, and persists in exercising his office in defiance of the sentence passed upon him, he thereby cuts himself off from all rights of appeal (*nullo modo liceat ei nec in alia Synodo restitutionis spem, aut locum habere satisfactionis*). This Canon was read out, and quoted as authoritative at the Council of Chalcedon, and is founded on the 29th Apostolic Canon. The 5th Canon provides that a Priest who sets up an Altar and holds private assem-

---

[1] "Huius (Concilii) Canones . . . in Concilio Chalcedonensi, et deinceps in ecclesia universa sunt in auctoritatem admissi." (Du Pin, *De Antiq. Eccl. Discip.*, p. 101.)

blies, "setting at nought his own Bishop," shall be wholly deposed after he has had due warning. The 6th Canon is virtually a repetition of the 5th Nicene Canon. The 9th Canon touches upon the rights of Metropolitans, and is an expansion of the 35th Apostolical Canon. It is as follows:—

Τοὺς καθ' ἑκάστην ἐπαρχίαν ἐπισκόπους εἰδέναι χρὴ τὸν ἐν τῇ μητροπόλει προεστῶτα ἐπίσκοπον καὶ τὴν φροντίδα ἀναδέχεσθαι πάσης τῆς ἐπαρχίας, διὰ τὸ ἐν τῇ μητροπόλει πανταχόθεν συντρέχειν πάντας τοὺς τὰ πράγματα ἔχοντας, ὅθεν ἔδοξε καὶ τῇ τιμῇ προηγεῖσθαι αὐτόν, μηδέν τε πράττειν περιττὸν τοὺς λοιποὺς ἐπισκόπους ἄνευ αὐτοῦ, κατὰ τὸν ἀρχαιότερον κρατήσαντα ἐκ τῶν πατέρων ἡμῶν κανόνα ἢ ταῦτα μόνα ὅσα τῇ ἑκάστου ἐπιβάλλει παροικίᾳ, καὶ ταῖς ὑπ' αὐτὴν χώραις· ἕκαστον γὰρ ἐπίσκοπον ἐξουσίαν ἔχειν τῆς ἑαυτοῦ παροικίας, διοικεῖν τε κατὰ τὴν ἑκάστῳ ἐπιβάλλουσαν εὐλάβειαν, καὶ πρόνοιαν ποιεῖσθαι πάσης τῆς χώρας τῆς ὑπὸ τὴν ἑαυτοῦ πόλιν, ὡς καὶ χειροτονεῖν πρεσβυτέρους καὶ διακόνους, καὶ μετὰ κρίσεως ἕκαστα διαλαμβάνειν· περαιτέρω δὲ μηδὲν πράττειν ἐπιχειρεῖν δίχα τοῦ τῆς μητροπόλεως ἐπισκόπου, μηδὲ αὐτὸν ἄνευ τῆς τῶν λοιπῶν γνώμης.

"It is necessary that the Bishops in each Eparchy (Province) should know that the Bishop presiding in the Metropolis has charge of the whole Province, because all who have business come together from all quarters to the Metropolis. For this reason it is decided that he should also hold the foremost rank, and that without him the other Bishops (according to the ancient and recognised Canon of our Fathers) should do nothing out of the common, save such things alone as belong to their respective Dioceses, and the districts belonging thereto. For every Bishop has authority in his own Diocese, and must govern it according to his own conscience, and take charge of the whole region around his Episcopal city; for instance, the ordaining of Priests and Deacons, and discharging all his duties with due judgment. Further than this, he may not venture without the Metropolitan, nor the latter without taking the opinion of the other Bishops."

We notice, first of all, that this Canon clearly lays down the principle of Primacy as the 35th Apostolic Canon has done. It also upholds Professor Ramsay's view, that the ecclesiastical organisation followed the civil organisation of the Empire, for the common-sense reason that the civil Metropolis of the Province was the best place for the residence of the Metropolitan, because it was the centre of business for the whole Province. Most writers on ecclesiastical antiquities take the same view, as we have already seen, and notably Beveridge and Bingham.[1] The right of the in-

---

[1] See Note E., Chap. i., and Bingham, vol. i. p. 342.

dividual Bishop to rule his own Diocese is carefully maintained, whilst at the same time he cannot take action outside the ordinary routine without the assent of his Metropolitan, nor can the Metropolitan act as an arbitrary ruler without consulting the Bishops of his Province.[1] Canon xiv. of Antioch is very important. It assumes that an appeal from the Synod of a Province to a higher Synod is a recognised procedure of ecclesiastical law. It forbids a Bishop, condemned by the Synod of his Province, from appealing to the civil power in the person of the Emperor, except by the permission (accorded under Canon xi.) of the Metropolitan or Bishops of the Province. He ought rather to appeal to a greater Synod of Bishops (*ad maius Episcoporum Concilium*), who shall deal with the matter. Du Pin's interpretation of this Canon is coloured by his view that the sentence of a Provincial Synod is final.[2] He tries to explain away its force by saying that it means that the

---

[1] A Metropolitan, or Archbishop, cannot inhibit a Bishop of his Province absolutely without reference to the Synod of Bishops of his Province. As a modern instance we may refer to Canon ii. of the South African Church, which states that the inhibition of a Bishop by the Metropolitan must be referred to the Synod of Bishops at its next session, who shall decide whether his reasons for so doing were sufficient.

[2] Yet Du Pin is constrained to admit that controversies of faith cannot be thus finally dealt with. "Observavimus controversias fidei primum iudicatas ubi nascebantur; quod si de isto iudicio Ecclesiæ secum invicem dissentirent, ultimum ac supremum iudicium fuisse penes Ecclesiam et Synodum Universalem." (*De Antiq. Eccl. Disc.*, p. 241.)

Bishops of the Province who condemned their com-provincial Bishop shall go to a higher Synod to get their condemnation confirmed.[1] But this is special pleading. The 14th Canon rules that, if the judgment of the Bishops of a Province in the trial of a Bishop is not unanimous, the Metropolitan of a neighbouring Province shall be called in to assist the Bishops of the Province to rehear the case with the assistance of his Bishops. ("Metropolitanus Episcopus a vicina Provincia iudices alios convocet . . . ut per eos, simul et per comprovinciales Episcopos, quod iustum visum fuerit approbetur.") No clearer testimony than this could be adduced in favour of the Cyprianic maxim, "Episcopatus est unus;" and no clearer proof could be adduced against the theory that each Province is an autocephalous unit, whose judgment is final. The only instance of such finality is in a criminal case, where (by Canon xv.) if a Bishop be found guilty of definite moral offences, and is unanimously condemned by all the Bishops of his Province, the matter is terminated. ("Si quis Episcopus de certis criminibus accusatus condemnetur ab omnibus Episcopis eiusdem Provinciæ," &c.) The reason of this is plain. The facts of a crime are best dealt with by those on the spot, who know the details and circumstances of the case. Therefore the Bishops of

---

[1] Du Pin, *De Antiq. Eccl. Disc.*, p. 103.

the Province, if unanimous, are trusted with the plenary authority of the Universal Episcopate in dealing with crime. Cases involving faith and doctrine stand on a different basis. The Canons of Antioch clearly set forth the universal law of the Church, which rules that a Bishop cannot be tried by his Metropolitan *alone*, but that he must be tried by the Metropolitan and his com-provincial Bishops. These Canons formed a strong portion of the arguments in favour of the Bishop of Lincoln's protest against his trial by the Archbishop of Canterbury sitting as *iudex solus*.

We may admire the juridical and dialectical skill of Archbishop Benson's judgment, in which he decided that he could judge one of his com-provincial Bishops as *iudex solus*. But his reasoning and his conclusions do not commend themselves as being in accordance with the Canon Law of the undivided Church. It cannot be proved that a Patriarch or Metropolitan ever sat as *iudex solus* to hear appeals, and such powers as Archbishop Benson claimed do not flow from the Patriarchal or Metropolitical position of the Throne of Canterbury, but rather from the mediæval prerogatives which the Hildebrandine Papacy granted to the Archbishop of Canterbury, as *Legatus natus* of the Pope. The 16th Canon of Antioch determines that

[1] *The Guardian*, May 15th, 1889.

if a Bishop without a See is elected to a vacant See even by the whole Diocese, he shall be deposed unless his appointment is confirmed by a *regular* Synod, and a *regular* Synod is one over which the Metropolitan presides. The 18th Canon provides for the case of a Bishop who has been consecrated for a Diocese which will not receive him, in the same way as the 18th Canon of Ancyra. The 19th Canon is practically a combination of the 4th and 6th Nicene Canons. The 22nd Canon forbids the intrusion of a Bishop into another Bishop's Diocese, and the 23rd forbids a Bishop to appoint his own successor.

The Council of Sardica was assembled in A.D. 344 at Sardica, the metropolis of Dacia, which was a part of Illyricum Orientale, and, as such, reckoned to be within the Roman Patriarchate.[1] It was assembled by the two Emperors, at the desire of Pope Julius, S. Athanasius, and Hosius of Cordova, to finally settle the dissensions that had arisen out of the Arian controversy.

It was intended to be an Œcumenical Synod, but it has never been accepted as such by the whole Church. Its great importance, as regards our present subject, lies in the fact that it definitely gave an appellate jurisdiction to the Roman Patriarch. The question to be determined is, first

[1] Sardica still exists under the name of Traditza, and is about sixty miles west of Constantinople.

of all, whether the Council of Sardica conferred novel privileges on the Roman Patriarch or merely formularised certain rights which were inherent in his office. Then comes the further question as to the exact nature of those privileges, and the manner in which they differed, if they differed at all, from the privileges accorded to other Patriarchs.

Before quoting the Canons of Sardica we must bear in mind that the See of Rome was the great supporter of S. Athanasius and the faith of Nicæa during the whole of the Arian controversy. The fall of Liberius was a personal lapse, which was subsequently condoned when he repented. The Roman Church was not turned from the path of orthodoxy by the defection of her Patriarch. The Roman Church did not consider the successor of S. Peter an infallible guide, whose leading was to be implicitly followed. The Imperial position and leadership of the Roman Church was rather accentuated than diminished by the removal of the chief seat of civil government to Constantinople. And so we find that Roman orthodoxy, and the prestige of the "Cathedra Petri," coupled with the fact of the dissensions at Alexandria and Antioch, caused the Sardican Fathers to feel that in Rome they had a centre that could be trusted. We must now quote the Sardican Canons dealing with appeals to Rome.

The third Canon of Sardica is divided into three parts. The first part is a repetition of the 13th Antiochene Canon, and says that a Bishop can perform Episcopal functions in another Diocese if called upon to do so by the Metropolitan and Bishops of the Province. The second part is in consonance with the fifth Nicene Canon in ordering causes to be settled in the Synod of each Province without the intervention of the Bishops of another Province. The third part deals with the exception to this usual method of allowing matters to be settled, if possible, by the Bishops of the Province. The Eusebians had been insolent to Pope Julius, and had in his person disparaged the Roman Primacy. The Sardican Fathers determined to redress the insult by mentioning Pope Julius by name in the first of their enactments concerning appeals to the Roman Patriarch. Hosius presided at Sardica, and S. Julius was represented by two legates. Every Canon proposed from the chair by the President is announced by the formula "Osius episcopus dixit," and confirmed by the response "Synodus respondit: Placet." The Canons appear in Greek and in Latin. We quote the Greek and Latin of the third part of Canon iii.

Εἰ δὲ ἄρα τις ἐπισκόπων ἔν τινι πράγματι δόξῃ κατακρίνεσθαι καὶ ὑπολαμβάνει ἑαυτὸν μὴ σαθρὸν ἀλλὰ καλὸν ἔχειν τὸ πρᾶγμα, ἵνα καὶ αὖθις ἡ κρίσις

ἀνανεωθῇ· εἰ δοκεῖ ὑμῶν τῇ ἀγάπῃ, Πέτρου τοῦ ἀποσ-
τόλου τὴν μνήμην τιμήσωμεν καὶ γραφῆναι παρὰ τούτων τῶν κρινάντων Ἰουλίῳ τῷ ἐπισκόπῳ Ῥώμης, ὥστε
διὰ τῶν γειτνιώντων τῇ ἐπαρχίᾳ ἐπισκόπων, εἰ δέοι,
ἀνανεωθῆναι τὸ δικαστήριον καὶ ἐπιγνώμονας αὐτὸς
παράσχοι· εἰ δὲ μὴ συστῆναι δύναται τοιοῦτον αὐτοῦ
εἶναι τὸ πρᾶγμα, ὡς παλινδικίας χρῄζειν, τὰ ἅπαξ
κεκριμένα μὴ ἀναλύεσθαι, τὰ δὲ ὄντα βέβαια τυγχάνειν.
"Quod si aliquis episcoporum iudicatus fuerit in aliqua causa, et putat se bonam causam habere, ut iterum concilium renovetur; si vobis placet, Sancti Petri Apostoli memoriam honoremus, ut scribatur ab his, qui causam examinarunt, Iulio Romano Episcopo, et si iudicaverit renovandum esse iudicium renovetur et det iudices; si autem probaverit, talem causam esse, ut non refricentur ea, quae acta sunt, quae decreverit confirmata erunt. Si hoc omnibus placet? Synodus respondit: Placet." The variations between the Greek and Latin versions may be combined in the following rendering: " If any of the Bishops shall have been condemned in any matter, and considers that he has a good and valid cause, so that his case should be reheard: if it please you, let us honour the memory of S. Peter the Apostle, and let the Bishops who have judged the case write to Julius, the Roman Bishop, and if he shall decide that the cause be reheard, it shall be reheard, and he shall appoint judges

from the Bishops in the neighbourhood of the Province ; but if he shall be unable to allow that the cause is of such a nature as to demand a rehearing, the previous decision shall not be undone, but shall remain as it has been originally decreed."

The fourth Canon of Sardica may be thus rendered in harmony with the Greek and Latin texts :—

"Bishop Gaudentius said, If pleasing to you, it shall be added to this judgment which you, Hosius, have brought forward, and which is full of pure love, that if a Bishop has been deposed by sentence of those Bishops who are in the neighbourhood (*i.e.* his com-provincials), and he desires again to defend himself, no other shall be appointed to his See until the Bishop of Rome has taken cognisance of the matter and decided thereon" (ἐὰν μὴ ὁ τῆς Ῥωμαίων ἐπίσκοπος ἐπιγνοὺς περὶ τούτου ὅρον ἐξενέγκῃ).

The fifth Canon decrees "that if a Bishop, who has been accused, and condemned, and deposed by his com-provincial Bishops, has appealed to the Bishop of the Roman Church (ἐπὶ τὸν μακαριώτατον τῆς Ῥωμαίων ἐκκλησίας ἐπίσκοπον), and the said Bishop considers that the matter shall be reheard : he shall write to the Bishops living nearest to the Province in question that they may thoroughly investigate the matter, and give sentence according to the truth. But if he who desires his cause to be reheard can induce the Bishop of the Romans to send from his side (ἀπὸ τοῦ ἰδίου πλευροῦ) priests, who shall judge with the Bishops, holding his authority by whom they were sent forth (*i.e.* as presiding at the second trial), it shall be in the power of the aforesaid Bishop to do so (εἶναι ἐν τῇ ἐξουσίᾳ αὐτοῦ τοῦ ἐπισκόπου). But should he think the Bishops alone sufficient for the Court of Appeal, he shall do what seems to him good."

These three Canons have caused a fierce controversy between Ultramontane and Gallican Canonists.

To begin with we may state plainly that the permissive powers which the Sardican Fathers held to reside in the Roman Patriarch cannot in any way be fitted into the huge fabric of Papal domination that was built upon the foundation of the Pseudo-Isidorian Decretals, and reached its culmination in the Vatican Decrees of 1870. Neither, on the other hand, can we admit the absolute truth of the minimising arguments of the Gallicans and some of their Anglican followers.[1]

These arguments fall into three main divisions.

(i.) That the Sardican Fathers created a new right of appeal to Rome which never existed, even in germ, before the passing of these Canons.

---

[1] De Marca (*De Concord.*, vii. 3); Richer (*Hist. Conc. Gen.*, i. 3); Du Pin (*De Antiq. Eccl. Discp.*, pp. 109-114); Puller (*Primitive Saints and the See of Rome*, p. 152); Robertson (*Growth of Papal Power*, p. 68), and others.

(ii.) That the right thus created was a temporary privilege accorded to S. Julius of Rome, on account of his firmness in the matter of S. Athanasius, and was not intended to apply to his successors.

(iii.) That these Sardican Canons do not involve a real appeal to the Roman Patriarch, but only the right of ordering a revision of the first sentence passed by a Provincial Synod.

An impartial examination of these Canons will show that none of these three positions can be maintained intact.

(i.) It is reasonable enough to maintain that the Sardican Fathers gave formal shape to ideas which had previously been undefined. It was impossible to maintain in any way the finality of the decisions of Provincial Synods. The Antiochene Canons witness plainly enough to this fact, although they were purely Eastern in their origin. They forbade the too frequent appeals to the Emperor by Bishops condemned by Provincial Synods. A remedy was needed, and the idea of a "higher," or Patriarchal, Synod was definitely set forth by the Council of Antioch. The question before the Sardican Fathers was this. Could all Patriarchal Synods be trusted? The influence of Alexandria and Antioch had been weakened by dissensions and conflicts with heresy. Rome alone had proved a centre of orthodoxy, and the interdependence of the great Sees was somewhat merged into the sole influence of Rome, by reason of this fact. The initiative of the Roman Patriarch in Christendom was an admitted fact, and the Sardican Fathers deemed that they were "honouring the memory of S. Peter" in a legitimate way by providing that this Primatial initiative should take form in certain cases as a right of intervention to prevent injustice. To appeal to Cæsar was to appeal to Rome as the centre of civil justice, until Cæsar moved from Rome to Byzantium. The idea of appealing to Rome as the ecclesiastical centre of Catholic unity was fostered by the custom of regarding Rome as the Imperial centre of justice. S. Julius had practically shown that his See and Church had become the centre of justice and equity for a distracted Christendom by his support of S. Athanasius and Marcellus, who had been unjustly deposed. The Sardican Fathers desired to stereotype and perpetuate the good work he had accomplished. It has been argued that the formula of the Canon, "if it please you," denotes a fresh departure and the definition of a new right. This lays too much stress upon the phrase, and it is impossible to build a solid argument on so slender a foundation. It is enough to conclude that the Sardican Fathers considered that they were applying in a special way for the benefit of the whole Church certain privileges which in a lesser degree belonged to all

Patriarchs but pre-eminently to the Primate of Christendom. S. Julius held that "all Bishops" (*i.e.* the Universal Episcopate) were the ultimate Court of Appeal, so that any action taken by any Patriarch, however eminent, was not unreformable or irreversible. The Patriarchs were, in a sense, the trustees of the Universal Episcopate, and the intermediaries of its inter-communion and inter-communication when an Œcumenical Council was not in session. The Roman Patriarch was the chief trustee, and the Sardican Fathers regulated the discharge of one function of his office in a way which they considered beneficial to the Church.

(ii.) The fact that the fourth and fifth Sardican Canons mention "the Bishop of the Romans" and not S. Julius by name is argument enough against the idea of Richer (of the Sorbonne) that these Canons were temporary provisions *ad personam*, and not *ad rem*.[1] The phrase, "the Bishop of the Church of the Romans," reminds us of the earlier style of the Roman Patriarchs, from S. Clement downwards, when the authoritative emphasis is laid on "the Church of the Romans," rather than the personality of its Bishop.

(iii.) We cannot accept the view that these Canons only contemplate a revision of the sentence by those who had previously judged the matter, and not an

---

[1] This view is stated also by Canon Robertson, *vide supra*.

actual appeal to Rome. It is true that the appeal was to be heard on the spot, and that the hearing of the cause was not to be carried to Rome itself; but the right of appointing fresh judges, if he saw fit, was contemplated as forming part of the Pope's duty in these Sardican Canons, and that right involves a true appellate jurisdiction.

Having determined negatively the true scope of these Canons, let us define their meaning as positive enactments. We must construe the three Canons together. They provide (i.) that when a Bishop has been deposed by the Synod of his Province, he may appeal to the Roman Patriarch, either personally (Canon v.) or through the Bishops of the Synod who have judged him as a Court of First Instance (Canon iii.).

(ii.) The Roman Patriarch now decides whether his appeal shall be allowed or not. If it is allowed the Roman Patriarch appoints a Second Court to rehear the case (Canon iii.). This Second Court may be composed solely of Bishops from the neighbourhood of the Province to which the appellant Bishop belongs, or, if he thinks fit, the Roman Patriarch may send in addition legates of his own, who shall preside in his name (Canons iii. and v.).

(iii.) Until the decision of the Roman Patriarch has been given, and the appeal disallowed, or duly heard, the appellant Bishop's See shall not be filled up (Canon iv.).

The Council of Sardica was meant to be Œcumenical. But its decrees were never received in the East, and consequently its Œcumenical character was not established. The great majority of its Bishops were Westerns, and the heretical Eusebian Bishops who seceded from its deliberations, and held a conclave of their own in the neighbouring town of Philippopolis, were very clever in veiling their heresy by a published letter, in which they complain that the Sardican Fathers decreed that Eastern Bishops should be judged by Westerns,[1] evidently referring to the Canons we have been discussing. The African Church also declined to accept the appellate jurisdiction of the Roman Patriarch in the case of Apiarius,[2]

---

[1] Ut Orientales Episcopi ab Occidentalibus iudicarentur. (Hefele, . p. 169.)

[2] Apiarius was a priest who was deposed and excommunicated by Urban, Bishop of Sicca, in A.D. 418. Apiarius appealed directly from his Bishop to the Roman Patriarch Zosimus. The legates of Zosimus appeared before the African Council, under Archbishop Aurelius of Carthage, and based the appellate jurisdiction of Rome upon the Canons of Sardica, which they thought were Nicene. The Africans provisionally accepted their statement, but the matter came up again, when Boniface succeeded Zosimus, in a General African Council, where the claim of the Sardican Canons to be Nicene was investigated, and the matter was again suspended, until the final letter of the African Bishops to Pope Celestine in A.D. 424, when the genuine Canons of Nicæa concerning appeals and trials of clergy were emphatically alluded to, and the Sardican permission to the Pope to send legates *a latere* to assist in trials in Africa was repudiated.

when the issues were complicated by a mistake on the part of the Roman legates, who believed the Sardican Canon to have been Nicene. The way in which the Canons of different Councils were mingled together in the then extant collections of Canon Law was sufficiently confusing to account for the error, which the African Bishops subsequently were able to point out. But the Decrees of Sardica won their way in the West, and their provisions were very wisely framed as affording a true basis for the appellate jurisdiction of a Patriarch. We shall see that similar rights were accorded to the Patriarch of Constantinople. Some such provision for appeals as the Fathers of Sardica made in these Canons was necessary for the just administration of ecclesiastical discipline. It is true that the whole Church never accepted the appeal to Rome which the Sardican Canons provide. But the whole Church accepted the general principles laid down at Sardica, and applied them to the Patriarchate, as an institution which lay behind the authority of Provincial Synods, and stood between them and the ultimate finality of the decision of the Universal Episcopate, expressed in an Œcumenical Council.

But the Roman Patriarch Damasus, in A.D. 378, without doubt acquired legal rights, as Ecclesiastical Judge of Appeals, with coercive jurisdiction throughout the whole Western Empire. He held a Synod at Rome in that year, and, conjointly with his Synod, requested the Emperor Gratian to enforce, by the coercion of the civil power, the Patriarchal jurisdiction of the Roman See. Damasus did not venture to ask the Emperor of the West to use his influence to compel the East to accept the Canons of Sardica. This was outside the sphere of practical politics, and one great secret of the commanding influence of the Roman See has always been its practical sagacity in statecraft.

Damasus and his Synod asked that the earlier enactment of Gratian, which conferred coercive jurisdiction on the See of Rome in the case of contumacious Bishops within the civil jurisdiction of the "Præfectus Prætorii" and the "Vicarius Urbis," should be rigidly enforced.[1] This applied to the Bishops of Italy and Illyricum. The Emperor Gratian, in his reply, gave Damasus more than he had asked for. He added to the coercive jurisdiction over Italy and Illyricum, which Damasus claimed, a further grant of coercive jurisdiction over Africa, Spain, Gaul, and Britain, and thus established the Western Patriarchate by State authority.

[1] The Roman Synod says, "Idcirco statuti imperialis non novitatem sed firmitudinem postulamus." (Coleti., ii. 1188.)

The effect of this action was an abnormal increase in the Roman claims. In process of time the jurisdiction thus granted by the civil power in the West was claimed to exist *iure divino* over the whole Catholic Church as the legitimate "Petri privilegium." The case of Apiarius shows that the African Church was not in all cases compelled by the civil power to obey the Emperor Gratian's decree, and in the 17th Canon of the African General Council of A.D. 418, which appears as Canon xxviii. of the "Codex Canonum Ecclesiæ Africanæ," appeals to Rome were forbidden, and ordered to be carried to the African General Council, on account of the Patriarchal position of the Archbishop of Carthage. "Non provocent ad transmarina iudicia, sed ad Primates suarum Provinciarum, *aut ad universale concilium, sicut et de episcopis sæpe constitutum est.*" The words in italics did not appear in the original draft of the Canon of A.D. 418, but were added subsequently, and are explained by the seventh Canon of the Synod of Hippo in A.D. 393, which applies the phrase "Concilium universale"[1] to the African General Council, which was held from time to time under the Primate of Carthage. The African Church upheld its own Patriarch and its own system of

---

[1] "Si autem ad Concilium universale anniversarium occurrerit," &c. (*Conc. Hipp. Can.*, 7.)

Patriarchal appeals, notwithstanding its temporary acceptance of the Sardican Canons as Nicene till it had proved the contrary. During this period of temporary acceptance, Anthony, Bishop of Fussala, appealed to Rome against the decision of the Primate and Synod of Numidia. S. Augustine wrote to Pope Celestine to dissuade him from restoring Anthony. Celestine inherited the case from his predecessor Boniface, who had threatened the people of Fussala with the secular power if they did not obey the Roman decision. The point of the case is that S. Augustine's letter has been used by modern controversialists to prove that he accepted the full Roman claims to jurisdiction. The real fact was that he, as an African Bishop, was loyally carrying out the compromise whereby appeals to Rome were temporarily allowed. In justice to Boniface, who threatened to use the power given him by Gratian's rescript in this case, it must be remembered that he loyally upheld the authority of the Metropolitan of Narbonne in accordance with the Nicene Canons, and in so doing he annulled a decree of his predecessor Zosimus in favour of the See of Arles.[1]

The desire of the Emperor Theodosius to banish Arianism from the East caused him to assemble a General Council of Eastern Christendom at Con-

---

[1] Labbe (*Conc.*, ii. p. 1585), and also Giesler (*Eccl. Hist.*, i. par. 92).

stantinople in A.D. 381. S. Meletius of Antioch was its first President, and no Roman legates were present. It is evident that the Roman Patriarch was not consulted, for S. Meletius was not in communion with the Roman See, which acknowledged Paulinus as the lawful Patriarch of Antioch. S. Meletius was himself orthodox, but the Arian party aided in his election, and so the small body of Catholics, who declined to recognise him, set up a rival orthodox Patriarch who was recognised by Rome. This breach of communion was not healed after the death of S. Meletius, which took place during the session of the Council of Constantinople, and during its continuance neither the Westerns, who recognised Paulinus, nor the Easterns, who recognised S. Meletius,[1] and after him Flavian, were considered to be cut off from the communion of the Catholic Church. Although S. Meletius died out of communion with Rome, he was afterwards honoured by the Roman Church as a Saint.

We must now deal with those Canons of the

[1] S. Basil the Great was very indignant when Pope Damasus recognised Paulinus in A.D. 375, and spoke of his letters recognising Paulinus as "defrauding of his due that most admirable Bishop of the true Church of God, Meletius." Παραλογιζόμενα δὲ τὸν θαυμασιώτατον ἐπίσκοπον τῆς ἀληθινῆς τοῦ Θεοῦ ἐκκλησίας Μελέτιον. (S. Basil, *Ep. ad Terent.*) This great Doctor of the Church pronounces very definitely against the idea that communion with the Roman See was necessary in order to be in communion with "the true Church of God."

Council of Constantinople which bear upon our special subject. Its Canons gradually won acceptance when the Council became Œcumenical by the general consent of Christendom. The second Canon of Constantinople deals with the jurisdiction of Patriarchs, and forbids the interference of one Patriarch with the jurisdiction of another.

Τοὺς ὑπὲρ διοίκησιν ἐπισκόπους ταῖς ὑπερορίοις ἐκκλησίαις μὴ ἐπιέναι, μηδὲ συγχέειν τὰς ἐκκλησίας· ἀλλὰ κατὰ τοὺς κανόνας τὸν μὲν Ἀλεξανδρείας ἐπίσκοπον τὰ ἐν Αἰγύπτῳ μόνον οἰκονομεῖν, τοὺς δὲ τῆς ἀνατολῆς ἐπισκόπους τὴν ἀνατολὴν μόνην διοικεῖν, φυλαττομένων τῶν ἐν τοῖς κανόσι τοῖς κατὰ Νικαίαν πρεσβείων τῇ Ἀντιοχέων ἐκκλησίᾳ, καὶ τοὺς τῆς Ἀσιανῆς διοικήσεως ἐπισκόπους τὰ κατὰ τὴν Ἀσίαν μόνον οἰκονομεῖν, καὶ τοὺς τῆς Ποντικῆς τὰ τῆς Ποντικῆς μόνον, καὶ τοὺς τῆς Θρᾴκης τὰ τῆς Θρᾳκικῆς μόνον οἰκονομεῖν. Ἀκλήτους δὲ ἐπισκόπους ὑπὲρ διοίκησιν μὴ ἐπιβαίνειν ἐπὶ χειροτονίαις ἤ τισιν ἄλλαις οἰκονομίαις ἐκκλησιαστικαῖς. Φυλαττομένου δὲ τοῦ προγεγραμμένου περὶ τῶν διοικήσεων κανόνος, εὔδηλον ὡς τὰ καθ' ἑκάστην ἐπαρχίαν ἡ τῆς ἐπαρχίας σύνοδος διοικήσει, κατὰ τὰ ἐν Νικαίᾳ ὡρισμένα. Τὰς δὲ ἐν τοῖς βαρβαρικοῖς ἔθνεσι τοῦ Θεοῦ ἐκκλησίας οἰκονομεῖσθαι χρὴ κατὰ τὴν κρατήσασαν συνήθειαν παρὰ τῶν πατέρων. "The Bishops of another 'Diocese' (Patriarchate) shall not pass over to Churches out of their defined limits and introduce confusion amongst them, but, in accordance with the Canons, the Bishop of Alexandria shall govern the affairs of Egypt only, and the Eastern Bishops (*i.e.* the Patriarchs of Constantinople) shall have charge of the affairs of the East only, whilst the rights of the Church of Antioch, as declared in the sixth Canon of Nicæa, shall be preserved, and the Bishops of the 'Diocese' of Asia shall only have jurisdiction over Asia, those of the 'Diocese' of Pontus over Pontus, and those of the 'Diocese' of Thrace over Thrace. Unless summoned, the Bishops shall not go beyond their own 'Dioceses' for the purpose of ordination or any other ecclesiastical function. While, however, the existing Canon with regard to the 'Dioceses' is observed, it is clear that the Provincial Synod must rule in each Province in accordance with the decisions of Nicæa. But the Churches of God among the barbarous nations shall be governed according to the custom prevailing from the times of the Fathers."

The third Canon of Constantinople must be read with the second Canon. It erects the See of Constantinople into a Patriarchate with a " Primacy of honour" next to Rome. Archbishop De Marca thought that the Patriarchate was not constituted until A.D. 451, by the 28th Canon of the Council of Chalcedon.[1] But it is evident that Canon ii.

---

[1] He says that the Primacy of honour alone was given by the Council of Constantinople (honorem verum solum in Synodo Constantinopolitana). (De Marca, *De Concord. Sac. et Imp.*, App. p. 155.)

means to imply that the " Diocese " of Thrace was transferred to Constantinople, because its former Primatial See, Heraclea (of which Constantinople was formerly a subordinate See), is not mentioned. Socrates dates the delimitation of the Patriarchates and their rearrangement from the General Council of Constantinople.[1] The Canon in question is as follows: Τὸν μέντοι Κωνσταντινουπόλεως ἐπίσκοπον ἔχειν τὰ πρεσβεῖα τῆς τιμῆς μετὰ τὸν τῆς Ῥώμης ἐπίσκοπον, διὰ τὸ εἶναι αὐτὴν νέαν Ῥώμην. " The Bishop of Constantinople shall hold the first rank after the Bishop of Rome, because Constantinople is New Rome."

This Canon naturally was not received in the West, when the decisions of the Council of Constantinople on the doctrinal question of the Godhead and Personality of the Holy Ghost were universally accepted, and caused the Council itself to rank as Œcumenical. It was not accepted at Rome until the Fourth Lateran Council, in A.D. 1215, allowed this second rank to the Latin Patriarchate of Constantinople that had been founded in 1204, after the Crusaders' conquest of that city.

The precedence thus accorded to Constantinople was immediately accorded in the East after some protest, although it needed the 28th Canon of Chalcedon

[1] Socrates, v. 8. Bishop Hefele considers the witness of Socrates in this passage an important confirmation of his view of the matter, which is opposite to De Marca's opinion.

to set the Patriarchal position of Constantinople upon a wider basis.

The second Canon of Constantinople sets the territorial arrangements of the Patriarchates and Primatial Sees upon a securer basis by an expansion of the Nicene Canons on the same subject. The word "Diocese" is paralleled in the civil "Dioceses" of the Empire, whose organisation is adopted territorially by the Church. This, as we have already seen, was the case from the earliest days, when Church and Empire stood face to face as bitter foes. By this Canon the Bishops of each Patriarchate were ordered to keep to their own borders. The Patriarch must not trespass, or allow any of his Bishops to trespass, upon the jurisdiction of another Patriarch. This Canon applies solely to the Eastern Church, using the term in its widest sense. It allows of no appeal from one Patriarchate to another, and by implication proves that the Sardican Canons did not gain acceptance in the East. It guards the rights of Provincial Synods, as secured by the Nicene Council, although it does not assert their finality. The last clause deals with Missionary Churches outside the civil "Dioceses" of the Roman Empire, which were to continue dependent upon the Patriarch from whom they originally received the Episcopate, as the Abyssinian Church had been on

Alexandria, since S. Athanasius had consecrated Frumentius as its first Bishop, and as certain missionary dioceses in Africa and elsewhere hold in the present day direct Mission from the See of Canterbury.

The sixth Canon of Constantinople is thought by some to belong to a subsequent Council, held at Constantinople in the year A.D. 382.[1] It is chiefly important as re-enacting with greater definiteness the appeal to the Greater Synod of the Patriarchate, which the Council of Antioch had already provided in its 14th Canon. It also draws a clear distinction between criminal and civil offences committed by Bishops and offences ecclesiastical. In the former case, any one, whoever he may be, or whatever may be his religion ($\theta\rho\eta\sigma\kappa\epsilon\iota\alpha\nu$), can be heard against a Bishop. In like manner the Council of Hippo (A.D. 393) ruled that no one whose personal conduct was culpable could accuse a Bishop "*nisi proprias causas, non tamen ecclesiasticas dicere voluerit.*"[2] But in ecclesiastical cases, where no civil offence or personal wrong was concerned, the accusers of a Bishop, and therefore *a fortiori* of a priest, must themselves be of

---

[1] Canon Bright accepts it as genuine. (See *Notes on Canons of General Councils*, p. 100.) Bishop Beveridge takes the view that it belongs properly to the Council of A.D. 382. (*Pandect. Canon. II. Ann.*, p. 98.)

[2] Mansi, iii. p. 920.

good standing. Accusations could not be received from heretics, persons formerly excommunicated, persons excommunicated "by ourselves" (under Canon i. of the Council of Constantinople, if we accept this Canon vi. as genuine), persons professing orthodoxy who have formed schismatic congregations, persons excommunicated, or, finally, persons under accusation. Persons who are not thus disqualified could bring their accusations against a Bishop before the Provincial Synod : εἰ δὲ συμβαίη ἀδυνατῆσαι τοὺς ἐπαρχιώτας πρὸς διόρθωσιν τῶν ἐπιφερομένων ἐγκλημάτων τῷ ἐπισκόπῳ· τότε αὐτοὺς προσιέναι μείζονι συνόδῳ τῶν τῆς διοικήσεως ἐκείνης ἐπισκόπων. "But if it happens that the Bishops of the Province are unable to set right the charges alleged against the Bishop, then let them have recourse to the Greater Synod of the Patriarchate to which they belong." Here is the appellate jurisdiction of Eastern Christendom. The appeal lies from the Provincial Synod, presided over by the Metropolitan, to the Patriarchal Synod, presided over by the Patriarch; and the Canon closes by ordering this course to be adopted, and forbidding an appeal from a Provincial Synod to the Emperor direct, or to a civil Court, or even to an Œcumenical Council,[1] since

---

[1] The fact that an Œcumenical Council was above all Patriarchs, as the ultimate Court of final appeal for the whole of the Catholic Church, was virtually admitted by one so tenacious of the claims of his See as Leo the Great. In his letter to Theodosius on the subject

the appellant, by passing over the Patriarchal Synod, would bring it into contempt (πάντας ἀτιμάσας τοὺς τῆς διοικήσεως ἐπισκόπους).

We are not to read into this Canon any idea that it meant to imply that an Œcumenical Council (as representing the Universal Episcopate) was not the final Court of Appeal. The plain meaning is that the Appeal must proceed in regular stages, and that it would be irregular to appeal direct from a Provincial Synod to an Œcumenical Council, without the previous resort to the Synod of the Patriarchate.

The African Code of Canons embodies a series of Canons which were passed by various African Councils at Hippo and at Carthage between the years A.D. 393 and A.D. 418. They were collected by Dionysius Exiguus in A.D. 419. Canons x. and xi. provide that a priest can appeal from the sentence of his Bishop to the Bishops of the Province (apud vicinos episcopos conqueri). Canon xiii. provides that no new Bishop can be appointed

---

of the Council of Ephesus, S. Leo states that the decisions of the Council will suffice to remove the evils of the Church, though he cannot himself be present. (S. Leo, *Ep.* 43.) After the Council of Chalcedon, which accepted his Tome, he writes; "Gloriamini . . . quod prius a prima omnium sede firmatum, totius Christiani orbis recepisset." (S. Leo, *Ep. ad Theod.*) He thus, as Du Pin observes, expresses his joy that his judgment had been confirmed by an Œcumenical Synod, "et eam non posse ullatenus convelli aut labefactari." (*De Antiq. Eccl. Disc.*, p. 388.)

without the consent of the Primate. Canon xix. provides for the trial of Bishops before the Metropolitan and Bishops of the Province, with an appeal to the General African Synod, which sat yearly under the presidency of the Archbishop of Carthage. Canon xxxiii. forbids Bishops to alienate any Church property without the knowledge of their Diocesan Synods. The Canons quoted as of the fourth Council of Carthage are probably a collection of various African enactments of early date. The 22nd of these Canons enacts that a Bishop shall not ordain persons without the advice of his clergy, and that he is bound also to seek for the "testimonium" of the laity (civium conniventiam et testimonium quærere). The 23rd Canon orders a Bishop to exercise his office as Judge with his clergy as assessors, otherwise his sentence is invalid. This Canon is a strong testimony against the theory of Episcopal autocracy.

Into the complex and chequered history of the Œcumenical Council of Ephesus (A.D. 431) it will not be necessary for us to enter. We have already touched upon the subject of its Presidency, and there is one other point with which it dealt that concerns our present inquiry. The Bishops of Cyprus petitioned the Council to preserve their independence against the claim of the Patriarch of Antioch to include the Province of

Cyprus within his Patriarchate, by exercising the Patriarchal right of consecrating their Archbishop.

The Council inquired whether this right belonged to the Patriarch of Antioch before the passing of the sixth Nicene Canon, which reserved the ancient Patriarchal rights of Antioch. The Patriarch John of Antioch was at this time in an attitude of hostility to the Council of Ephesus, and so his side of the case was not heard. The Cypriote Bishops stated that from the Apostolic age no Bishop outside Cyprus had consecrated their Metropolitan. The Council gave a judgment to which a saving clause was annexed: καὶ μάλιστα εἰ μηδὲ ἔθος ἀρχαῖον παρηκολούθησεν, ὥστε τὸν ἐπίσκοπον τῆς Ἀντιοχέων πόλεως, τὰς ἐν Κύπρῳ ποιεῖσθαι χειροτονίας, καθὰ διὰ τῶν λιβέλλων καὶ τῶν οἰκείων φωνῶν ἐδίδαξαν οἱ εὐλαβέστατοι ἄνδρες οἱ τὴν πρόσοδον τῇ ἁγίᾳ συνόδῳ ποιησάμενοι, κ.τ.λ.

"If it has not been a continuous ancient custom for the Bishop of Antioch to hold ordinations in Cyprus, as is asserted by memorials and by word of mouth by the religious men who have sought access to the Holy Synod," then the Council proceeded to lay down that the independence of the Province of Cyprus from the See of Antioch was to be maintained; and further, that the principle was to be laid down that no Patriarch is to take possession of any Province that has not from the first been subject to his own See. Some time after this decision was given, Alexander, Patriarch of Antioch, wrote to Innocent of Rome, and maintained that the Cypriote Bishops had begun this practice of consecrating their own Metropolitan as a safeguard against Arianism, when the See of Antioch was in Arian hands, and that the custom remained when the excuse for it had passed away.[1] Balsamon the Canonist, himself a Patriarch of Antioch, admits the claim of the Bishops of Cyprus.[2] When Peter "the Father" revived the claim of Antioch, the discovery of the body of S. Barnabas the Apostle was opportunely alleged as a conclusive proof that the Church of Cyprus was Apostolic, and could claim independence on that account. The 39th Canon of the Council in Trullo recognised the autocephalous position of the Church of Cyprus. The real position of the matter in dispute seems to be this. The Cypriotes claimed that their Church was founded by the Apostle S. Barnabas, and that on this account it was independent of Antioch. But it was not independent of the Universal Church, even if the "Ius Cyprium" was founded on right. No National Church or Province could be autonomous in the sense that it was not under the jurisdiction of an Œcumenical

---

[1] Innoc. (*Ep.* 18, 2).
[2] Balsam. (*in Conc. Constant.*, Can. 2).

Council. The Metropolitan of Cyprus claimed a similar independence to that of the Archbishop of Carthage, who was practically a Patriarch. The "Ius Cyprium" has been applied to the attitude of the English Church towards the Roman See. It is only partially true to compare the autocephalous position claimed by the British Bishops in their dispute with S. Augustine of Canterbury to the rights claimed by the Church of Cyprus. The British Bishops had suffered isolation from the Christianity and civilisation of the West, owing to the Saxon invasion and conquest. The Christianity of the British was of the same type as that of Gaul and the rest of the West when it was first planted amongst the Romanised Celts of that part of the island which was then included in the Roman Empire. The local usages of Celtic Christianity were mainly peculiarities caused by long isolation from their Continental fellow-Christians. At the Reformation the orderly abolition of the usurped Papal jurisdiction was neither schismatic nor an assertion of independence such as is involved in the "Ius Cyprium." The action of Convocation and Parliament in abolishing Roman usurpations was not intended to deprive the Roman Patriarch of any lawful spiritual power.[1] "They did not deny the precedence of the Bishop of Rome in the

[1] *Vide* Archbishop Bramhall. (*Works*, p. 340.)

Universal Church, nor his right (in conjunction with Christian Princes) of summoning and presiding in General Councils, nor his power of defining questions of faith in conjunction with the Catholic Church, nor his right to exhort all Bishops to observe the Canons, nor his being the centre of Catholic unity when he is in communion with all the Catholic Church."[1] We now quit the subject with the remark that the importance of the so-called "Ius Cyprium," regarded in its bearing upon questions pending between Canterbury and Rome, is much exaggerated.

We close our inquiry with the Council of Chalcedon in A.D. 451. This Council is the last of the undisputed Œcumenical Councils, and it closes an epoch in the history and life of the Church which marks the final settlement, not only of vital controversies concerning the Faith, but of very many points of procedure and constitutional law, which have never since been seriously questioned or disturbed.[2] There is a vast difference in the authority of the Canon Law when we consider the *date* of its several enactments. The authority of the Canon Law of the undivided Church naturally is greater than the authority of Western Canon Law that was

---

[1] Palmer on the Church (vol. i. 433).

[2] We have already noted the fact that the first Canon of Chalcedon stamped with its œcumenical authority a body of existing Canon Law which included the Antiochene Canons of A.D. 341.

not current in the East, or Eastern Canon Law which was not current in the West. And the Council of Chalcedon, in its 9th and 28th Canons, sets forth with clear precision the position of the great Patriarchs and their jurisdiction. Its legislation forms a fitting conclusion to our investigations into the constitutional authority of the Bishops of the Catholic Church.

Canon ix. forbids clergy to go to law in secular courts, and provides a graduated system of appeals to the Patriarch, or, in the case of the Eastern Empire, to its senior Patriarch, who sat on the throne of Constantinople. εἰ δὲ καὶ κληρικὸς πρᾶγμα ἔχοι πρὸς τὸν ἴδιον ἐπίσκοπον ἢ πρὸς ἕτερον, παρὰ τῇ συνόδῳ τῆς ἐπαρχίας δικαζέσθω· εἰ δὲ πρὸς τὸν τῆς αὐτῆς ἐπαρχίας μητροπολίτην ἐπίσκοπος, ἢ κληρικός, ἀμφισβητοίη, καταλαμβανέτω ἢ τὸν ἔξαρχον τῆς διοικήσεως,[1] ἢ τὸν τῆς βασιλευούσης Κωνσταντινουπόλεως Θρόνον, καὶ ἐπ᾽ αὐτῷ δικασέσθω. "But if a cleric has any matter against his own Bishop, or against another Bishop, let it be decided by the Synod of the Province. But if any Bishop or cleric has a controversy with the Metropolitan of his Province, let him appeal to the Exarch[2] of his Diocese (*i.e.*

---

[1] In commenting upon this Canon, the Greek Canonist Balsamon says: "Διοίκησίς ἐστιν ἡ πολλὰς ἐπαρχίας ἔχουσα ἐν ἑαυτῇ."—"A Diocese is that which contains many Provinces within itself."

[2] The title "Exarch" was derived from the official nomenclature of the officers of the Empire, such as "the Exarch of Ravenna," who

the Patriarch of his Patriarchate) or to the Throne (Patriarchal) of the Imperial city of Constantinople, and there let the cause be decided."

The alternative appeal which this Canon provides to the Patriarch of Constantinople for the East, was of wider scope than the appeal to Rome which was provided by the Canons of Sardica. The Roman legates did not object to this 9th Canon, for they did not apparently believe that the Primacy of Rome militated against Patriarchal jurisdiction elsewhere. They did not venture to apply the Sardican Canons to the whole Church in this instance. But they objected to the 28th Canon of Chalcedon, which amplified the Canon of Constantinople by further defining the powers of the Patriarch of New Rome. The wording of this Canon is significant, and is given in the following extract:
καὶ γὰρ τῷ Θρόνῳ τῆς πρεσβυτέρας Ῥώμης, διὰ τὸ βασιλεύειν τὴν πόλιν ἐκείνην, οἱ πατέρες εἰκότως ἀποδεδώκασι τὰ πρεσβεῖα καὶ τῷ αὐτῷ σκοπῷ κινούμενοι οἱ ἑκατὸν πεντήκοντα θεοφιλέστατοι ἐπίσκοποι τὰ ἴσα πρεσβεῖα ἀπένειμαν τῷ τῆς νέας Ῥώμης ἁγιωτάτῳ Θρόνῳ, εὐλόγως κρίναντες τὴν βασιλείᾳ καὶ συγκλήτῳ τιμηθεῖσαν πόλιν, καὶ τῶν ἴσων ἀπολαύουσαν πρεσβείων

---

governed the civil "Diocese" of Italy and represented the Imperial power. The ecclesiastical use of the title seems to have involved a certain inferiority to the title "Patriarch," which was reserved for the greater Sees, although the jurisdiction of the Patriarch and the Exarch was virtually the same.

τῇ πρεσβυτέρᾳ βασιλίδι ‛Ρώμῃ, καὶ ἐν τοῖς ἐκκλησιαστικοῖς ὡς ἐκείνην μεγαλύνεσθαι πράγμασι δευτέραν μετ' ἐκείνην ὑπάρχουσαν, κ.τ.λ. "For the Fathers have reasonably conceded its primatial rights to the Throne of Old Rome, because it was the Imperial City; and influenced by the same consideration, the hundred and fifty most religious Bishops have awarded the like privileges to the most holy See of New Rome, judging, with good reason, that the city which is honoured by the Imperial Power and the Senate (as the capital), and which enjoys the same privileges as the Elder Imperial Rome, should also in its ecclesiastical relations be exalted, and hold the second place after that city," &c.

The Fathers of Chalcedon could not very well expect S. Leo the Great to accept this Canon without protest. Into the details of the controversy we need not enter. The principle here laid down, that the civil rank of the city should find its counterpart in the ecclesiastical rank of its Bishop, was accepted without question in the East, and, as we have already seen, was a chief factor in the Roman Primacy in the West. But it did not account for all the influence exercised by Rome as a centre. The fact of the "Cathedra Petri," with its traditions of the Primate Apostle, counted for a great deal in the thoughts and imaginations of Christendom. Besides which, New Rome could never be what Old Rome was. The traditions of Imperial rule, law, and order could not be divorced from the "Eternal City," and the gradual decay of the Western Empire transferred these traditions from the Roman Emperor to the Roman Patriarch.

We may note here that the word Patriarch was officially employed in the Acts of Chalcedon where allusion was made to the "most holy Patriarchs" of each Diocese (ὁσιώτατοι Πατριάρχαι διοικήσεως ἑκάστης).[1] S. Leo the Great is called "the Patriarch of Great Rome," and also, in Canon xxx. of Chalcedon, the Tome of S. Leo is described as "the Epistle of the most holy Archbishop Leo" (τοῦ ὁσιωτάτου Ἀρχιεπισκόπου Λέοντος). The titles of "Patriarch" and "Archbishop" did not long remain thus interchangeable. The title of "Archbishop" was reserved for the chief Metropolitans as a title of honour, and in course of time it was in certain cases used as a title of honour for certain Bishops who were not actually Metropolitans of Provinces. In the Anglican Communion the title of Archbishop belongs exclusively to the Primatial See of Canterbury, and to the principal Metropolitans who own its Primacy.[2] The ecclesiastical

---

[1] *Conc. Chalced.*, Act 2, p. 338.

[2] The Archbishops of the Anglican Communion are the Archbishop of Canterbury, who is acknowledged by the South African Church as

laws concerning the Patriarchs and their powers afterwards received civil authority in the East by the Laws of Justinian, much in the same way as the Edict of Gratian had given civil authority to the jurisdiction of the Roman Patriarch. Justinian enacted that a Patriarch should be consecrated by the Bishops of his Patriarchal Synod.[1] He also provided for the trial of a Metropolitan before his Patriarch.[2]

A modern instance of this procedure may be found in the 20th Canon of the Church of the Province of South Africa, which commits the trial of the Archbishop of Capetown, in a matter of faith, doctrine, or discipline, to the Archbishop of Canterbury and Bishops selected by him. This is a direct recognition on the part of the South African Church of the *de facto* Patriarchate of Canterbury. A like recognition of a carefully guarded and canonical Patriarchate of Canterbury

"Primate of Archbishops, Primates, and Metropolitans," and the Archbishops of York, Armagh, Dublin, Rupertsland, Ontario, Sydney, Capetown, and the West Indies.

[1] "Ipsum vero (patriarcham) a proprio ordinari concilio." (Justin. Novel. 131.)

[2] "Quoties quidem sacerdotum accusabuntur, vel de fide, aut turpi vita, aut ob aliquid aliud contra sacros canones admissum ; si quidem episcopus est is qui accusatus est, eius Metropolitanus examinet ea quæ dicta sunt : si vero Metropolitanus sit, eius beatissimus Archiepiscopus sub quo degit." (Ibid., 37, 5.) The Laws of Justinian on the subject of ecclesiastical trials and appeals need not be considered as Erastian. We may look upon them as intended to prevent direct appeals to the Emperor and Secular Courts.

by the various Churches and Provinces who own its Primacy is the sole solution whereby the unity and solidarity of the Anglican Communion can be maintained.

Our investigation closes at this point. We may claim that it has been directed exclusively to the authority of the undivided Church of Christ. To that authority the Anglican Reformers made their constant appeal. If some who profess an exaggerated regard for the opinions of the Anglican Reformers as individuals would look beyond them and behind them to that Primitive Church which their mediæval training hindered them from following as closely as they intended to do, it would be of good omen for all Catholics in communion with the See of Canterbury. An insular and dry Anglicanism would be broadened to grasp the needs of Anglo-Saxon Christianity as a whole, and our Episcopate would gain in influence far more than it would lose in the eyes of those who view it as a mediæval Prelacy, by frankly foregoing the methods of autocracy, and of its own free will adopting that position of constitutional authority which is its legitimate inheritance from the Day of Pentecost.

NOTE A.

Chorepiscopi.

A controversy has arisen as to whether these "country Bishops" who were assistants to the Diocesan Bishops were in Episcopal orders or not. Van Espen, the great Canonist, Bishop Beveridge, Hammond, Cave, and Bingham maintain that they were really Bishops; against Morinus and others, who hold them to have been merely Priests. The learned Sorbonnist Witasse goes very fully into the question, and agrees with the view that they were Bishops. They set apart men for the minor orders of readers, exorcists, and sub-deacons, while the ordination of Deacons and Priests was reserved, as a rule, to the Diocesan Bishop. They were not coadjutor Bishops *cum iure successionis*, which is contrary to primitive Canon law. They were "Assistant Bishops" in the same sense as retired Colonial Bishops, who have been commissioned by Bishops in England to aid them in Diocesan work.

The appointment of a Coadjutor Bishop, *cum iure successionis*, by the Diocesan Bishop was forbidden by the 5th Council of Paris (A.D. 577): "Nullus episcoporum se vivente alium in loco suo eligat," with the apparent saving clause "nisi certæ conditiones extiterint ut ecclesiam suam et clerum regere non possit" (Can. ii.). S. Gregory the Great permits an infirm Bishop to have a coadjutor, but without right of succession. (S. Greg., Ep. ix. 4.) The Chorepiscopi of the early Church were meant to meet such cases, as well as to assist Bishops whose Dioceses were too large.

NOTE B.

The Authority of Law and Custom.

S. Athanasius writes of the authority of Canon Law as follows:—

Οὐ γὰρ νῦν κανόνες καὶ τύποι ταῖς ἐκκλησίαις ἐδόθησαν, ἀλλ' ἐκ τῶν πατέρων ἡμῶν καλῶς καὶ βεβαίως παρεδόθησαν· οὐδὲ νῦν ἡ πίστις ἤρξατο, ἀλλ' ἐκ τοῦ Κυρίου διὰ τῶν μαθητῶν εἰς ἡμᾶς διαβέβηκεν. (S. Ath., *Encyc. ad Epis.*, cap. i.) "For the Canons and patterns were not now for the first time given to the Churches, but were handed down well and firmly from our fathers, nor did the Faith begin nowadays, but it hath been handed down to us from the Lord and His disciples." This comparison between the Faith once delivered to the Saints, and then carefully handed down as a sacred deposit by the Church, and the similar authoritative tradition of the Laws and Usages of the Church, is significant as coming from the pen of the greatest theologian of his age.

The authority of custom, as well as of the written Canons, which the 18th Nicene Canon alleges, may perhaps be paralleled with the "patterns" or authorised forms and usages which S. Athanasius couples with the "Canons."

The Canon Law is best described as *Ius Canonicum*, rather than *Lex Canonica*. *Ius* is a general term which includes both *laws* and *customs* of the Church. The authority of custom is appealed to by S. Paul when he says "we have no such custom, neither the Churches of God" (1 Cor. xi. 16).

There is an authority of custom which finds admission

into our ordinary English jurisprudence which will serve as a useful illustration of our meaning. The Statute Law of England is supplemented by the Common Law, which receives its authority from usage and universal reception. (See Stephens' ed. of Blackstone, vol. i. p. 41.)

So in the Canon Law of the Church, ancient customs (ἀρχαῖα ἔθη) and long-established usage (*mos*) have a binding obligation equally with the written Canons of the Church (*leges*).

So great is the obligation of *mos*, that its contrary, namely, Desuetude, can in certain cases be pleaded with sufficient authority to abrogate even a *lex scripta*. (Devoti. Instit., i. 4.) It is needless to add that the greatest caution is needed in applying this principle. It is difficult to prove Desuetude, even in such cases as may occur when a law has been for many years only partially observed. The *Ius Canonicum* thus includes *leges*, the written and codified Laws of the Church, and *maxims* of Fathers, which, like the decrees of Councils, acquire authority by universal acceptance and customs. An instance of an authoritative *maxim* is the saying of Pope Celestine, "Nullus detur invitis." An instance of an authoritative *custom* is the use of the Mixed Chalice, which we find cited as the ordinary usage by Justin Martyr. (*Apol.*, i. 67.)

It is useful to note the distinction made by the Gallican Canonists between *Ius Antiquum* and *Ius Novum*. (See Schram., *Instit. Iuris Eccl.*, i. p. 4.)

The Ancient Canon Law is that which dates before the Pseudo-Isidorian Decretals; the "new Canon Law" is the mediæval code which incorporated them into its authoritative "Corpus Iuris," and which modified ancient laws and customs to suit the changes necessitated by the development of the Papal despotism.

In the foregoing pages our inquiry has shown that the *Ius Antiquum* is so full in its provisions, and so marvellously adapted to after ages, that the novelties of the *Ius Novum* are superfluous excrescences upon the sacred jurisprudence of the Catholic Church, which will one day be abrogated either by direct enactment or Desuetude.

NOTE C.

S. Gregory the Great on the Interdependence of the Chief Patriarchates.

Although the mediæval period of Church History, which may be said to begin with the Pontificate of Gregory the Great, lies outside the scope of the present inquiry, it is interesting to note that a strong Pope, such as Gregory the Great undoubtedly was, held views with regard to the interdependence of the chief Patriarchates which recall primitive times, and which are quite irreconcilable with modern Ultramontane claims. In A.D. 587, in a Synod held at Constantinople against a certain Bishop Gregorius, the Patriarch John the Faster adopted the title of "Œcumenical Bishop" (οἰκουμενικὸς ἐπίσκοπος), which had previously been allowed to John the Cappadocian in another Synod held at Constantinople. (*Concil. Const. sub Menna et Anthimo*, iv. 7 and novell. 16.) It was not intended to apply to the whole world, but only to the region which owned the Primacy of New Rome. In a Synod at Constantinople held in A.D. 536 it is applied both to the Patriarchs of Old and New Rome. (Mansi, vol. viii. col. 895, 956.) But the Council of A.D. 587 is reckoned by the Eastern Church as having conferred this title on the Patriarch of Constantinople by a formal act, and Pelagius of Rome refused on this account to recognise the Acts of the Council. The Epistle of Pelagius which protested against the assumption of this title is one of the Pseudo-Isidorian forgeries. His genuine objection is preserved in Pope Gregory's letter. (S. Greg., Epp. iv. No. 38.) Even so convinced a Gallican as Du Pin seems to have been unconsciously influenced by Pseudo-Isidore, when he says that Pelagius "ob elationis huius vocabulum . . . huius concilii *acta dissolvit.*" (*De Antiq. Eccl. Disc.*, p. 328.) When S. Gregory succeeded Pelagius he wrote to the Patriarch of Constantinople in A.D. 595, and also to the Patriarchs of Alexandria and Antioch, protesting against this title of "Universal Bishop." Alexandria and Antioch naturally were in sympathy with Rome in resisting the encroachments of Constantinople. It was evident to S. Gregory that, although the Patriarch of Constantinople did not claim authority over other Patriarchs, he was yet claiming precedence, because civilly Constantinople was before Rome as the Imperial capital. It is very interesting to note S. Gregory's line in objecting to this claim. "No one of my predecessors," he says, "has ever consented to so profane a title, since, if one Patriarch is called Universal, the name is derogated in the case of the others." (Epp. v. 43.) Eulogius of Alexandria replied that he would never again use the title in addressing the Patriarch of Constantinople, and he thought to please S. Gregory by applying it to him instead. But S. Gregory emphatically repudiated it. He was a strong Primate of Christendom, and claimed by virtue of his Primacy to interpose when anything went wrong in the East as well as in his own Western Patriarchate. He replies, "I beg you will not speak of *commanding*, since I know who I am and who you are. In dignity you are my brothers, in character you are my fathers. I never commanded, but only wished to indicate what was useful. . . . You have thought fit to make use of the proud title, calling me Universal Bishop. I beg your most sweet Holiness to do so no more. . . . I do not regard that as an honour whereby I know that my brethren's honour is taken away. For the honour of the Universal Church is my honour, the stable welfare of my brethren is my honour, I am truly honoured when the honour due to each and all is not denied them. And when your Holiness calls me Universal Pope, you deny that you are yourself what you call me universally." (Epp. viii. 30.)

The Primate of Christendom declined to rob the "Pope" of Alexandria of his due honour. We have already noted S. Gregory's reason for the link between Rome and Alexandria. In a very remarkable passage he amplifies this reason, and conjoins Antioch with Alexandria and Rome in mutual interdependence as the threefold See of S. Peter. The passage is so interesting that we quote the original. "Itaque cum multi sint Apostoli, pro ipso tamen principatu sola Apostolorum Principis sedes in auctoritate convaluit, quæ in tribus locis unius est. Ipse enim sublimavit sedem, in qua etiam quiescere et præsentem vitam finire dignatus est. Ipse decoravit sedem, in qua evangelistam discipulum misit. Ipse firmavit sedem, in qua septem annis, quamvis decessurus, sedit. Cum ergo unius atque una est sedes, cui ex auctoritate divina tres nunc episcopi præsident, quicquid ergo de vobis boni audio, hoc mihi imputo." (Epp. vii. 40.) "Though there be many Apostles, yet the See of the Prince of the Apostles alone has become strong in its authority, as regards the principality itself, since this See, although in three places, is the See of one. For he himself (S. Peter) exalted the See in which he both dwelt and abode to the end of this present life (the See of Rome). He himself adorned the See to which he sent his disciple the Evangelist (S. Mark to Alexandria). He himself established the See in which he, though he afterwards left it, sat for seven years (the See of Antioch). Since therefore it is the See of One, and One See, over which preside three Bishops by Divine authority, whatever good I hear of you, I reckon as belonging to me also."

This remarkable linking together of the three Chief Patriarchates as joint inheritors of the succession of S. Peter, was not merely a clever argument on S. Gregory's part against Constantinople, which could claim no link with S. Peter. It was a true assertion of the mutual interdependence of the Chief Patriarchates upon the common basis of Apostolic descent and Catholic communion, and a true assertion of the legitimate Primacy of the Roman Patriarch as "Primus inter pares."

CONCLUSION

A BRIEF summary of the results obtained by the investigation undertaken in the foregoing pages, may prove helpful in applying it to the circumstances of the Church in our own day. We are not unmindful of the fact that the guidance of the Holy Spirit is as much the heritage of the Church of to-day, as it was in the first five centuries of her life. Neither are we unmindful of the fact that questions of procedure and ecclesiastical discipline stand upon a different footing from doctrinal definitions. We are bound by the definitions of the first four Œcumenical Councils in matters of Faith. The Established Provinces of Canterbury and York are bound to something more by the standard of Heresy set up by 1 Eliz. i. 36, where the standards for judging heresy are defined to be "the Canonical Scriptures, the first four General Councils ... or by any other General Council wherein the same was declared Heresy by the express and plain words of the said Canonical Scriptures." The first General Council of the Anglican Communion, assembled under the name of the Lambeth Conference in 1867, adopted the standard of the Elizabethan Reformation as a body of Catholic Bishops acting in complete independence of the State. The Archbishops and Bishops sent forth the following clear statement in the Introduction of their Resolutions: "We, Bishops of Christ's Holy Catholic Church ... do here solemnly record our conviction that unity will be most effectually promoted by maintaining the Faith in its purity and integrity, as taught in the Holy Scriptures, held by the Primitive Church, summed up in the Creeds, and affirmed by the undisputed General Councils." But though questions of Canonical procedure and discipline do not stand on the same level as doctrinal definitions, we must remember that the Canon Law of the undivided Church, as expressed in its Œcumenical Councils and "ancient customs," comes to us with a preponderant weight of authority, as the expression of the regal power of Christ in His Church. Some principles of procedure and discipline are invariable, and come to us with plenary authority. We do not ordain women to the Priesthood, nor do we suffer Deacons to consecrate the Blessed Sacrament of the Altar. There are again other matters pertaining to discipline, where the living voice of the Church from age to age frames the details of her life and her procedure to fit the needs and special circumstances of the people and times, to whose varying necessities she must adapt her methods. There is room for an ordered freedom and elasticity. The true canonist is not narrowed to precedents, which in their application might tend to that "*summum ius summa iniuria,*" which sometimes disfigures the administration of Statute Law. But when we make the largest possible allowance for the freedom of adaptation, it is manifest that the root-principles of procedure and discipline are to be sought in the Canon Law of the undivided Church, and that it is our bounden duty to place them second only to its doctrinal definitions in the authority which we admit in them. One of the most striking results of a careful study of the Canon Law of the undivided Church, is that it provides beforehand for almost every conceivable case of procedure and discipline that can possibly arise in the Church of the present day. If Hildebrand had grasped this fact, and had not been misled by the huge superstructure of the False Decretals, the Council of Trent would have escaped assenting to some dubious definitions, and the Vatican Council would never have robbed Christendom of its ancient and historic centre of unity, by erecting around the Eternal City a barrier, made impassable by the thorns and briars of unlawful and un-Catholic terms of communion. The ancient Churches of the East have maintained with unwavering fidelity the procedure and discipline of the Primitive Church, save in the few points where an undue subservience to Byzantine Cæsarism, and its modern Russian counterpart, has deflected their Church polity from the primitive standard.

The recovery of primitive procedure and discipline by Anglican Christendom is capable of ready accomplishment, save in England itself. The Anglo-Saxon mind is eminently practical, and the practical wisdom of the primitive discipline readily commends itself to Churchmen of the United States and the British Colonies. On the whole, the Free Churches of the Anglican Communion have manifested a loyal adherence to primitive principles of Church order. But much remains to be done. We have to combine freedom with solidarity, unity with diversity, the formation of a strong centre at Canterbury with the ordered liberty of Provincial action. The chief obstacle to the consolidation of the Anglican Communion on lines of primitive and Catholic order lies with the unconstitutional traditions of mediæval Prelacy, which hamper the English Episcopate even more than its alliance with the State. It is with a view to set forth a truer and more primitive standard that the investigation contained in the foregoing pages has been undertaken.

We have now reviewed the evidence which bears upon the constitutional position of a Bishop in the Catholic Church, from the Apostolic Age to the Council of Chalcedon. We claim to have shown conclusively that the modern idea of an English Bishop as the autocratic *Persona Ecclesiæ*, who can act independently of his Priests, without the counsel of his Laity, is feudal and mediæval rather than primitive. We have shown that a Bishop does not exercise his judicial functions without some Priests, as assessors, to represent his Synod of Priests. Nor does he rule his Diocese apart from his Diocesan Synod, in which he sits as President, as representing his order. The Diocese is subordinate to the Province of which it is a unit, so that the Synod of the Province can re-examine and disallow any act of a Diocesan Synod to which the Bishop has given his assent. *A fortiori* it can examine the reasons for his dissent from the conclusions of his Diocesan Synod, since the veto of the Bishop is suspensory, and not absolute. This is plain when we consider the Cyprianic definition of the Episcopate, whereby each individual Bishop is viewed as a joint shareholder in the common trust which is vested in the united Episcopate as a whole. Each Bishop is thus responsible for all his actions, judicial and administrative, to the Universal Episcopate of the Catholic Church.

This responsibility finds its due and orderly development in the principle of Primacy in its regular gradations. And this very principle of Primacy does not involve, any more than Episcopacy itself, an irresponsible or autocratic individualism. As the Diocesan Bishop rules, with the counsel of his Priests and the assent of his Laity, in his Diocesan Synod, so does the Metropolitan rule his Province. In cases of appeal the Bishops of the Province sit with the Metropolitan as judges and not merely as assessors. If an appeal should be made from the Metropolitan and his com-provincial Bishops to the Patriarch, the same process is repeated. The chief Bishops of the Patriarchate aid him in deciding the appeal.

Although the Roman Patriarchate ultimately degenerated into an ecclesiastical despotism, the frequent Roman Synods, which were held during the period of Church history which we have been considering, show that, notwithstanding the Sardican Canons, and the coercive jurisdiction conferred on the Roman Patriarch by Imperial authority, it is fair to consider these Synods as occupying to some degree the position in the West which the regular Patriarchal Synods occupied in the East. But behind the Patriarch and his Synod lay an appeal to the Universal Episcopate of the Church in Œcumenical Council assembled. Notwithstanding the vast claims of the Hildebrandine Papacy, which had for so long dominated Western Christendom, we find the Councils of Constance and Basle laying down the doctrine that an Œcumenical Council was an authority superior to that of the Pope. Thus we see that, however it was at times obscured or overlaid, the true position of a Bishop is that of a constitutional ruler, and the true theory of the unity and solidarity of the Church is not involved in the absolute monarchy of a single Patriarch, but in an ordered system of reference to higher authority. Whether matters concerned doctrine or discipline, they were referred first to the constitutional tribunal of the Bishop in his Diocese. Thence an appeal lay to the Metropolitan and his Synod, with a further appeal to the Patriarch and his Synod, and an ultimate appeal could be lodged with an Œcumenical Council. We do not allege that this graduated system of appeals was ever practically adopted throughout Christendom without let or hindrance.

The human element so interpenetrates the Divine Order of the Catholic Church, that hindrances must of necessity arise which mar the perfection of its ideal law and order. The tares and wheat must both grow together until the harvest. But this fact need not cause us to lose sight of the Divine ideal, or hinder us from attempting to fashion our Church polity after the pattern of the Mount.

We Catholics in communion with the See of Canterbury have a unique opportunity of fulfilling primitive ideals. We are free from the doctrinal fetters of the Vatican Council. We are also free from the undue conservatism of Eastern Christendom. We have begun to walk upon the ancient paths of Church order and consolidation, and have met with no lions in the way. Our history does not stamp us as mere revolters from the unlawful claims of modern Rome. Whatever may have been the link between the Western Patriarch and the Romano-Celtic Christianity of the early British Church, it is evident that the title of " Basileus," used by the Anglo-Saxon Kings, and that independence of the Holy Roman Empire, which was always asserted as a right by their Norman and Angevin successors, placed England outside the European mediæval system in which Pope and Emperor claimed supreme rule in their respective spheres. The claim of Henry VIII. in the famous Statute of Appeals that the realm of England is an Empire, is an undisputed historical fact.[1]

And so the Church of England, though owing so much to the mission of S. Augustine, and so little

[1] "Where by dyvers sundrie olde autentike histories and cronicles it is manifestly declared and expressed that this realme of Englond is an Impire, and so hath been accepted in the worlde, governed by one suprem hed and King having the dignitie and roiall estate of the imperiall crowne of the same," &c. (Preamble of Act xxiv. Henry VIII.)

to its Romano-Celtic predecessor, could logically and historically claim for itself, despite occasional lapses, a less subordinate position with regard to the Roman Patriarchate than any of the Churches of the Continent.

The complimentary phrase, "alterius orbis Papa," implies the exclusion of the realm of England from the Holy Roman Empire, and also implies an independence, more or less definite, for the Archbishop of Canterbury, as "Pope of the other worlds" which lay beyond those Imperial boundaries within which Imperial law enforced the submission of all Prelates to the Roman Patriarch.

It is instructive to compare Canterbury with Carthage, as we have already done in the previous chapter. The parallel is incomplete in one sense, because North Africa was within the Roman Empire. But the position of the Archbishop of Carthage, as Primate of Metropolitans, was virtually that of a Patriarch who showed to Rome a sturdy forefront of independence, whilst acknowledging, as S. Cyprian did, the legitimate rights of the Patriarch of the West. There was courteous communion between Carthage and Rome, without any sense of undue subservience.

After three hundred years of a silence, which was caused by the excommunication of Queen Elizabeth by the Pope, courteous communications have passed between Rome and Canterbury which have lost none of their courtesy in the revelation of a mutual "non possumus" with regard to terms of re-union.

We may carry the parallel even further. The virtual Patriarchate of the Archbishop of Carthage, although never acknowledged *eo nomine* by the Church, finds its modern counterpart in the virtual Patriarchate of Canterbury.

The procedure adopted by the Archbishop of Carthage, as Primate of the North African Church, has been already, in a measure, adopted by the Archbishop of Canterbury, as Primate of the whole Anglican Communion. The Primates of the North African Provinces dealt with affairs in their Provincial Synods, and great questions which were incapable of being decided by the Synod of a single Province were brought before the General Council of the African Churches in which the Archbishop of Carthage presided, as Primate of Primates. In like manner the General and Provincial Synods of the American and Colonial Churches deal with questions under the leadership of their own Archbishops, Primates, and Metropolitans. But by common consent the greater and more important questions are referred to that General Council of the whole Anglican Communion which assembles under the name and style of the Lambeth Conference.

The Archbishop of Canterbury, as the President and convener of this great Council, exercises his office as a virtual Patriarch over a far wider sphere than any Archbishop of Carthage ever did. A truer parallel to his present position of influence might perhaps be sought in the great office of the Patriarch of "New Rome" in its palmiest days. It may be said that a good deal of what has been done at present in the direction of consolidating the Anglican Communion is somewhat shadowy and indefinite. But the Anglo-Saxon mind is more tolerant of anomalies in detail, and more given to regard the practical working-out of matters, than to legislate with logical precision and accuracy. The question of the canonical limits and due scope of the Canterbury Patriarch will be tentatively and practically worked out by experience.

Solvitur ambulando. And it must be admitted that the question has moved forward since the first Lambeth Council of 1867. The need of union and of a strong centre is felt at the extremities more than at the centre itself. English Churchmen are so insular, and so much wrapped up in their own burning questions, that they do not often trouble to find out what American and Colonial Churchmen are thinking on such a question as the Canterbury Patriarchate and the true functions of the Lambeth Councils.

We have, however, gained much. The General and Provincial Synods of a portion of the Colonial Church submitted the important question of the adoption of the title of "Archbishop" by Colonial Metropolitans to the Council holders at Lambeth in 1897. That Council also took some definite steps to shape itself, and made provision for its periodical meeting upon the summons of the Primate of the Anglican Communion. The establishment of a Consultative Body, to be formed by the Archbishop of Canterbury, for the purpose of aiding him to give his decisions (under the name of "Advice") upon questions submitted to him from any Church or Province of the Anglican Communion, is a step in accordance with primitive precedent. It is also a step which will have far-reaching consequences in the direction of unity when it has justified itself by results. What has already been done to consolidate the Anglican Communion has been framed on right lines, and in accordance with primitive precedent. We have in outline our Canterbury Patriarchate, our General Council of the Anglican Communion, and our organisation of Churches and Provinces under their own Metropolitans. That outline will one day be filled in. It may be necessary for the Established Provinces of Canterbury and York to be severed from their State connection before the ideal conveyed by that outline is fully realised. It may be that the Archbishops, Primates, and Metropolitans of the Anglican Communion will demand a consultative voice in the appointment of their Primate and Patriarch. But one conclusion alone can satisfy the aspirations of those who desire to set forth peace and unity as the ministers of strength and power. The model of Primitive Church organisation and order must be followed as far as human frailty doth permit. If we take the Vincentian maxim, "Quod semper, quod ubique, quod ab omnibus," as our watchword in matters of faith and doctrine, we must adhere none the less closely in matters of procedure and discipline to the maxim of Nicæa, τὰ ἀρχαῖα ἔθη κρατείτω.

THE END

Printed by BALLANTYNE, HANSON & Co.
Edinburgh & London

August 1898.

A Selection of Works
IN
THEOLOGICAL LITERATURE
PUBLISHED BY

MESSRS. LONGMANS, GREEN, & CO.

London : 39 PATERNOSTER ROW, E.C.
New York : 91 and 93 FIFTH AVENUE.
Bombay : 32 HORNBY ROAD.

Abbey and Overton.—THE ENGLISH CHURCH IN THE EIGHTEENTH CENTURY. By CHARLES J. ABBEY, M.A., Rector of Checkendon, Reading, and JOHN H. OVERTON, D.D., Canon of Lincoln. *Crown 8vo. 7s. 6d.*

Adams.—SACRED ALLEGORIES. The Shadow of the Cross—The Distant Hills—The Old Man's Home—The King's Messengers. By the Rev. WILLIAM ADAMS, M.A. *Crown 8vo. 3s. 6d.*
The four Allegories may be had separately, with Illustrations. *16mo. 1s. each.*

Aids to the Inner Life.
Edited by the Venble. W. H. HUTCHINGS, M.A., Archdeacon of Cleveland, Canon of York, Rector of Kirby Misperton, and Rural Dean of Malton. *Five Vols. 32mo, cloth limp, 6d. each; or cloth extra, 1s. each.*
OF THE IMITATION OF CHRIST. By THOMAS À KEMPIS.
THE CHRISTIAN YEAR
THE DEVOUT LIFE. By ST. FRANCIS DE SALES.
THE HIDDEN LIFE OF THE SOUL.
THE SPIRITUAL COMBAT. By LAURENCE SCUPOLI.

Barnett.—THE SERVICE OF GOD : Sermons, Essays, and Addresses. By SAMUEL A. BARNETT, Warden of Toynbee Hall, Whitechapel ; Canon of Bristol Cathedral ; Select Preacher before Oxford University. *Crown 8vo. 6s.*

Bathe.—Works by the Rev. ANTHONY BATHE, M.A.
A LENT WITH JESUS. A Plain Guide for Churchmen. Containing Readings for Lent and Easter Week, and on the Holy Eucharist. *32mo, 1s.; or in paper cover, 6d.*
AN ADVENT WITH JESUS. *32mo, 1s.; or in paper cover, 6d.*
WHAT I SHOULD BELIEVE. A Simple Manual of Self-Instruction for Church People. *Small 8vo, limp, 1s. ; cloth gilt, 2s.*

Bathe and Buckham.—THE CHRISTIAN'S ROAD BOOK.
2 Parts. By the Rev. ANTHONY BATHE and Rev. F. H. BUCKHAM.
Part I. DEVOTIONS. *Sewed, 6d. ; limp cloth, 1s. ; cloth extra, 1s. 6d.*
Part II. READINGS. *Sewed, 1s. ; limp cloth, 2s. ; cloth extra, 3s. ; or complete in one volume, sewed, 1s. 6d. ; limp cloth, 2s. 6d. ; cloth extra, 3s. 6d.*

Benson.—Works by the Rev. R. M. BENSON, M.A., Student of Christ Church, Oxford.

THE FINAL PASSOVER: A Series of Meditations upon the Passion of our Lord Jesus Christ. *Small 8vo.*

Vol. I.—THE REJECTION. 5s.
Vol. II.—THE UPPER CHAMBER.
  Part I. 5s.
  Part II. 5s.
Vol. III.—THE DIVINE EXODUS. Parts I. and II. 5s. each.
Vol. IV.—THE LIFE BEYOND THE GRAVE. 5s.

THE MAGNIFICAT; a Series of Meditations upon the Song of the Blessed Virgin Mary. *Small 8vo.* 2s.

SPIRITUAL READINGS FOR EVERY DAY. 3 *vols. Small 8vo. 3s. 6d. each.*

I. ADVENT.   II. CHRISTMAS.   III. EPIPHANY.

BENEDICTUS DOMINUS: A Course of Meditations for Every Day of the Year. Vol. I.—ADVENT TO TRINITY. Vol. II.—TRINITY, SAINTS' DAYS, etc. *Small 8vo. 3s. 6d. each ; or in One Volume, 7s.*

BIBLE TEACHINGS: The Discourse at Capernaum.—St. John vi. *Small 8vo. 3s. 6d.*

THE WISDOM OF THE SON OF DAVID: An Exposition of the First Nine Chapters of the Book of Proverbs. *Small 8vo. 3s. 6d.*

THE MANUAL OF INTERCESSORY PRAYER. *Royal 32mo.; cloth boards, 1s. 3d. ; cloth limp, 9d.*

THE EVANGELIST LIBRARY CATECHISM. Part I. *Small 8vo.* 3s.

PAROCHIAL MISSIONS. *Small 8vo.* 2s. 6d.

Bickersteth.—YESTERDAY, TO-DAY, AND FOR EVER: a Poem in Twelve Books. By EDWARD HENRY BICKERSTETH, D.D., Lord Bishop of Exeter. *One Shilling Edition,* 18mo. *With red borders,* 16mo, 2s. 6d.

The Crown 8vo Edition (5s.) *may still be had.*

Blunt.—Works by the Rev. JOHN HENRY BLUNT, D.D.

THE ANNOTATED BOOK OF COMMON PRAYER: Being an Historical, Ritual, and Theological Commentary on the Devotional System of the Church of England. *4to.* 21s.

THE COMPENDIOUS EDITION OF THE ANNOTATED BOOK OF COMMON PRAYER: Forming a concise Commentary on the Devotional System of the Church of England. *Crown 8vo.* 10s. 6d.

IN THEOLOGICAL LITERATURE. 3

Blunt.—Works by the Rev. JOHN HENRY BLUNT, D.D.—*contd.*

DICTIONARY OF DOCTRINAL AND HISTORICAL THEOLOGY. By various Writers. *Imperial 8vo.* 21*s.*

DICTIONARY OF SECTS, HERESIES, ECCLESIASTICAL PARTIES AND SCHOOLS OF RELIGIOUS THOUGHT. By various Writers. *Imperial 8vo.* 21*s.*

THE REFORMATION OF THE CHURCH OF ENGLAND: its History, Principles, and Results. 1574-1662. Two Vols. 8*vo.* 34*s.*

THE BOOK OF CHURCH LAW. Being an Exposition of the Legal Rights and Duties of the Parochial Clergy and the Laity of the Church of England. Revised by Sir WALTER G. F. PHILLIMORE, Bart., D.C.L., and G. EDWARDES JONES, Barrister-at-Law. *Crown 8vo.* 7*s.* 6*d.*

A COMPANION TO THE BIBLE: Being a Plain Commentary on Scripture History, to the end of the Apostolic Age. Two Vols. small 8*vo. Sold separately.*
THE OLD TESTAMENT. 3*s.* 6*d.* THE NEW TESTAMENT. 3*s.* 6*d.*

HOUSEHOLD THEOLOGY: a Handbook of Religious Information respecting the Holy Bible, the Prayer Book, the Church, etc., etc. *Paper cover,* 16*mo.* 1*s. Also the Larger Edition,* 3*s.* 6*d.*

Body.—Works by the Rev. GEORGE BODY, D.D., Canon of Durham.

THE LIFE OF LOVE. A Course of Lent Lectures. 16*mo.* 2*s.* 6*d.*

THE SCHOOL OF CALVARY; or, Laws of Christian Life revealed from the Cross. 16*mo.* 2*s.* 6*d.*

THE LIFE OF JUSTIFICATION. 16*mo.* 2*s.* 6*d.*

THE LIFE OF TEMPTATION. 16*mo.* 2*s.* 6*d.*

THE PRESENT STATE OF THE FAITHFUL DEPARTED. *Small 8vo. sewed,* 6*d.* 32*mo. cloth,* 1*s.*

Boultbee.—A COMMENTARY ON THE THIRTY-NINE ARTICLES OF THE CHURCH OF ENGLAND. By the Rev. T. P. BOULTBEE, formerly Principal of the London College of Divinity, St. John's Hall, Highbury. *Crown 8vo.* 6*s.*

Bright.—Works by WILLIAM BRIGHT, D.D., Regius Professor of Ecclesiastical History in the University of Oxford, and Canon of Christ Church, Oxford.

THE ROMAN SEE IN THE EARLY CHURCH: And other Studies in Church History. *Crown 8vo.* 7*s.* 6*d.*

WAYMARKS IN CHURCH HISTORY. *Crown 8vo.* 7*s.* 6*d.*

MORALITY IN DOCTRINE. *Crown 8vo.* 7*s.* 6*d.*

LESSONS FROM THE LIVES OF THREE GREAT FATHERS. St. Athanasius, St. Chrysostom, and St. Augustine. *Crown 8vo.* 6*s.*

THE INCARNATION AS A MOTIVE POWER. *Crown 8vo.* 6*s.*

Bright and Medd.—LIBER PRECUM PUBLICARUM ECCLESIÆ ANGLICANÆ. A GULIELMO BRIGHT, S.T.P., et PETRO GOLDSMITH MEDD, A.M., Latine redditus. *Small 8vo.* 7*s.* 6*d.*

Browne.—WEARIED WITH THE BURDEN: A Book of Daily Readings for Lent. By ARTHUR HEBER BROWNE, M.A., LL.D., Rector of St. John's, Newfoundland. *Crown 8vo.* 4s. 6d.

Browne.—AN EXPOSITION OF THE THIRTY-NINE ARTICLES, Historical and Doctrinal. By E. H. BROWNE, D.D., sometime Bishop of Winchester. 8vo. 16s.

Campion and Beamont.—THE PRAYER BOOK INTERLEAVED. With Historical Illustrations and Explanatory Notes arranged parallel to the Text. By W. M. CAMPION, D.D., and W. J. BEAMONT, M.A. *Small 8vo.* 7s. 6d.

Carter.—Works edited by the Rev. T. T. CARTER, M.A., Hon. Canon of Christ Church, Oxford.

THE TREASURY OF DEVOTION: a Manual of Prayer for General and Daily Use. Compiled by a Priest.
    18mo. 2s. 6d.; cloth limp, 2s.
    Bound with the Book of Common Prayer, 3s. 6d.
    Red-Line Edition. *Cloth extra, gilt top.* 18mo, 2s. 6d. net.
    Large-Type Edition. *Crown 8vo.* 3s. 6d.

THE WAY OF LIFE: A Book of Prayers and Instruction for the Young at School, with a Preparation for Confirmation. Compiled by a Priest, 18mo. 1s. 6d.

THE PATH OF HOLINESS: a First Book of Prayers, with the Service of the Holy Communion, for the Young. Compiled by a Priest. With Illustrations. 16mo. 1s. 6d.; *cloth limp*, 1s.

THE GUIDE TO HEAVEN: a Book of Prayers for every Want. (For the Working Classes.) Compiled by a Priest. 18mo. 1s. 6d.; *cloth limp*, 1s. *Large-Type Edition. Crown 8vo.* 1s. 6d.; *cloth limp*, 1s.

THE STAR OF CHILDHOOD: a First Book of Prayers and Instruction for Children. Compiled by a Priest. With Illustrations. 16mo. 2s. 6d.

SIMPLE LESSONS; or, Words Easy to be Understood. A Manual of Teaching. I. On the Creed. II. The Ten Commandments. III. The Sacrament. 18mo. 3s.

A BOOK OF PRIVATE PRAYER FOR MORNING, MID-DAY, AND OTHER TIMES. 18mo. limp cloth, 1s.; *cloth, red edges*, 1s. 3d.

NICHOLAS FERRAR: his Household and his Friends. With Portrait engraved after a Picture by CORNELIUS JANSSEN at Magdalene College, Cambridge. *Crown 8vo.* 6s.

THE LIFE AND TIMES OF JOHN KETTLEWELL. With Details of the History of the Non-Jurors. With Portrait. *Crown 8vo.* 6s.

MANUAL OF DEVOTION FOR SISTERS OF MERCY. 8 parts in 2 vols. 32mo. 10s. Or separately, as follows:—Part I. Prayers for Daily Use, 1s. 6d. Part II. For Different Necessities, 1s. Part III. For Forgiveness of Sins, 1s. Part IV. On the Holy Communion, 2s. Part V. Acts of Adoration, etc., 1s. Part VI. Prayers to our Lord Jesus Christ, 1s. Part VII. Devotions on the Passion. Part VIII. Devotions for the Sick, 1s. 6d.

SHORT OFFICE OF THE HOLY GHOST. 32mo. 1s.

Conybeare and Howson.—THE LIFE AND EPISTLES OF ST. PAUL. By the Rev. W. J. CONYBEARE, M.A., and the Very Rev. J. S. HOWSON, D.D. With numerous Maps and Illustrations.
LIBRARY EDITION. *Two Vols.* 8*vo.* 21*s.* STUDENTS' EDITION. *One Vol.* Crown 8*vo.* 6*s.* POPULAR EDITION. *One Vol.* Crown 8*vo.* 3*s.* 6*d.*

Creighton.—A HISTORY OF THE PAPACY FROM THE GREAT SCHISM TO THE SACK OF ROME (1378-1527). By Right Hon. and Right Rev. MANDELL CREIGHTON, D.D., Lord Bishop of London. *Six volumes. Crown* 8*vo.* 6*s. each.*

DAY-HOURS OF THE CHURCH OF ENGLAND, THE. Newly Revised according to the Prayer Book and the Authorised Translation of the Bible. *Crown* 8*vo. sewed,* 3*s.* ; *cloth,* 3*s.* 6*d.*

SUPPLEMENT TO THE DAY-HOURS OF THE CHURCH OF ENGLAND, being the Service for certain Holy Days. *Crown* 8*vo. sewed,* 3*s.* ; *cloth,* 3*s.* 6*d.*

Devotional Series, 16mo, Red Borders. *Each* 2*s.* 6*d.*
BICKERSTETH'S YESTERDAY, TO-DAY, AND FOR EVER.
CHILCOT'S TREATISE ON EVIL THOUGHTS.
THE CHRISTIAN YEAR.
FRANCIS DE SALES' (ST.) THE DEVOUT LIFE.
HERBERT'S POEMS AND PROVERBS.
KEMPIS' (À) OF THE IMITATION OF CHRIST.
WILSON'S THE LORD'S SUPPER. *Large type.*
*TAYLOR'S (JEREMY) HOLY LIVING.
*——— ——— HOLY DYING.
   * *These two in one Volume.* 5*s.*

Devotional Series, 18mo, without Red Borders. *Each* 1*s.*
BICKERSTETH'S YESTERDAY, TO-DAY, AND FOR EVER.
THE CHRISTIAN YEAR.
FRANCIS DE SALES' (ST.) THE DEVOUT LIFE.
HERBERT'S POEMS AND PROVERBS.
KEMPIS (À) OF THE IMITATION OF CHRIST.
WILSON'S THE LORD'S SUPPER, *Large type.*
*TAYLOR'S (JEREMY) HOLY LIVING.
*——— ——— HOLY DYING.
   * *These two in one Volume.* 2*s.* 6*d.*

Edersheim.—Works by ALFRED EDERSHEIM, M.A., D.D., Ph.D.
THE LIFE AND TIMES OF JESUS THE MESSIAH. *Two Vols.* 8*vo.* 24*s.*
JESUS THE MESSIAH : being an Abridged Edition of 'The Life and Times of Jesus the Messiah.' *Crown* 8*vo.* 7*s.* 6*d.*
HISTORY OF THE JEWISH NATION AFTER THE DESTRUCTION OF JERUSALEM UNDER TITUS. 8*vo.* 18*s.*

Ellicott.—Works by C. J. Ellicott, D.D., Bishop of Gloucester.
A CRITICAL AND GRAMMATICAL COMMENTARY ON ST. PAUL'S EPISTLES. Greek Text, with a Critical and Grammatical Commentary, and a Revised English Translation. 8vo.

Galatians. 8s. 6d.	Philippians, Colossians, and Philemon. 10s. 6d.
Ephesians. 8s. 6d.	Thessalonians. 7s. 6d.

Pastoral Epistles. 10s. 6d.

HISTORICAL LECTURES ON THE LIFE OF OUR LORD JESUS CHRIST. 8vo. 12s.

ENGLISH (THE) CATHOLIC'S VADE MECUM: a Short Manual of General Devotion. Compiled by a Priest. 32mo. 1s.

Epochs of Church History.—Edited by Right Hon. and Right Rev. Mandell Creighton, D.D., Lord Bishop of London. *Small 8vo.* 2s. 6d. *each.*

- THE ENGLISH CHURCH IN OTHER LANDS. By the Rev. H. W. Tucker, M.A.
- THE HISTORY OF THE REFORMATION IN ENGLAND. By the Rev. Geo. G. Perry, M.A.
- THE CHURCH OF THE EARLY FATHERS. By the Rev. Alfred Plummer, D.D.
- THE EVANGELICAL REVIVAL IN THE EIGHTEENTH CENTURY. By the Rev. J. H. Overton, D.D.
- THE UNIVERSITY OF OXFORD. By the Hon. G. C. Brodrick, D.C.L.
- THE UNIVERSITY OF CAMBRIDGE. By J. Bass Mullinger, M.A.
- THE ENGLISH CHURCH IN THE MIDDLE AGES. By the Rev. W. Hunt, M.A.
- THE CHURCH AND THE EASTERN EMPIRE. By the Rev. H. F. Tozer, M.A.
- THE CHURCH AND THE ROMAN EMPIRE. By the Rev. A. Carr, M.A.
- THE CHURCH AND THE PURITANS, 1570-1660. By Henry Offley Wakeman, M.A.
- HILDEBRAND AND HIS TIMES. By the Rev. W. R. W. Stephens, M.A.
- THE POPES AND THE HOHENSTAUFEN. By Ugo Balzani.
- THE COUNTER REFORMATION. By Adolphus William Ward, Litt.D.
- WYCLIFFE AND MOVEMENTS FOR REFORM. By Reginald L. Poole, M.A.
- THE ARIAN CONTROVERSY. By H. M. Gwatkin, M.A.

EUCHARISTIC MANUAL (THE). Consisting of Instructions and Devotions for the Holy Sacrament of the Altar. From various sources. 32mo. *cloth gilt, red edges.* 1s. *Cheap Edition, limp cloth.* 9d.

Farrar.—Works by Frederick W. Farrar, D.D., Dean of Canterbury.

THE BIBLE: Its Meaning and Supremacy. 8vo. 15s.

'ALLEGORIES.' With 25 Illustrations by Amelia Bauerle. *Crown 8vo.* 6s.

Contents.—The Life Story of Aner—The Choice—The Fortunes of a Royal House—The Basilisk and the Leopard.

Fosbery.—Works edited by the Rev. THOMAS VINCENT FOSBERY, M.A., sometime Vicar of St. Giles's, Reading.

VOICES OF COMFORT. *Cheap Edition. Small 8vo.* 3s. 6d.
The Larger Edition (7s. 6d.) may still be had.

HYMNS AND POEMS FOR THE SICK AND SUFFERING. In connection with the Service for the Visitation of the Sick. Selected from Various Authors. *Small 8vo.* 3s. 6d.

Geikie.—Works by J. CUNNINGHAM GEIKIE, D.D., LL.D., late Vicar of St. Martin-at-Palace, Norwich.

HOURS WITH THE BIBLE: the Scriptures in the Light of Modern Discovery and Knowledge. *New Edition, largely rewritten.* Complete in Twelve Volumes. *Crown 8vo.* 3s. 6d. *each.*

OLD TESTAMENT.

In Six Volumes. Sold separately. 3s. 6d. *each.*

CREATION TO THE PATRIARCHS. *With a Map and Illustrations.*

MOSES TO JUDGES. *With a Map and Illustrations.*

SAMSON TO SOLOMON. *With a Map and Illustrations.*

REHOBOAM TO HEZEKIAH. *With Illustrations.*

MANASSEH TO ZEDEKIAH. *With the Contemporary Prophets. With a Map and Illustrations.*

EXILE TO MALACHI. *With the Contemporary Prophets. With Illustrations.*

NEW TESTAMENT.

In Six Volumes. Sold separately. 3s. 6d. *each.*

THE GOSPELS. *With a Map and Illustrations.*

LIFE AND WORDS OF CHRIST. *With Map.* 2 vols.

LIFE AND EPISTLES OF ST. PAUL. *With Maps and Illustrations.* 2 vols.

ST. PETER TO REVELATION. *With* 29 *Illustrations.*

LIFE AND WORDS OF CHRIST.
Cabinet Edition. With Map. 2 vols. *Post 8vo.* 12s.
Cheap Edition, without the Notes. 1 vol. *8vo.* 5s.

A SHORT LIFE OF CHRIST. *With numerous Illustrations. Crown 8vo.* 3s. 6d. ; *gilt edges,* 4s. 6d.

OLD TESTAMENT CHARACTERS. *With many Illustrations. Crown 8vo.* 3s. 6d.

LANDMARKS OF OLD TESTAMENT HISTORY. *Crown 8vo.* 3s. 6d.

THE ENGLISH REFORMATION. *Crown 8vo.* 3s. 6d.

[continued.

Geikie.—Works by J. CUNNINGHAM GEIKIE, D.D., LL.D., late Vicar of St. Martin-at-Palace, Norwich—*continued.*

ENTERING ON LIFE. A Book for Young Men. *Crown 8vo.* 2s. 6d.

THE PRECIOUS PROMISES. *Crown 8vo.* 2s.

GOLD DUST: a Collection of Golden Counsels for the Sanctification of Daily Life. Translated and abridged from the French by E.L.E.E. Edited by CHARLOTTE M. YONGE. Parts I. II. III. Small Pocket Volumes. *Cloth, gilt, each* 1s. Parts I. and II. in One Volume. 1s. 6d. Parts I., II., and III. in One Volume. 2s.

*** The two first parts in One Volume, *large type,* 18mo. *cloth, gilt.* 2s. 6d. Parts I. II. and III. are also supplied, bound in white cloth, with red edges, in box, price 3s.

Gore.—Works by the Rev. CHARLES GORE, M.A., D.D., Canon of Westminster.

THE MINISTRY OF THE CHRISTIAN CHURCH. *8vo.* 10s. 6d.

ROMAN CATHOLIC CLAIMS. *Crown 8vo.* 3s. 6d.

GREAT TRUTHS OF THE CHRISTIAN RELIGION. Edited by the Rev. W. U. RICHARDS. *Small 8vo.* 2s.

Hall.—Works by the Right Rev. A. C. A. HALL, D.D., Bishop of Vermont.

THE VIRGIN MOTHER: Retreat Addresses on the Life of the Blessed Virgin Mary as told in the Gospels. With an appended Essay on the Virgin Birth of our Lord. *Crown 8vo.* 4s. 6d.

CHRIST'S TEMPTATION AND OURS. *Crown 8vo.* 3s. 6d.

Harrison.—Works by the Rev. ALEXANDER J. HARRISON, B.D., Lecturer of the Christian Evidence Society.

PROBLEMS OF CHRISTIANITY AND SCEPTICISM. *Crown 8vo.* 7s. 6d.

THE CHURCH IN RELATION TO SCEPTICS: a Conversational Guide to Evidential Work. *Crown 8vo.* 3s. 6d.

THE REPOSE OF FAITH, IN VIEW OF PRESENT DAY DIFFICULTIES. *Crown 8vo.* 7s. 6d.

Hatch.—THE ORGANIZATION OF THE EARLY CHRISTIAN CHURCHES. Being the Bampton Lectures for 1880. By EDWIN HATCH, M.A., D.D., late Reader in Ecclesiastical History in the University of Oxford. *8vo.* 5s.

Heygate.—THE MANUAL: a Book of Devotion. Adapted for General Use. By the Rev. W. E. HEYGATE, M.A., Rector of Brighstone. 18mo. *cloth limp,* 1s.; *boards,* 1s. 3d. *Cheap Edition,* 6d. *Small 8vo. Large Type,* 1s. 6d.

Holland.—Works by the Rev. HENRY SCOTT HOLLAND, M.A., Canon and Precentor of St. Paul's.
    GOD'S CITY AND THE COMING OF THE KINGDOM. *Cr. 8vo.* 3s. 6d.
    PLEAS AND CLAIMS FOR CHRIST. *Crown 8vo.* 3s. 6d.
    CREED AND CHARACTER : Sermons. *Crown 8vo.* 3s. 6d.
    ON BEHALF OF BELIEF. Sermons. *Crown 8vo.* 3s. 6d.
    CHRIST OR ECCLESIASTES. Sermons. *Crown 8vo.* 2s. 6d.
    LOGIC AND LIFE, with other Sermons. *Crown 8vo.* 3s. 6d.

Hollings.—Works by the Rev. G. S. HOLLINGS, Mission Priest of the Society of St. John the Evangelist, Cowley, Oxford.
    THE HEAVENLY STAIR ; or, A Ladder of the Love of God for Sinners. *Crown 8vo.* 3s. 6d.
    PORTA REGALIS ; or, Considerations on Prayer. *Crown 8vo. limp cloth,* 1s. 6d. *net* ; *cloth boards,* 2s. *net.*
    MEDITATIONS ON THE DIVINE LIFE, THE BLESSED SACRAMENT, AND THE TRANSFIGURATION. *Crown 8vo.* 3s. 6d.
    CONSIDERATIONS ON THE SPIRITUAL LIFE. Suggested by Passages in the Collects for the Sundays in Lent. *Crown 8vo.* 2s. 6d.
    CONSIDERATIONS ON THE WISDOM OF GOD. *Crown 8vo.* 4s.
    PARADOXES OF THE LOVE OF GOD, especially as they are seen in the way of the Evangelical Counsels. *Crown 8vo.* 4s.
    ONE BORN OF THE SPIRIT ; or, the Unification of our Life in God. *Crown 8vo.* 3s. 6d.

Hutchings.—Works by the Ven. W. H. HUTCHINGS, M.A. Archdeacon of Cleveland, Canon of York, Rector of Kirby Misperton, and Rural Dean of Malton.
    SERMON SKETCHES from some of the Sunday Lessons throughout the Church's Year. *Vols. I and II. Crown 8vo.* 5s. *each.*
    THE LIFE OF PRAYER : a Course of Lectures delivered in All Saints' Church, Margaret Street, during Lent. *Crown 8vo.* 4s. 6d.
    THE PERSON AND WORK OF THE HOLY GHOST : a Doctrinal and Devotional Treatise. *Crown 8vo.* 4s. 6d.
    SOME ASPECTS OF THE CROSS. *Crown 8vo.* 4s. 6d.
    THE MYSTERY OF THE TEMPTATION. Lent Lectures delivered at St. Mary Magdalene, Paddington. *Crown 8vo.* 4s. 6d.

Hutton.—THE CHURCH OF THE SIXTH CENTURY. Six Chapters in Ecclesiastical History. By WILLIAM HOLDEN HUTTON, B.D., Birkbeck Lecturer in Ecclesiastical History, Trinity College, Cambridge. *With 11 Illustrations. Crown 8vo.* 6s.

INHERITANCE OF THE SAINTS ; or, Thoughts on the Communion of Saints and the Life of the World to come. Collected chiefly from English Writers by L. P. With a Preface by the Rev. HENRY SCOTT HOLLAND, M.A. *Seventh Edition. Crown 8vo.* 7s. 6d.

Jameson.—Works by Mrs. JAMESON.

SACRED AND LEGENDARY ART, containing Legends of the Angels and Archangels, the Evangelists, the Apostles. With 19 Etchings and 187 Woodcuts. *2 vols. 8vo.* 20s. *net.*

LEGENDS OF THE MONASTIC ORDERS, as represented in the Fine Arts. With 11 Etchings and 88 Woodcuts. *8vo.* 10s. *net.*

LEGENDS OF THE MADONNA, OR BLESSED VIRGIN MARY. With 27 Etchings and 165 Woodcuts. *8vo.* 10s. *net.*

THE HISTORY OF OUR LORD, as exemplified in Works of Art. Commenced by the late Mrs. JAMESON ; continued and completed by LADY EASTLAKE. With 31 Etchings and 281 Woodcuts. *2 Vols. 8vo.* 20s. *net.*

Jennings.—ECCLESIA ANGLICANA. A History of the Church of Christ in England from the Earliest to the Present Times. By the Rev. ARTHUR CHARLES JENNINGS, M.A. *Crown 8vo.* 7s. 6d.

Jukes.—Works by ANDREW JUKES.

THE NEW MAN AND THE ETERNAL LIFE. Notes on the Reiterated Amens of the Son of God. *Crown 8vo.* 6s.

THE NAMES OF GOD IN HOLY SCRIPTURE : a Revelation of His Nature and Relationships. *Crown 8vo.* 4s. 6d.

THE TYPES OF GENESIS. *Crown 8vo.* 7s. 6d.

THE SECOND DEATH AND THE RESTITUTION OF ALL THINGS. *Crown 8vo.* 3s. 6d.

THE ORDER AND CONNEXION OF THE CHURCH'S TEACHING, as set forth in the arrangement of the Epistles and Gospels throughout the Year. *Crown 8vo.* 2s. 6d.

THE CHRISTIAN HOME. *Crown 8vo.* 3s. 6d.

Knox Little.—Works by W. J. KNOX LITTLE, M.A., Canon Residentiary of Worcester, and Vicar of Hoar Cross.

> THE HOPES AND DECISIONS OF THE PASSION OF OUR MOST HOLY REDEEMER. *Crown 8vo.* 2s. 6d.
>
> CHARACTERISTICS AND MOTIVES OF THE CHRISTIAN LIFE. Ten Sermons preached in Manchester Cathedral, in Lent and Advent. *Crown 8vo.* 2s. 6d.
>
> SERMONS PREACHED FOR THE MOST PART IN MANCHESTER. *Crown 8vo.* 3s. 6d.
>
> THE MYSTERY OF THE PASSION OF OUR MOST HOLY REDEEMER. *Crown 8vo.* 2s. 6d.
>
> THE WITNESS OF THE PASSION OF OUR MOST HOLY REDEEMER. *Crown 8vo.* 2s. 6d.
>
> THE LIGHT OF LIFE. Sermons preached on Various Occasions. *Crown 8vo.* 3s. 6d.
>
> SUNLIGHT AND SHADOW IN THE CHRISTIAN LIFE. Sermons preached for the most part in America. *Crown 8vo.* 3s. 6d.

Lear.—Works by, and Edited by, H. L. SIDNEY LEAR.

> FOR DAYS AND YEARS. A book containing a Text, Short Reading, and Hymn for Every Day in the Church's Year. *16mo.* 2s. 6d. *Also a Cheap Edition,* 32mo. 1s.; *or cloth gilt,* 1s. 6d.; *or with red borders,* 2s. 6d.
>
> FIVE MINUTES. Daily Readings of Poetry. *16mo.* 3s. 6d. *Also a Cheap Edition,* 32mo. 1s.; *or cloth gilt,* 1s. 6d.
>
> WEARINESS. A Book for the Languid and Lonely. *Large Type. Small 8vo.* 5s.
>
> JOY: A FRAGMENT. With a slight sketch of the Author's life. *Small 8vo.* 2s. 6d.
>
> CHRISTIAN BIOGRAPHIES. *Nine Vols. Crown 8vo.* 3s. 6d. *each.*
>
> MADAME LOUISE DE FRANCE, Daughter of Louis XV., known also as the Mother Térèse de St. Augustin.
>
> A DOMINICAN ARTIST: a Sketch of the Life of the Rev. Père Besson, of the Order of St. Dominic.
>
> HENRI PERREYVE. By PÈRE GRATRY.
>
> ST. FRANCIS DE SALES, Bishop and Prince of Geneva.
>
> THE REVIVAL OF PRIESTLY LIFE IN THE SEVENTEENTH CENTURY IN FRANCE.
>
> A CHRISTIAN PAINTER OF THE NINETEENTH CENTURY.
>
> BOSSUET AND HIS CONTEMPORARIES.
>
> FÉNELON, ARCHBISHOP OF CAMBRAI.
>
> HENRI DOMINIQUE LACORDAIRE.

[continued.

Lear.— Works by, and Edited by, H. L. SIDNEY LEAR— *continued.*

DEVOTIONAL WORKS. Edited by H. L. SIDNEY LEAR. *New and Uniform Editions. Nine Vols. 16mo. 2s. 6d. each.*

FÉNELON'S SPIRITUAL LETTERS TO MEN.

FÉNELON'S SPIRITUAL LETTERS TO WOMEN.

A SELECTION FROM THE SPIRITUAL LETTERS OF ST. FRANCIS DE SALES. Also *Cheap Edition*, 32mo, 6d. cloth limp; 1s. cloth boards.

THE SPIRIT OF ST. FRANCIS DE SALES.

THE HIDDEN LIFE OF THE SOUL.

THE LIGHT OF THE CONSCIENCE. Also *Cheap Edition*, 32mo, 6d. cloth limp; and 1s. cloth boards.

SELF-RENUNCIATION. From the French.

ST. FRANCIS DE SALES' OF THE LOVE OF GOD.

SELECTIONS FROM PASCAL'S 'THOUGHTS.'

Liddon.—Works by HENRY PARRY LIDDON, D.D., D.C.L., LL.D.

LIFE OF EDWARD BOUVERIE PUSEY, D.D. By HENRY PARRY LIDDON, D.D., D.C.L., LL.D. Edited and prepared for publication by the Rev. J. O. JOHNSTON, M.A., Principal of the Theological College, and Vicar of Cuddesdon, Oxford; the Rev. R. J. WILSON, D.D., late Warden of Keble College; and the Rev. W. C. E. NEWBOLT, M.A., Canon and Chancellor of St. Paul's. *With Portraits and Illustrations. Four Vols. 8vo. Vols. I. and II., 36s. Vol. III., 18s. Vol. IV. 18s.*

SERMONS ON SOME WORDS OF ST. PAUL. *Crown 8vo. 5s.*

SERMONS PREACHED ON SPECIAL OCCASIONS, 1860-1889. *Crown 8vo. 5s.*

EXPLANATORY ANALYSIS OF ST. PAUL'S FIRST EPISTLE TO TIMOTHY. *8vo. 7s. 6d.*

CLERICAL LIFE AND WORK: Sermons. *Crown 8vo. 5s.*

ESSAYS AND ADDRESSES: Lectures on Buddhism—Lectures on the Life of St. Paul—Papers on Dante. *Crown 8vo. 5s.*

EXPLANATORY ANALYSIS OF ST. PAUL'S FIRST EPISTLE TO TIMOTHY. *8vo. 7s. 6d.*

EXPLANATORY ANALYSIS OF PAUL'S EPISTLE TO THE ROMANS. *8vo. 14s.*

SERMONS ON OLD TESTAMENT SUBJECTS. *Crown 8vo. 5s.*

SERMONS ON SOME WORDS OF CHRIST. *Crown 8vo. 5s.*

THE DIVINITY OF OUR LORD AND SAVIOUR JESUS CHRIST. Being the Bampton Lectures for 1866. *Crown 8vo. 5s.*

ADVENT IN ST. PAUL'S. *Two Vols. Crown 8vo. 3s. 6d. each. Cheap Edition in one Volume. Crown 8vo. 5s.*

CHRISTMASTIDE IN ST. PAUL'S. *Crown 8vo. 5s.*

PASSIONTIDE SERMONS. *Crown 8vo. 5s.*

[continued.

Liddon.—Works by HENRY PARRY LIDDON, D.D., D.C.L., LL.D.—*continued*.

EASTER IN ST. PAUL'S. Sermons bearing chiefly on the Resurrection of our Lord. *Two Vols. Crown 8vo. 3s. 6d. each. Cheap Edition in one Volume. Crown 8vo. 5s.*

SERMONS PREACHED BEFORE THE UNIVERSITY OF OXFORD. *Two Vols. Crown 8vo. 3s. 6d. each. Cheap Edition in one Volume. Crown 8vo. 5s.*

THE MAGNIFICAT. Sermons in St. Paul's. *Crown 8vo. 2s. 6d.*

SOME ELEMENTS OF RELIGION. Lent Lectures. *Small 8vo. 2s. 6d.* [*The Crown 8vo. Edition* (5s.) *may still be had.*]

SELECTIONS FROM THE WRITINGS OF. *Crown 8vo. 3s. 6d.*

MAXIMS AND GLEANINGS. *Crown 16mo. 1s.*

Luckock.—Works by HERBERT MORTIMER LUCKOCK, D.D., Dean of Lichfield.

THE HISTORY OF MARRIAGE, JEWISH AND CHRISTIAN, IN RELATION TO DIVORCE AND CERTAIN FORBIDDEN DEGREES. *Crown 8vo. 6s.*

AFTER DEATH. An Examination of the Testimony of Primitive Times respecting the State of the Faithful Dead, and their Relationship to the Living. *Crown 8vo. 3s. 6d.*

THE INTERMEDIATE STATE BETWEEN DEATH AND JUDGMENT. Being a Sequel to *After Death*. *Crown 8vo. 3s. 6d.*

FOOTPRINTS OF THE SON OF MAN, as traced by St. Mark. Being Eighty Portions for Private Study, Family Reading, and Instruction in Church. *Crown 8vo. 3s. 6d.*

FOOTPRINTS OF THE APOSTLES, as traced by St. Luke in the Acts. Being Sixty Portions for Private Study, and Instruction in Church. A Sequel to 'Footprints of the Son of Man, as traced by St. Mark.' *Two Vols. Crown 8vo. 12s.*

THE DIVINE LITURGY. Being the Order for Holy Communion, Historically, Doctrinally, and Devotionally set forth, in Fifty Portions. *Crown 8vo. 3s. 6d.*

STUDIES IN THE HISTORY OF THE BOOK OF COMMON PRAYER. The Anglican Reform—The Puritan Innovations—The Elizabethan Reaction—The Caroline Settlement. With Appendices. *Crown 8vo. 3s. 6d.*

THE BISHOPS IN THE TOWER. A Record of Stirring Events affecting the Church and Nonconformists from the Restoration to the Revolution. *Crown 8vo. 3s. 6d.*

LYRA GERMANICA. Hymns translated from the German by CATHERINE WINKWORTH. *Small 8vo. 5s.*

MacColl.—Works by the Rev. MALCOLM MACCOLL, M.A., Canon Residentiary of Ripon.
 CHRISTIANITY IN RELATION TO SCIENCE AND MORALS. *Crown 8vo.* 6s.
 LIFE HERE AND HEREAFTER : Sermons. *Crown 8vo.* 7s. 6d.

Mason.—Works by A. J. MASON, D.D., Lady Margaret Professor of Divinity in the University of Cambridge and Canon of Canterbury.
 THE CONDITIONS OF OUR LORD'S LIFE UPON EARTH. Being the Bishop Paddock Lectures, 1896. To which is prefixed part of a First Professorial Lecture at Cambridge. *Crown 8vo.* 5s.
 THE PRINCIPLES OF ECCLESIASTICAL UNITY. Four Lectures delivered in St. Asaph Cathedral. *Crown 8vo.* 3s. 6d.
 THE FAITH OF THE GOSPEL. A Manual of Christian Doctrine. *Crown 8vo.* 7s. 6d. *Cheap Edition. Crown 8vo.* 3s. 6d.
 THE RELATION OF CONFIRMATION TO BAPTISM. As taught in Holy Scripture and the Fathers. *Crown 8vo.* 7s. 6d.

Maturin.—Works by the Rev. B. W. MATURIN, sometime Mission Priest of the Society of St. John the Evangelist, Cowley.
 SOME PRINCIPLES AND PRACTICES OF THE SPIRITUAL LIFE. *Crown 8vo.* 4s. 6d.
 PRACTICAL STUDIES ON THE PARABLES OF OUR LORD. *Crown 8vo.* 5s.

Medd.—THE PRIEST TO THE ALTAR; or, Aids to the Devout Celebration of Holy Communion, chiefly after the Ancient English Use of Sarum. By PETER GOLDSMITH MEDD, M.A., Canon of St. Alban's. Fourth Edition, revised and enlarged. *Royal 8vo.* 15s.

Mortimer.—Works by the Rev. A. G. MORTIMER, D.D., Rector of St. Mark's, Philadelphia.

JESUS AND THE RESURRECTION: Thirty Addresses for Good Friday and Easter. *Crown 8vo.* 5s.

CATHOLIC FAITH AND PRACTICE: A Manual of Theological Instruction for Confirmation and First Communion. *Crown 8vo.* 7s. 6d.

HELPS TO MEDITATION: Sketches for Every Day in the Year.
 Vol. I. ADVENT to TRINITY. 8vo. 7s. 6d.
 Vol. II. TRINITY to ADVENT. 8vo. 7s. 6d.

STORIES FROM GENESIS: Sermons for Children. *Crown 8vo.* 4s.

THE LAWS OF HAPPINESS; or, The Beatitudes as teaching our Duty to God, Self, and our Neighbour. 18mo. 2s.

THE LAWS OF PENITENCE: Addresses on the Words of our Lord from the Cross. 16mo. 1s. 6d.

SERMONS IN MINIATURE FOR EXTEMPORE PREACHERS: Sketches for Every Sunday and Holy Day of the Christian Year. *Crown 8vo.* 6s.

NOTES ON THE SEVEN PENITENTIAL PSALMS, chiefly from Patristic Sources. *Fcp. 8vo.* 3s. 6d.

THE SEVEN LAST WORDS OF OUR MOST HOLY REDEEMER: with Meditations on some Scenes in His Passion. *Crown 8vo.* 5s.

LEARN OF JESUS CHRIST TO DIE: Addresses on the Words of our Lord from the Cross, taken as Teaching the way of Preparation for Death. 16mo. 2s.

IN THEOLOGICAL LITERATURE. 15

Mozley.—Works by J. B. MOZLEY, D.D., late Canon of Christ Church, and Regius Professor of Divinity at Oxford.

ESSAYS, HISTORICAL AND THEOLOGICAL. *Two Vols.* 8vo. 24s.

EIGHT LECTURES ON MIRACLES. Being the Bampton Lectures for 1865. *Crown* 8vo. 3s. 6d.

RULING IDEAS IN EARLY AGES AND THEIR RELATION TO OLD TESTAMENT FAITH. 8vo. 6s.

SERMONS PREACHED BEFORE THE UNIVERSITY OF OXFORD, and on Various Occasions. *Crown* 8vo. 3s. 6d.

SERMONS, PAROCHIAL AND OCCASIONAL. *Crown* 8vo. 3s. 6d.

A REVIEW OF THE BAPTISMAL CONTROVERSY. *Crown* 8vo. 3s 6d.

Newbolt.—Works by the Rev. W. C. E. NEWBOLT, M.A., Canon and Chancellor of St. Paul's Cathedral.

PRIESTLY IDEALS; being a Course of Practical Lectures delivered in St. Paul s Cathedral to 'Our Society' and other Clergy, in Lent, 1898. *Crown* 8vo. 3s. 6d.

THE GOSPEL OF EXPERIENCE; or, the Witness of Human Life to the truth of Revelation. Being the Boyle Lectures for 1895. *Crown* 8vo. 5s.

COUNSELS OF FAITH AND PRACTICE: being Sermons preached on various occasions. *New and Enlarged Edition*. *Crown* 8vo. 5s.

SPECULUM SACERDOTUM; or, the Divine Model of the Priestly Life. *Crown* 8vo. 7s. 6d.

THE FRUIT OF THE SPIRIT. Being Ten Addresses bearing on the Spiritual Life. *Crown* 8vo. 2s. 6d.

THE MAN OF GOD. *Small* 8vo. 1s. 6d.

THE PRAYER BOOK: Its Voice and Teaching. *Crown* 8vo. 2s. 6d.

Newman.—Works by JOHN HENRY NEWMAN, B.D., sometime Vicar of St. Mary's, Oxford.

LETTERS AND CORRESPONDENCE OF JOHN HENRY NEWMAN DURING HIS LIFE IN THE ENGLISH CHURCH. With a brief Autobiography. Edited, at Cardinal Newman's request, by ANNE MOZLEY. 2 *vols.* *Crown* 8vo. 7s.

PAROCHIAL AND PLAIN SERMONS. *Eight Vols.* *Cabinet Edition*. *Crown* 8vo. 5s. *each*. *Cheaper Edition*. 3s. 6d. *each*.

SELECTION, ADAPTED TO THE SEASONS OF THE ECCLESIASTICAL YEAR, from the 'Parochial and Plain Sermons,' *Cabinet Edition*. *Crown* 8vo. 5s. *Cheaper Edition*. 3s. 6d.

FIFTEEN SERMONS PREACHED BEFORE THE UNIVERSITY OF OXFORD *Cabinet Edition*. *Crown* 8vo. 5s. *Cheaper Edition*. 3s. 6d.

SERMONS BEARING UPON SUBJECTS OF THE DAY. *Cabinet Edition*. *Crown* 8vo. 5s. *Cheaper Edition*. *Crown* 8vo. 3s. 6d.

LECTURES ON THE DOCTRINE OF JUSTIFICATION. *Cabinet Edition*. *Crown* 8vo. 5s. *Cheaper Edition*. 3s. 6d.

** A Complete List of Cardinal Newman's Works can be had on Application.

Osborne.—Works by EDWARD OSBORNE, Mission Priest of the Society of St. John the Evangelist, Cowley, Oxford.

    THE CHILDREN'S SAVIOUR. Instructions to Children on the Life of Our Lord and Saviour Jesus Christ. *Illustrated.* 16mo. 2s. 6d.

    THE SAVIOUR KING. Instructions to Children on Old Testament Types and Illustrations of the Life of Christ. *Illustrated.* 16mo. 2s. 6d.

    THE CHILDREN'S FAITH. Instructions to Children on the Apostles' Creed. *Illustrated.* 16mo. 2s. 6d.

Ottley.—ASPECTS OF THE OLD TESTAMENT: being the Bampton Lectures for 1897. By ROBERT LAWRENCE OTTLEY, M.A., Vicar of Winterbourne Bassett, Wilts; sometime Principal of the Pusey House. 8vo. 16s.

OUTLINES OF CHURCH TEACHING: a Series of Instructions for the Sundays and chief Holy Days of the Christian Year. For the Use of Teachers. By C. C. G. With Preface by the Very Rev. FRANCIS PAGET, D.D., Dean of Christ Church, Oxford. *Crown 8vo.* 3s. 6d.

Oxenden.—Works by the Right Rev. ASHTON OXENDEN, sometime Bishop of Montreal.

    PLAIN SERMONS, to which is prefixed a Memorial Portrait. *Crown 8vo.* 5s.

    PEACE AND ITS HINDRANCES. *Crown 8vo.* 1s. sewed; 2s. cloth.

    THE PATHWAY OF SAFETY; or, Counsel to the Awakened. *Fcap. 8vo, large type.* 2s. 6d. *Cheap Edition. Small type, limp,* 1s.

    THE EARNEST COMMUNICANT. *New Red Rubric Edition.* 32mo, cloth. 2s. *Common Edition.* 32mo. 1s.

    OUR CHURCH AND HER SERVICES. *Fcap.* 8vo. 2s. 6d.

    FAMILY PRAYERS FOR FOUR WEEKS. First Series. *Fcap. 8vo.* 2s. 6d. Second Series. *Fcap. 8vo.* 2s. 6d.

        LARGE TYPE EDITION. Two Series in one Volume. *Crown 8vo.* 6s.

    COTTAGE SERMONS; or, Plain Words to the Poor. *Fcap. 8vo.* 2s. 6d.

    THOUGHTS FOR HOLY WEEK. 16mo, cloth. 1s. 6d.

    DECISION. 18mo. 1s. 6d.

    THE HOME BEYOND; or, A Happy Old Age. *Fcap. 8vo.* 1s. 6d.

    THE LABOURING MAN'S BOOK. 18mo, *large type,* cloth. 1s. 6d.

Oxenham.—THE VALIDITY OF PAPAL CLAIMS: Lectures delivered in Rome. By F. NUTCOMBE OXENHAM, D.D., English Chaplain at Rome. With a Letter by His Grace the ARCHBISHOP OF YORK. *Crown 8vo.* 2s. 6d.

Paget.—Works by FRANCIS PAGET, D.D., Dean of Christ Church.
STUDIES IN THE CHRISTIAN CHARACTER: Sermons. With an Introductory Essay. *Crown 8vo.* 6*s.* 6*d.*
THE SPIRIT OF DISCIPLINE: Sermons. *Crown 8vo.* 6*s.* 6*d.*
FACULTIES AND DIFFICULTIES FOR BELIEF AND DISBELIEF. *Crown 8vo.* 6*s.* 6*d.*
THE HALLOWING OF WORK. Addresses given at Eton, January 16-18, 1888. *Small 8vo.* 2*s.*

Percival.—SOME HELPS FOR SCHOOL LIFE. Sermons preached at Clifton College, 1862-1879. By J. PERCIVAL, D.D., LL.D., Lord Bishop of Hereford. New Edition, with New Preface. *Crown 8vo.* 3*s.* 6*d.*

Percival.—THE INVOCATION OF SAINTS. Treated Theologically and Historically. By HENRY R. PERCIVAL, M.A., D.D., Author of 'A Digest of Theology,' 'The Doctrine of the Episcopal Church,' etc. *Crown 8vo.* 5*s.*

POCKET MANUAL OF PRAYERS FOR THE HOURS, ETC. With the Collects from the Prayer Book. *Royal 32mo.* 1*s.*

Powell.—THE PRINCIPLE OF THE INCARNATION. With especial Reference to the Relation between our Lord's Divine Omniscience and His Human Consciousness. By the Rev. H. C. POWELL, M.A. of Oriel College, Oxford; Rector of Wylye and Prebendary of Salisbury Cathedral. *8vo.* 16*s.*

PRACTICAL REFLECTIONS. By a CLERGYMAN. With Prefaces by H. P. LIDDON, D.D., D.C.L., and the LORD BISHOP OF LINCOLN. *Crown 8vo.*
THE BOOK OF GENESIS. 4*s.* 6*d.*
THE PSALMS. 5*s.*
ISAIAH. 4*s.* 6*d.*
THE MINOR PROPHETS. 4*s.* 6*d.*
THE HOLY GOSPELS. 4*s.* 6*d.*
ACTS TO REVELATIONS. 6*s.*

PRIEST'S (THE) PRAYER BOOK. Containing Private Prayers and Intercessions; Occasional, School, and Parochial Offices; Offices for the Visitation of the Sick, with Notes, Readings, Collects, Hymns, Litanies, etc. With a brief Pontifical. By the late Rev. R. F. LITTLEDALE, LL.D., D.C.L., and Rev. J. EDWARD VAUX, M.A., F.S.A. *New Edition, Revised.* 20*th Thousand. Post 8vo.* 6*s.* 6*d.*

Pullan.—LECTURES ON RELIGION. By the Rev. LEIGHTON PULLAN, M.A., Fellow of St. John's College, Lecturer in Theology at Oriel and Queen's Colleges, Oxford. *Crown 8vo.* 6*s.*

Pusey.—LIFE OF EDWARD BOUVERIE PUSEY, D.D. By HENRY PARRY LIDDON, D.D., D.C.L., LL.D. Edited and prepared for publication by the Rev. J. O. JOHNSTON, M.A., Principal of the Theological College, and Vicar of Cuddesdon, Oxford; the Rev. R. J. WILSON, D.D., late Warden of Keble College; and the Rev. W. C. E. NEWBOLT, M.A., Canon and Chancellor of St. Paul's. *With Portraits and Illustrations. Four Vols. 8vo. Vols. I. and II.*, 36s. *Vol. III.*, 18s. *Vol. IV.* 18s.

Randolph.—Works by B. W. RANDOLPH, M.A., Principal of the Theological College and Hon. Canon of Ely.

> THE THRESHOLD OF THE SANCTUARY: being Short Chapters on the Inner Preparation for the Priesthood. *Crown 8vo.* 3s. 6d.
>
> THE LAW OF SINAI: being Devotional Addresses on the Ten Commandments delivered to Ordinands. *Crown 8vo.* 3s. 6d.

Rede.—Works by WYLLYS REDE, D.D., Rector of the Church of the Incarnation, and Canon of the Cathedral, Atalanta, Georgia.

> STRIVING FOR THE MASTERY: Daily Lessons for Lent. *Cr. 8vo.* 5s.
>
> THE COMMUNION OF SAINTS: a Lost Link in the Chain of the Church's Creed. With a Preface by LORD HALIFAX. *Crown 8vo.* 3s. 6d.

Reynolds.—THE SUPERNATURAL IN NATURE: A Verification by Free Use of Science. By JOSEPH WILLIAM REYNOLDS, M.A., Past President of Sion College, Prebendary of St. Paul's Cathedral. *New and Cheaper Edition, Revised. Crown 8vo.* 3s. 6d.

Sanday.—INSPIRATION: Eight Lectures on the Early History and Origin of the Doctrine of Biblical Inspiration. Being the Bampton Lectures for 1893. By W. SANDAY, D.D., Margaret Professor of Divinity and Canon of Christ Church, Oxford. *New and Cheaper Edition, with New Preface. 8vo.* 7s. 6d.

Scudamore.—STEPS TO THE ALTAR: a Manual of Devotion for the Blessed Eucharist. By the Rev. W. E. SCUDAMORE, M.A. *Royal 32mo.* 1s.

> On toned paper, with red rubrics, 2s: The same, with Collects, Epistles, and Gospels, 2s. 6d; Demy 18mo. cloth, 1s; Demy 18mo. cloth, large type, 1s. 3d; Imperial 32mo. limp cloth, 6d.

Simpson.—THE CHURCH AND THE BIBLE. By the Rev. W. J. SPARROW SIMPSON, M.A., Vicar of St. Mark's, Regent's Park. *Crown 8vo.* 3s. 6d.

Strong.—CHRISTIAN ETHICS : being the Bampton Lectures for 1895. By THOMAS B. STRONG, M.A., Student of Christ Church, Oxford, and Examining Chaplain to the Lord Bishop of Durham. *New and Cheaper Edition.* 8vo. 7s. 6d.

Tee.—THE SANCTUARY OF SUFFERING. By ELEANOR TEE, Author of 'This Everyday Life,' etc. With a Preface by the Rev. J. P. F. DAVIDSON, M.A., Vicar of St. Matthias', Earl's Court; President of the 'Guild of All Souls.' *Crown 8vo.* 7s. 6d.

Williams.—Works by the Rev. ISAAC WILLIAMS, B.D.

A DEVOTIONAL COMMENTARY ON THE GOSPEL NARRATIVE. *Eight Vols. Crown 8vo.* 5s. *each.*

THOUGHTS ON THE STUDY OF THE HOLY GOSPELS.
A HARMONY OF THE FOUR GOSPELS.
OUR LORD'S NATIVITY.
OUR LORD'S MINISTRY (Second Year).
OUR LORD'S MINISTRY (Third Year).
THE HOLY WEEK.
OUR LORD'S PASSION.
OUR LORD'S RESURRECTION.

FEMALE CHARACTERS OF HOLY SCRIPTURE. A Series of Sermons. *Crown 8vo.* 5s.

THE CHARACTERS OF THE OLD TESTAMENT. *Crown 8vo.* 5s.

THE APOCALYPSE. With Notes and Reflections. *Crown 8vo.* 5s.

SERMONS ON THE EPISTLES AND GOSPELS FOR THE SUNDAYS AND HOLY DAYS. *Two Vols. Crown 8vo.* 5s. *each.*

PLAIN SERMONS ON CATECHISM. *Two Vols. Cr. 8vo.* 5s. *each.*

Wilson.—THOUGHTS ON CONFIRMATION. By Rev. R. J. WILSON, D.D., late Warden of Keble College. 16mo. 1s. 6d.

Wirgman.—THE DOCTRINE OF CONFIRMATION CONSIDERED IN RELATION TO HOLY BAPTISM AS A SACRAMENTAL ORDINANCE OF THE CATHOLIC CHURCH: with a Preliminary Historical Survey of the Doctrine of the Holy Spirit. By A. THEODORE WIRGMAN, B.D., D.C.L., Vice-Provost of St. Mary's Collegiate Church, Port Elizabeth, South Africa. *Cr. 8vo.* 7s. 6d.

Wordsworth.—Works by CHRISTOPHER WORDSWORTH, D.D., sometime Bishop of Lincoln.

THE HOLY BIBLE (the Old Testament). With Notes, Introductions, and Index. *Imperial 8vo.*

Vol. I. THE PENTATEUCH. 25s. Vol. II. JOSHUA TO SAMUEL. 15s. Vol. III. KINGS to ESTHER. 15s. Vol. IV. JOB TO SONG OF SOLOMON. 25s. Vol. V. ISAIAH TO EZEKIEL. 25s. Vol. VI. DANIEL, MINOR PROPHETS, and Index. 15s.
Also supplied in 12 Parts. Sold separately.

[continued.

Wordsworth.—Works by Christopher Wordsworth, D.D., sometime Bishop of Lincoln—*continued.*

THE NEW TESTAMENT, in the Original Greek. With Notes, Introductions, and Indices. *Imperial 8vo.*
   Vol. I. Gospels and Acts of the Apostles. 23s. Vol. II. Epistles, Apocalypse, and Indices. 37s.
   Also supplied in 4 Parts. Sold separately.

LECTURES ON INSPIRATION OF THE BIBLE. *Small 8vo.* 1s. 6d. cloth. 1s. sewed.

A CHURCH HISTORY TO A.D. 451. *Four Vols. Crown 8vo.*
   Vol. I. To the Council of Nicæa, A.D. 325. 8s. 6d. Vol. II. From the Council of Nicæa to that of Constantinople. 6s. Vol. III. Continuation. 6s. Vol. IV. Conclusion, To the Council of Chalcedon, A.D. 451. 6s.

THEOPHILUS ANGLICANUS: a Manual of Instruction on the Church and the Anglican Branch of it. *12mo.* 2s. 6d.

ELEMENTS OF INSTRUCTION ON THE CHURCH. *16mo.* 1s. cloth. 6d. sewed.

ON UNION WITH ROME. *Small 8vo.* 1s. 6d. Sewed, 1s.

THE HOLY YEAR: Original Hymns. *16mo.* 2s. 6d. and 1s. Limp, 6d.
   ,,   ,,   With Music. Edited by W. H. Monk. *Square 8vo.* 4s. 6d.

MISCELLANIES, Literary and Religious. *Three Vols. 8vo.* 36s.

ON THE INTERMEDIATE STATE OF THE SOUL AFTER DEATH. *32mo.* 1s.

Wordsworth.—Works by John Wordsworth, D.D., Lord Bishop of Salisbury.

THE HOLY COMMUNION: Four Visitation Addresses. 1891. *Crown 8vo.* 3s. 6d.

THE ONE RELIGION: Truth, Holiness, and Peace desired by the Nations, and revealed by Jesus Christ. Eight Lectures delivered before the University of Oxford in 1881. *Second Edition. Crown 8vo.* 7s. 6d.

UNIVERSITY SERMONS ON GOSPEL SUBJECTS. *Sm. 8vo.* 2s. 6d.

PRAYERS FOR USE IN COLLEGE. *16mo.* 1s.

10,000/8/98.

www.ingramcontent.com/pod-product-compliance
Lightning Source LLC
Chambersburg PA
CBHW030013240426
43672CB00007B/930